GRANDMA'S HOUSE

A Memoir

Shirley Dawson Johnson

ISBN:
978-1-916622-80-7 eBook
978-1-916622-81-4 Paperback
978-1-916622-82-1 Hardcover

Published by
Amazon Publishing Agency

Dedicated to my dear grandmother,

Mrs. Florence Reid Daugherty

For your love, care, and encouragement. For all the good things that you taught me by example.

And for teaching me to have confidence in myself.

I love you, Grandma.

Table of Contents

Introduction

For a long time, President Franklin Delano Roosevelt had been saying he was determined to keep the United States out of war. Grandma would listen to the news on the radio twice a day and read the two daily newspapers delivered to the house. Then she would say, "I'm mighty afraid the country will go to war."

In January of 1938, President Roosevelt still said he didn't want war, but he thought it would be wise to prepare for it. He asked Congress to appropriate one billion dollars to begin preparing for war in case we were forced to become involved in it.

New jobs were created at the Norfolk Naval Base in Norfolk, Virginia, and the Norfolk Naval Shipyard. The Norfolk Naval Shipyard was not in Norfolk. It was in Portsmouth, Virginia. It was called the navy yard by nearly everyone. The navy yard had a bus that drove around Norfolk to pick up workers every morning to take them to their jobs at the navy yard in Portsmouth and return them to their homes in the afternoon. At the Naval Base, workers made improvements to old structures, and they constructed new ships and submarines at the navy yard.

President Roosevelt said he thought we should be prepared because trouble in Europe and Asia had been brewing since 1932, when the Nazis led the German elections and the United States protested Japanese aggression in Manchuria.

In 1933, Adolf Hitler was appointed German chancellor. He gained the powers of a dictator, and the Nazi terror began. The Holocaust, a word defined in a dictionary as vast or total destruction, began in March of 1933 when the first concentration camp for Jews was established. Boycotts of Jews began in April of 1933. In this same year, Germany and Japan withdrew from the League of Nations, an agreement signed by the Allies and Germany after World War I.

By September of 1935, anti-Semitic laws were passed, and Jews lost their citizenship and civil rights.

Another concentration camp opened in July of 1937. By November, Jewish institutions in Germany and Austria were destroyed, and 26,000 Jews were sent to concentration camps. Jewish children were expelled from schools. In December, Jewish property and businesses were taken by the Nazis.

The Nazis continued to invade and conquer other countries and send Jews to concentration camps. By 1939, newspapers reported that Hitler planned to get rid of all Jews in Germany and the countries that the Nazis conquered, such as Poland. In September 1939, Britain and France declared war on Germany. Newspapers in Germany denounced President Roosevelt and threatened our country with war, but Roosevelt proclaimed American neutrality.

During this time, Japan was regularly dropping bombs on China.

In May 1940, the Nazis invaded Belgium and Luxembourg. Italy declared war on France and Britain and invaded France. There was an alliance of Germany, Italy, Japan, Hungary, Romania, and Bulgaria. They became known as the Axis powers.

There was eventually another alliance, known as the Allies, which included the United States, Britain, France, U.S.S.R., Australia, Belgium, Brazil, Canada, China, Denmark, Greece, Netherlands, New Zealand, Norway, Poland, South Africa, and Yugoslavia.

With more and more Allies becoming involved, there was little wonder that President Roosevelt continued to ask Congress to appropriate money just in case the United States was drawn into the war.

In May 1940, after the Nazis invaded Belgium and Luxembourg, President Roosevelt asked for enough money to construct 50,000 planes a year.

The Norfolk Naval Base and the Norfolk Naval Shipyard continued to add new workers. In July 1940, the government took over 1,000 acres of land for the expansion of the Norfolk Naval Base and the Norfolk Naval Air Station. The workers built more barracks, warehouses, and piers. They also dredged at the piers and improved the runways.

The Army moved into military reservations, which were named Camp Pendleton and Fort Story at Virginia Beach. Soldiers who were on leave boarded buses to downtown Norfolk, so the streets were often crowded with soldiers as well as sailors.

President Roosevelt came to the Norfolk Naval Shipyard on his yacht Potomac to observe the construction at the shipyard. Then, he was driven from Portsmouth through Norfolk, up Hampton Boulevard, to the Norfolk Naval Base. He said he was pleased with the progress being made.

President Roosevelt, a Democrat, had been overwhelmingly elected to his first term as president in 1932. The Great Depression, which began in 1929, occurred during President Hoover's administration and became worse each year, so the people were eager for a change.

President Roosevelt provided the necessary changes during the rest of the thirties. The threat of war hung over the United States during that time, but the country recovered and was on the road to prosperity by 1940.

Being three years old, I was too young to understand what was going on in the world, and I didn't know much about war; I just thought it was bad. We were looking forward to my Aunt Nita's high school graduation, but I didn't know if it was right for me to feel happy about it.

My grandma reassured me, "You should feel as happy as you want, honey. It's January 1940. If the United States has to go to war, it might be a long time away."

Part I — 1940 & 1941

High School Graduation

It was a cold winter day in January of 1940 when Grandma, Mama, BeeWee, and I bundled up in our woolen coats and stood shivering on Grandma's front porch to watch BeeWee, my grandfather, get ready to take pictures of Aunt Nita in her graduation cap and gown. I was even wearing tan woolen leggings and a hat that matched my coat. Since Nita couldn't wear a coat in the picture, she was waiting inside the house until BeeWee figured out the best spot for her to stand.

I was as fascinated by the picture-taking as if BeeWee had been a professional photographer with expensive equipment. He had two Kodak box cameras. They were exactly alike, except that one was red, and the other was black. They were plain and looked like boxes. He used his black one for Nita's picture and took his time, moving from place to place in the front yard to be sure he was standing in the best place for the best light.

Eventually, he said I could open the door and tell Nita he was ready. She came out looking pretty and sweet and stood on the porch.

We were proud, happy, and excited about Nita's graduation because she was about to become the first high school graduate in our family. Mama was four years older than Nita, so she could have been the first, but she quit school a week after her eighteenth birthday. Grandma had told me about that. She said BeeWee cried for two weeks after Mama got married because he had wanted her to finish high school and get a diploma.

He took several pictures of Nita and then took a picture of me wearing her graduation cap. I asked Nita if I could go inside and look in the mirror to see myself in the cap, and she said I could. I went upstairs to Grandma's and BeeWee's room, which everyone called the back bedroom. Their room had a large wardrobe, with two doors that each had a full-length mirror. It had belonged to Grandma's mother. When I saw the reflection of myself wearing the cap, I thought about the family's pride and happiness.

Grandma came into the room to put away the camera and smiled at me.

"You know what, Grandma? I want to graduate from high school, too, just like Nita."

"Well, I think that's very nice, honey. I hope you do because education is important. BeeWee and I didn't finish school because we had to go to work at an early age to help our families."

"Once you start school, the time will go by fast, too fast, and you'll be Juanita's age and graduating, too."

I was almost three years old, very young to be thinking so much about Nita's graduation, but when Grandma said those words to me, I could hardly believe it. I was in awe to think that Grandma believed I could also graduate from high school someday.

I felt confident, and I was determined to prove to everyone that Grandma was right about me. This was the first time I had confidence in myself.

Changes

We knew in January of 1941 that we were in a time of transition. Our city, Norfolk, Virginia, had recovered from The Great Depression, a time of extreme economic hardship that adversely affected the entire country. The city was experiencing the transition from old-fashioned customs to more modern trends. The older generation tended to hang on to what they had, and the younger generation seemed to prefer the changes.

My grandparents had lived through some hard times, including their hard-life childhoods, World War I, and The Great Depression. They were thankful that my grandfather had a steady job with the Norfolk and Western Railroad; they'd taken out a loan to buy the house and the furniture that belonged to Grandma's mother. They could pay their bills; they had enough food for their family and the clothes they needed to wear. They were thankful for what they had.

Aunt Nita liked her job as a long-distance operator at the telephone company and preferred the modern trends. She lived at home, as most single working girls did then. She dressed well and stayed downtown with her friends after work to eat at restaurants, go to movies, and go shopping.

As soon as she saved enough money, she bought a light walnut bedroom suite to replace the dark, old-fashioned furniture in her room. The suite included a four-poster bed with a new mattress and springs, a dresser with a large round mirror, a chest of drawers, and a dressing table. The dressing table was made like a kneehole desk, with a space for your feet and legs in the center and two drawers on each side. A large round mirror, like the one on the dresser, was attached, and there was a padded vanity bench with a low back to use for sitting at the dressing table.

The bed was covered with a pink and white chenille bedspread, and the tops of the furniture were covered with pink and white woven dresser scarves that fitted each piece of furniture perfectly. There was a small, pink, ceramic lamp shaped like a lady in a long, full-skirted dress with a white shade on each side of the dressing table.

The only thing in her room that wasn't modern was the Morris chair that once belonged to Grandma's mother. It was a large, high-back chair with a dark oak frame and soft, thick, burgundy-colored velvet cushions. I liked to sit on one of the wide arms of the chair and put my arm around Grandma's neck while she sat in the chair and read one of my little Whitman books she had bought for me. When she read the story of *The Three Bears*, I pretended we were sitting in Papa Bear's big chair.

On January 4th, which was Aunt Nita's nineteenth birthday, BeeWee moved the Morris chair to the back bedroom; Grandma swept and dusted where it had been, and a furniture store delivered a small, rose-flowered print boudoir chair to fill the space. They'd seen it advertised in the paper and surprised Aunt Nita with it when she came home from work.

Then, her room was completely modern. No other room in the house had modern furniture.

Mama and Daddy wanted to change from the old-fashioned to the modern, but they were limited to living in people's furnished rooms, so they couldn't buy any new furniture. Because of the housing shortage, there were no apartments available. The good apartments had waiting lists, and they could only add their names and telephone number and hope to get a call. Besides the housing shortage being a drawback, when some people found a good apartment, they stayed in it for the rest of their lives.

Aunt Nita didn't stop by, just making changes in her room, though. She actually convinced my grandparents to change the color of the living room mantle from its natural dark wood to ivory, the color of all the woodwork in the house.

"Everyone's doing it now. You'd be surprised how it brightens a room and makes it look more modern," Aunt Nita told Grandma and BeeWee.

"Who's doing it?" Grandma was anxious to know.

Aunt Nita informed them, "All my friends' parents have painted their mantles."

"I don't mind painting it," BeeWee offered. "But it'll take a few coats of paint to cover that dark wood."

Aunt Nita was so excited. "I'll be happy to buy all the paint!"

BeeWee turned to Grandma, "What do you say, Florence? I'll be glad to paint it, but it was your mother's house, so I think you should be the one to make the decision."

"Well, Juanita seems to think everyone's doing it, and that's what she wants, so I guess it'll be all right."

BeeWee and Aunt Nita were both considerate to consult Grandma about changing the color of the mantle. Nita was thoughtful to pay for the paint, and BeeWee was nice to agree to do the painting, even though he had a few other paint jobs to finish first. Grandma very wisely agreed. I could hardly wait to watch him paint.

A few days later, BeeWee got ready to paint the mantle ivory. Grandma helped him by taking everything off the two shelves and spreading newspapers on the floor. She kept a stack of newspapers on the back porch for things like BeeWee's painting projects, cleaning fish, Boy Scout paper drives, and dying eggs on Easter.

BeeWee put a coat of aluminum-colored paint on the mantle, which made it look awful.

"BeeWee, I thought you were going to paint the mantle ivory."

BeeWee chuckled. "I am, Sugie. This is just a primer coat to keep me from having to put on so many coats of ivory paint."

We all complimented BeeWee on the beautiful job he did of painting the mantle. It was tedious work, but he was remarkably good at it.

The Housing Shortage

Some evenings President Roosevelt gave speeches on the radio, which were called "Fireside Chats." When Grandma knew he was going to speak, she stopped everything she was doing, took the little Emerson radio to the living room, plugged it in, and the family sat around and listened intently to every word he said. He always said he didn't want our country to go to war, but he wanted us to be prepared, so he created jobs for defense workers to make the necessary preparations.

The Norfolk Naval Base, which was one of the largest naval bases in the world, was a ten-minute drive from Grandma's house. Numerous jobs were added there and at the Naval Shipyard. People came from all over the country to take jobs, and they had to have places to live.

Daddy was soon laid off from the railroad, and for a while, there were no auto mechanic jobs available. They couldn't even afford a furnished room, so they moved in with my grandparents. The only room not being used was the little room, which was all right for one adult with a high tolerance for cold and hot weather, but way too small for two people.

As you entered the little room on the left, there was a brown metal, twin-sized bed between the door and the wall, with a brown, metal-shaded reading light that hung over the high headboard. The one window in the room was on the front of the house. It had a translucent ivory-colored window shade raised halfway up the window and ivory lace curtains. There wasn't enough room for a chest of drawers to hold clothes, and the hook on the back of the door was already filled with black wire hangers that held our winter coats.

BeeWee put a hook on the inside of the closet door under the stairway. That was the only closet in the house. Grandma took the hangers with our coats on them off the little room door and hung them on the hook. The closet had a dark wooden door that opened into the back hall. Since we needed to use the woolen coats for extra bed covers on cold winter nights, it was not a convenient place to hang them. Only things like curtain stretchers and the iron Christmas tree stand were usually kept there.

Mama and Daddy Move In

I was born Shirley May Dawson on March 17, 1937. Grandma and BeeWee brought Mama and me to their house from the hospital. I was born when Daddy was working with his brother as an auto mechanic in North Carolina. Grandma said he came to the hospital that afternoon to see us, but he had to go right back.

BeeWee gave Daddy a good reference to get a railroad job. Mama and Daddy ended up moving so much to places that were single-furnished rooms in private homes with shared baths for all the tenants in the building.

Grandma wanted me to stay with her. Mama had to help Grandma to give me a bath and dress me because it gave her a backache to do things like that.

Daddy had to go on strike with the other railroad men numerous times. BeeWee didn't have to go on strike because he had seniority, having worked at the railroad much longer than Daddy. After that, Mama and Daddy came back to Grandma's to live.

Mama and Daddy didn't have anything to move into the house except their clothes and Daddy's guitar, which he said he'd bought from a pawn shop before he and Mama were married. He said one of his cousins played the guitar and taught him how to play.

He and Mama hung their coats in the hall closet and hung their clothes on the little room door hook. He propped his guitar in the corner.

It was the coldest time of the year, so they brought the little round electric space heater that they'd used when they rented rooms. They only used it when they got dressed because Grandma thought it was a fire hazard to have on while they were sleeping.

Daddy was as quiet as he always was. He got dressed every morning and stayed out all day, looking for a job as an auto mechanic. Grandma couldn't even persuade him to have a cup of coffee before he left the house. I don't think he felt comfortable living at my grandparents' house and not having a job because he was a hard worker.

It wasn't long before he came in one afternoon with an ear-to-ear grin that I'd never seen before. "I got a job, and I'm going back to work with my tools in the morning," he declared.

After working on automobiles all day, Daddy liked to take a bath and change his clothes before he and Mama went out to eat. Sometimes they went to a movie or visited Daddy's brother. By the time they got back to Grandma's house, it was time to go to bed. I was already asleep in my Aunt Nita's double bed in the next room.

Since Daddy was very quiet, we never knew when he was in the house unless we saw him. He got up early to go out for breakfast and go to work while Mama slept, so he was usually only in the house long enough to take a bath, shave, change clothes, and sleep. Mama sent his work clothes, pajamas, underwear, socks, and their sheets and pillowcase to the laundry, and he took their other clothes to a dry cleaner.

They weren't comfortable sleeping on a twin bed in that tiny, cold room, so they began to look for another place, which they thought would be nearby in a furnished room in someone's house so Daddy could drop off Mama at Grandma's every weekday morning and pick her up when he got off from work.

I liked the idea of Mama and Daddy moving in. It made us seem like a family.

Then, the day Daddy got his job, they moved to a newly furnished room, so our time together didn't last very long.

Mama and Daddy's New Apartment

One of the mechanics Daddy worked with knew he needed a place of his own and told him he had an apartment to sublet. Mama and Daddy could hardly believe it. They went to look at it and liked it better than any place they'd ever had. It was a second-floor apartment in a large brick building in Ghent. That neighborhood was near where Daddy worked and not too far from Grandma's house.

Daddy told the rental office that he'd paint all the rooms if they'd provide the paint. They provided gallon cans of ivory paint and a brush, and Daddy painted every night. Mama helped him by laying down old newspapers and cleaning up little paint spills. They decided to move in and take me with them because it was the first time they'd had a private bath and more than one room in any place they'd rented. I stayed with Grandma until Daddy finished painting all the rooms and letting them air out.

They were even able to buy some new bedroom furniture. They bought a light walnut bedroom suite similar to Aunt Nita's. Besides the bed, they had a dresser with a round mirror, a vanity with a round mirror and bench, a tall combination chest of drawers and a wardrobe, and a nightstand. They bought a big Philco console radio and a large green hassock, a footstool without legs, to set in front of it. Daddy liked to sit there, turning the knobs to tune it.

Mama kept the place clean and neat and got me ready every weekday afternoon to visit Grandma. We caught the bus across the street from the apartment building and rode as far as we could. Then we got off the bus and walked about four blocks to Grandma's. As we got closer to the house, I saw her standing at the front door, watching for us. She saw us coming up the walk and opened the screen door. I hurried up the steps, ran to Grandma, and she leaned over to hug me. "I certainly do miss my little sunshine," she said with tears in her eyes.

"I missed you, too, Grandma," I almost cried. Every time I went to Grandma's, I was so happy to see her that I climbed up on the sofa and jumped up and down. Next, I jumped down from the sofa and climbed up on a chair.

When I started jumping on the chair, Mama scolded me. "I want you to sit down on that chair and not move until I tell you it's all right to get up."

"She's just happy," defended Grandma.

"She can be happy without jumping on the furniture," Mama insisted.

Grandma explained to me. "Grandma's furniture is old. It's faded and worn, but I've always liked it because it belonged to my mother."

"I like your furniture, too, Grandma. It looks good to me."

"Well, thank you, honey; I appreciate that."

I didn't like living with Mama and Daddy. It was a nice apartment for them, but not for me. None of my toys were even there, and I had to share a bed with them. I don't like to say it, but I didn't feel any love from Mama and Daddy. I did feel the love from Grandma, BeeWee, and Aunt Nita.

Crying Over Spilled Milk

One afternoon when Mama and I went to Grandma's house, we went to the kitchen, and Grandma poured a small glass of milk for me.

As the three of us stood there, I accidentally spilled some of my milk on the floor.

Grandma didn't say anything, but Mama was mad.

"You wouldn't have spilled your milk if you'd paid attention to what you were doing," she said in a stern voice.

I became angry with her because I thought she should have known it was an accident. I'd never spilled anything on the floor or even on the kitchen or dining room table.

Being surprised at her reaction and not knowing how to handle my anger, I blurted out, "You made me do it."

It was a dumb thing for me to say because I knew she didn't make me do it, and it made her even madder at me. She raised her right hand to slap me on the top of my left arm.

Grandma, blaming herself for handing me the glass of milk, extended her arm to pull me toward her.

I tried to prevent Mama from slapping me by grabbing her arm and clamping my teeth on her wrist.

Grandma managed to keep me from being slapped, but I was shocked to see the imprint of my teeth on her wrist instead of Mama's. I grabbed the wrong wrist and hurt my wonderful grandmother, who was trying to help me.

I started sobbing and said, "I'm sorry, Grandma. I didn't mean to hurt you."

"Don't worry, honey. You didn't hurt me. The skin isn't even broken."

"Mama, you shouldn't take up for Shirley when she's done something wrong," said Mama disapprovingly.

"Florencie, she's just a child. She's only three years old. She couldn't help spilling the milk. I blame myself for not pouring the milk in her little cup so she could hold onto the handle," said Grandma.

After being with Grandma for twenty-four hours a day since I was born, I missed her when Mama and Daddy took me to live with them. I looked forward to seeing her every weekday afternoon, spending Saturday night with her, and going to Sunday school with her and BeeWee the next morning, the way I always did.

Mama told me to go into the living room and sit in the chair until I stopped crying. I curled up in a ball in the chair, cried myself to sleep, and woke up when Mama told me it was time for us to get ready to leave.

Daddy picked us up, and we went out to eat. I wasn't very hungry because of what had happened and because I was afraid Mama would tell Daddy, and he'd spank me.

Mama didn't tell him, but she and I barely spoke for the rest of the evening.

Shortly after we went to the apartment, I put on my pajamas and lay on my side of Mama's and Daddy's bed, hoping to fall asleep soon. I remembered something that Grandma often said about past mistakes that couldn't be changed. "There's no use in crying over spilled milk."

I realized I needed to stop worrying because I couldn't change what happened.

Mama took me to Grandma's house the next day, and we all had a nice time together, although I couldn't stop feeling guilty about Grandma's wrist. I looked at it every chance I got to see if it was better or worse. Within a couple of days, the marks were gone, but I knew I'd never forget them.

Living with Mama and Daddy

Although I was just as happy to see Grandma every time we visited her, I didn't jump on the living room furniture anymore. I did like to climb, though. I climbed on everything I could climb on, like the huge oak buffet at the back dining room wall. There was a brass-colored radiator beside it. I'd put a chair beside the radiator, step on the radiator, and then on the buffet. I liked to sit on the top shelf above the built-in mirror.

Mama sat at the kitchen table and listened to soap operas with Grandma while Grandma washed and dried dishes and put them away or washed clothes at the sink. They talked during the commercials.

BeeWee and Aunt Nita were always at work in the afternoons, so I hardly ever saw them anymore.

Each time I visited Grandma, I ran to the dining room doorway and looked up to see if the hooks were still there.

"Mama, will you hang up my swing?" I asked.

"It seems as though each time I hang up this swing, I have to raise it higher. You won't be able to use it much longer," she said.

Mama adjusted the swing so it would be higher, probably for the last time.

Daddy got off from work and picked up Mama and me. He was wearing the heavy white cotton shirt and heavy navy-blue pants that he worked in. He had a black coupe, which was a small two-door car. It had one seat that was wide enough for two people, but since I was just a small child and Mama was slim, they were able to squeeze me between them. We went to the apartment long enough for Daddy to take a bath and change into a sport shirt and slacks.

He drove to the Belmont Restaurant, which was less than a five-minute drive from the apartment. The restaurant was small, with some tables, chairs, and booths. We sat in a booth, with Mama and I on one side and Daddy on the other. I don't remember what we ordered, but we were very quiet. Mama left half of her food, so Daddy switched plates with her and finished it. They always did that.

Sometimes after supper, we went to see a movie at the Visulite Theater, which was across the street from the apartment. Mama said it had to be a movie with action because that's what Daddy liked to see. At first, I didn't sit still and watch the movies. I just watched the cartoons and played with the seats in our row in the nearly empty theater.

Humphrey Bogart and Edward G. Robinson were two of Daddy's favorite actors because they were often in crime movies. He also liked westerns and didn't mind seeing Tarzan movies. Daddy always sat on an aisle seat, Mama sat next to him, and I sat beside her. Within two or three minutes, Daddy fell asleep while Mama and I watched the movie. Mama nudged Daddy every time he snored.

I liked watching the Tarzan and western movies best because I could understand them. Even though I didn't understand parts of the other movies, they always ended by teaching that crime doesn't pay, which Mama and Daddy said was an important lesson for everyone to learn. I agreed with that.

While Daddy was working at the automobile dealership, he met some musicians who invited him and Mama to the place where they played music for Saturday night barn dances.

At first, Mama didn't want to go because there would be drinking there, and she didn't drink, but Daddy insisted that she go, at least to meet the musicians and listen to their music. She said she liked them and enjoyed listening to their music, but then Daddy insisted she join him in drinking, which she didn't want to do.

She went to BeeWee and told him she wanted to take me, leave Daddy, and go back to live with him and Grandma.

BeeWee said, "You made your bed; now you'll have to lie in it. You went with Bill from the time you were fourteen years old, and you knew he drank. If he wants you to drink with him when you go to a dance, it won't hurt you to have one drink just to be sociable."

Mama and Daddy continued going to the barn dances every Saturday night. They took me to Grandma's before they went, and I spent the night with her, which I looked forward to because I missed her.

My grandparents attended Sunday school at the Methodist church a few blocks from their house, and they said I was old enough to start going to a Sunday school class, too. Mama bought me a new dress, matching socks, and new black patent leather shoes. Grandma helped me to get ready. Grandma, BeeWee, and I went to separate classes, which we all liked very much. Grandma had taught me to say my prayers a long time ago, and we knelt beside the bed to say our prayers together every night.

Mama and Daddy picked me up on Sunday evenings.

I don't remember much about living in the apartment except for three incidents. One night while I was sleeping, I rolled off the bed and onto the floor. When I climbed back into bed, I noticed it was Mama's and Daddy's bed because Mama was sleeping in the middle, and Daddy was on the other side of her. Mama said she hung my clothes in her wardrobe, and I stood on a stool in front of it to reach the clothes that I wore when we went to Grandma's house, but I don't remember doing it. Then, there was the night that I lay on the bed thinking about the spilled milk. The apartment must have had only one bedroom since I didn't have a room.

The other thing I remember about the apartment is watching Mama scrubbing the kitchen floor. A box of Duz soap powder was sitting on the floor, and I decided I wanted to see how it smelled. The box top was open a little, and I opened it wider, stuck my nose as close to the powder as I could, and inhaled. Some of the powder went up my nose, and I nearly lost my breath. My nostrils kept stinging even after Mama wiped my nose with a wet washcloth. She was mad and told me never to do anything like that again.

Eventually, Mama and Daddy said they walked into their apartment after a Saturday night barn dance, turned on the lights, and saw roaches. Some of the roaches were flying. I'd never seen roaches.

Mama said Daddy was going to the rental office during his lunch hour on Monday to notify them about the roaches.

I was afraid of going back into the apartment and seeing flying roaches, so Grandma said I could stay with her on Sunday night.

Daddy brought Mama to Grandma's on Monday morning because I was there, and Mama was afraid to stay in the apartment by herself all day. When he got off from work and came to pick up Mama, he said the manager of the rental office said they were going to put roach powder around the baseboards of every room in the apartment on Tuesday.

Staying at Grandma's House

Grandma and Mama didn't think it was safe for me to inhale the roach powder. They also didn't trust me to stay out of it because I'd inhaled the Duz soap powder, so they agreed it would be best for me to stay with Grandma for a while. Part of the agreement was that Daddy would bring Mama to Grandma's every day before he went to work so she could take care of me during the day, the way she had done when they rented rooms. She would stay at her apartment on Saturdays and Sundays because she had to clean it, wash her hair, and get ready to go to the Saturday night barn dances. Daddy's only day off was Sunday, so she wanted to be with him on Sundays.

On Monday night, Mama and Daddy brought my clothes to Grandma's house. The large tricycle I'd gotten for Christmas was still in the corner of Grandma's dining room. From time to time, I got on it and stretched to try to reach the pedals, but I still couldn't ride it. After all, I wasn't quite three yet.

After Mama and Daddy left, Grandma and I sat side-by-side in the high back chair in the living room. The seven-and-a-half-watt bulb in the brass floor lamp cast just enough light over Grandma's left shoulder for her to see how to read one of my favorite stories, *Little Red Riding Hood*. I liked hearing that story over and over again because it was about a little girl going to visit her grandmother.

I'd always loved Grandma and felt comfortable being with her, but I was worried about being around BeeWee all the time because I knew he didn't want to be a grandfather, and I'd hated him for a while after he tried to hit Grandma. When he did that, I told him, "I hate you, BeeWee." He probably hadn't forgotten I'd said I hated him, either.

For a long time, I'd bitten my nails or my lower lip when I was worried about something. When I started to bite my nails that night, Grandma said, "Honey, please don't bite your nails anymore. You've already bitten them to the quick."

"What does that mean, Grandma?"

"It means you've bitten your nails down to the skin. If you bite any closer, the skin around your nails will bleed."

I stopped biting my fingernails, but I still bit my lower lip.

"We'll go upstairs at nine o'clock, but first, let's go back to the kitchen and listen to the radio." Grandma led the way into the kitchen, turned on the radio, and turned on the stove. She heated up water in a kettle for her cup of hot water and condensed milk and heated up milk in a Pyrex pan for my hot chocolate.

"Grandma, where am I going to sleep?"

"You're going to sleep in Juanita's bed."

The radio programs were funny, but I couldn't concentrate on them. Although I'd outgrown my crib and slept in Aunt Nita's bed every Saturday night for the past few months, I was worried that Aunt Nita wouldn't like the idea of my sleeping in her bed every night. "Grandma, I can sleep in the little room," I offered.

"Honey, it's winter, and there's no heat in the room."

"That's all right, Grandma. I can sleep under a lot of covers."

"You don't understand, honey. That room doesn't have a radiator, so it never gets any heat. It's as cold in there as it is outside."

"Grandma, I don't think Aunt Nita will want me to sleep with her all the time."

"Juanita won't mind," assured Grandma lovingly.

At nine o'clock, Grandma turned off the radio and gathered the things she took upstairs each night. She took a bottle of cold water from the refrigerator, the flat tin box of Bayer aspirins, the Baby Ben alarm clock that she kept on one of the top kitchen shelves during the day and two clear juice glasses. She made two trips upstairs to carry everything to Aunt Nita's room and set it on the ivory-colored mantle. When she came back for me, she turned off the oven and turned out the kitchen light. She'd already pressed the downstairs wall switch to turn on the front hall ceiling light so we could see how to walk up the steps. After we climbed all the steps, she pressed one of the upstairs wall switches to turn out the light.

The two front windows in Aunt Nita's room had translucent ivory-colored window shades raised halfway up the windows and ivory-colored lace curtains, the same as in every room of the house and the hall windows. Only the kitchen and bathroom windows didn't have lace curtains, just ivory window shades.

There was enough light shining in the room from the streetlight for me to see how to undress and put on my pajamas and my long, rose-colored chenille robe that I tied at the waist. Grandma took off her house dress and put her long white chenille robe over her plain white rayon slip. Her robe was made exactly like mine. It was cold in the room, and we slept in long robes to help to keep us warm.

Grandma said she let the fire go out in the coal stove every evening because she was afraid it would overheat while we were sleeping and catch the house on fire. When the fire went out in the stove, all the radiators in the house got cold and stopped heating the rooms. We weren't cold in the kitchen because Grandma turned on the oven and kept the oven door open until we were ready to go upstairs to go to bed.

Slipping in bed between the sheets was like slipping between two sheets of ice, and the pillowcase under my face felt freezing cold as I lay on my side and tried to draw myself into a ball by pulling my knees up under my chin. I wrapped my arms around my legs to hold myself in that position until Grandma finished piling enough woolen blankets and coats on the bed to warm me up. Then, I gradually slid my legs toward the foot of the bed.

Grandma laughed. "I guess you're warm enough for me to take the coats off now, so I'll hang them back on the little room door."

She'd taken the coats from the hall closet and hung them back in the little room after Mama and Daddy moved. Thank goodness she did because she had to go up and down the steps with the coats every night when they were here.

Trying to get warm took my mind off my worries about BeeWee's and Aunt Nita's reaction to my staying at Grandma's house all the time. Once I was warm and comfortable, I fell asleep.

By the time I woke up the next morning, it was fully daylight. Grandma had gotten up early and built a fire in the coal stove.

The room was getting warm, and she was standing by the bed. "Sit up, honey, so I can prop the pillows behind your back. I'm going to bring you something to drink to help you warm up and get your eyes open." She went downstairs and came back, holding my Peter Rabbit cup on a white saucer. "Try this and see if you like it," she said, handing the cup to me as she held the saucer.

The cup felt warm and was filled to about an inch from the top with a light tan drink that smelled good. I took one sip of the warm, creamy liquid and said, "It's delicious. What is it?"

"It's coffee with mostly milk, some pure cream, and a little sugar. There isn't too much coffee, just a little to flavor it. I've always brought BeeWee a cup of coffee every morning, and I think you're old enough now for me to bring a cup to you, too."

When I finished drinking it, she took the cup, and I thanked her. Before she went downstairs, she said I could get up, start putting on the clothes she'd set out for me, and come down for breakfast.

Grandma was loving, kind, and thoughtful. I loved her so much.

Aunt Nita must have come home after I fell asleep. She must have gotten ready for work before I woke up because I hadn't seen her. I'd often heard her say it was barely daylight when she left home in the morning. She said she liked to get to the telephone company early enough to eat breakfast in the cafeteria.

When I heard someone walking down the steps, I figured BeeWee must be going downstairs to eat his breakfast.

Even though I'd gotten dressed when Grandma asked me to, I didn't want to go downstairs yet because I thought if BeeWee saw me too often, he'd be reminded he was a grandfather and want me to leave.

The back door always had to be slammed so it would close all the way, so when I heard it slam, I thought BeeWee had gone out to the back yard, and I went downstairs to the kitchen. Grandma was standing at the stove, and Mama was sitting in a chair at the back of the table.

I was glad BeeWee wasn't in the kitchen, so he wouldn't have to see me.

"I thought you were still asleep," said Mama.

"No. I've been awake and dressed for a long time. I just wasn't ready to come down yet, Mama. What smells so good?"

"I've made coffee and fried eggs. Maybe that's what you smell," said Grandma. "Sit down, and I'll fry an egg for you. I'll get you a slice of nice fresh bread, and your mother can butter it for you while I'm frying the egg."

In a couple of minutes, Grandma put the fried egg on my plate and cut it into bite-sized pieces. The yolk was soft but not runny, and the white part of the egg was crispy around the edges. "I'm sorry I let the edges brown. I guess I had the burner turned up too high. I'll fry another egg for you," Grandma said apologetically.

"Can you fry it the same way? This is just the way I like it."

She laughed and made another cup of coffee for me, like the one she'd brought to the bed, and she set it beside my plate. I drank some of it as I was eating my buttered bread. Then I ate my second egg.

"I've never seen Shirley eat so much," remarked Mama.

"It makes me happy to see you enjoy eating something I've cooked," Grandma beamed.

I didn't want Grandma and BeeWee to think I was eating too much because they might not be able to afford for me to stay with them. In the future, I planned to eat what was first put on my plate and turn down any second helpings.

Grandma washed and dried breakfast dishes, and Mama put them on the shelves behind the glass doors of the cabinet. They talked for a while about the roach powder being put down in the apartment.

"I haven't seen one roach since they put down the powder."

"Well, that's good, Florencie." Grandma turned on the radio, and they listened to the news. After the newscast ended, Grandma turned off the radio, shook her head from side to side, and said, "I'm mighty afraid our country is going to war."

Mama pointed out, "We've heard all of President Roosevelt's 'Fireside Chats' and he has always said he doesn't want our country to go to war. President Roosevelt is a good man, and I believe he doesn't want our country to go to war, but he says he's preparing for war, just in case we're forced into it."

BeeWee came in, washed his hands at the sink, and said he was going upstairs to take his nap.

I went to the hall to swing.

Later, the wonderful aroma of Grandma's cooking filled the house again, so I went back to the kitchen to watch her cook. She stood in front of two black cast iron frying pans, holding a long turner in one hand and a long spoon in the other. The larger pan was filled with round steak ground patties and chopped onions in sizzling hot Fluffo shortening. Grandma turned the patties. Then, she used the long spoon to stir the potatoes and onions she was cooking in the smaller frying pan.

Mama sat at the table, adding mayonnaise, salt, and pepper to a clear glass bowl of lettuce and tomato salad. She stirred the salad with a silver-plated serving spoon and set the bowl in the middle of the table. Then, she took the white dishes from the cabinet and began setting the table. When the dishes were in place, she lifted the front side of the white oilcloth table cover and opened the drawer to get the knives, forks, and spoons to place beside the plates.

"I think everything's about ready, Florencie., so you can go upstairs and wake up your daddy." Grandma put the patties and lightly browned onions on a white platter trimmed with bluebirds and set it on top of the oven. Next, she filled a white bowl with potatoes and onions and set it on the table. Then, she placed the platter on the table.

Mama came back into the kitchen and poured coffee into the adults' cups. She poured milk into a small glass for me.

We sat down to eat before BeeWee came downstairs because Grandma said he liked for the food to cool before he ate it. Mama put food on my plate, but she didn't have to cut the meat because I could easily cut it with the edge of my fork as I ate. I'd had this meal at Grandma's before, so I knew it would taste as wonderful as it smelled.

We always bowed our heads and said grace before eating lunch. Grace was a short prayer that we said to thank God for our daily food and other blessings.

We were half-finished eating when BeeWee walked into the room dressed in his railroad clothes. He carried his railroad cap in his right hand and set it on the ledge of the cabinet beside his chair. Then, he sat down at the table, bowed his head to say grace silently, and ate his lunch. After finishing, he pulled a package of Camel cigarettes from his coat pocket, shook one out of the pack, and put it between his lips. He struck a match to light it and coughed as he inhaled and exhaled the smoke. When he finished smoking, he ground out the cigarette butt on his plate.

He pushed back in his chair, just far enough from the table to pull out his railroad watch, look at it, say it was time to go to work, push the chair back some more, and stand up. He picked up his cap from the shelf and walked toward the back door. As he passed the other side of the table, Grandma handed him his bag of sandwiches. He still carried his lunch in a brown paper lunch bag that was so wrinkled and thin it looked worn out.

"You have my two bean sandwiches in here, don't you?" he asked, raising the bag a little.

"They're in there," she said.

He kissed her on her forehead as usual, put on his cap, and said he'd see her tonight. She followed him to the back porch so she could hook the door when he left.

There had been no talking at the table from the time he entered the room because Grandma and Mama had always said he was grumpy when he first woke up from his nap.

Mama and Grandma talked as they cleared the table, and Grandma washed and rinsed the dishes. As Grandma set the rinsed dishes on the drain board, Mama dried them and put them on the shelves.

Then Mama said it was time for me to go upstairs for my bath and nap. She ran about two inches of warm water into the tub and handed me a washcloth and a bar of soap. It was so cold in the bathroom that I was shivering and getting goose bumps.

"Why is it so cold in here?" I asked.

"There's no radiator in the bathroom, so you'll have to bathe in a hurry and let me dry you quickly," said Mama as she stood beside the tub holding a bath towel. When I was dry, Mama opened the can of Johnson's baby powder, shook some into my cupped hands, and I rubbed it all over my body. "Run into the back bedroom and put on your clothes."

When I was dressed, Mama said I had to take a nap. She said I'd never taken a nap at the apartment because we'd slept late every morning, so I didn't need one. Now that I was getting up early again, I had to take a nap every afternoon. I lay on my back on the mauve-colored chenille bedspread, and she put a woolen blanket over me. I thought I'd lie there awake until Mama said it was time to get up, but I dozed off as soon as I closed my eyes.

Mama woke me up, and we went downstairs to the kitchen, where Mama and Grandma were listening to the afternoon soap operas and talking during commercials. Grandma was on her hands and knees, with a scrub bucket beside her and a big rag in her hand, scrubbing the blue patterned Congoleum rug on the kitchen floor. A Congoleum rug resembled linoleum, but it wasn't as expensive. The rugs came rolled up and were in different sizes. Grandma's rug was nine by twelve feet and covered the middle of the floor, with about a foot of dark oak wood showing around the edges.

Aunt Nita and Mama had often said that Grandma kept her floors so clean you could almost eat off of them. It was a joke, though. We would never eat food that fell on the floor. Grandma would be the first one to wash it off or throw it away, depending on what was dropped.

Grandma took the radio to the living room, and Mama plugged it into the wall outlet. They sat in there to listen to the soap operas while the kitchen floor was drying. Mama said soap operas were ongoing stories, and when you started listening to them, you had to listen every weekday, or you'd miss something. I went to the dining room to swing because I wanted to enjoy my swing as long as I could. I knew I'd outgrown it, but I wasn't ready to part with it yet.

Grandma's floor got dry, she took the radio back into the kitchen, and Daddy came for Mama.

I enjoyed talking with Grandma after we ate our Campbell's chicken noodle soup and bread and butter.

She told me BeeWee had been a streetcar conductor, and she was a cashier in a grocery store when they met. They were married when she was twenty-two, and he was twenty-four. He said he asked her to quit her job because he believed the man should be the breadwinner in the family. Like many men of his generation, he believed a married woman's place was in the home, cooking, cleaning, and caring for the children.

He eventually got a job as a pier car operator with the Norfolk and Western Railroad, and they had their first daughter, Florence Elizabeth. Grandma's mother's name was Mary Elizabeth. Their second daughter, Juanita Evelyn, was born four years later.

I liked listening to Grandma talk about her life.

Corner Markets, Supermarkets, and Milkmen

My grandparents bought their groceries from one of the locally owned grocery stores, a corner market a few blocks from their house. They bought a two weeks supply of groceries every payday, and Grandma sometimes called for a few items to be delivered before the next payday.

Before she dialed the number, she picked up the same yellow pencil that she always kept by the telephone. BeeWee kept it sharpened with his pocketknife. She jotted down a short grocery list on a small piece of paper and picked up the receiver.

"Grandma, can I dial the number," I asked.

"Sure, honey," she said as she slowly gave me one digit at a time.

If she ordered a loaf of bread, she said, "Mr. Dillard, be sure it's Nolde's bread and feel it to see if it's fresh because I don't want any stale bread."

Once, she ordered a small jar of sweet pickles and asked Mr. Dillard to be sure the pickles looked small and crisp because she couldn't stand soft pickles.

The groceries were delivered by a boy on a bicycle that had a big, wide wire basket on the front. Two delivery boys worked at the store. I liked both of them and always asked if they would give me a ride on their bikes. One boy, who appeared to be so young that he could barely maneuver the delivery bike looked scared to death of me and almost fell off his bike as he hurried from the yard. The other boy, who appeared to be a few years older, just smiled and said he had to get back to the store to make more deliveries. Grandma always gave them a tip, probably a nickel, which was enough to pay for a candy bar, a bottled soft drink, a small soda fountain drink, a single dip ice cream cone, and many other things.

The boys smiled and said, "Thank you."

Grandma said, "Don't mention it."

She always said that when anyone thanked her for something.

About two blocks away from that grocery store, the A and P supermarket chain store had already moved in. It was on a corner, but it was far larger than the local corner grocery stores. Including the large parking lot, it covered nearly half a city block. It had a large produce department, with a lot more room for fruits and vegetables than the market down the street had, so the larger store could sell more, especially since their prices were said to be lower. Grandma bought more potatoes and onions than any other fresh vegetables, so she could probably have saved money on them and on everything else, too, according to their newspaper ads.

Grandma and BeeWee actually drove a couple of blocks past the A and P store to get to Dillard's Market.

The supermarket also had a dairy case with all the dairy products, including bottles of milk, but Grandma ordered her milk from one of the several dairies in the area. Milkmen wore white uniforms and drove white trucks. They delivered milk in glass bottles that they placed on the porch beside the front door. After finishing a bottle of milk, Grandma washed the empty bottle and left it by the door the night before to be picked up when the new, full bottle was delivered. The milkmen came early in the morning while most people were still sleeping.

Mama didn't do much cooking, but she and Daddy shopped at the A and P store for all their groceries because they said the prices were lower. Sometimes Mama showed Grandma the A and P supermarket ads in the newspapers to prove that their prices were lower than the market's prices.

Grandma looked at the ads and said, "Uh huh, that's nice, but I can't shop there."

They were accustomed to shopping where the grocer knew them. When Grandma and BeeWee were "running short" of groceries and money a couple of days before payday, Grandma knew she could call the grocer, and he would deliver whatever she needed. They wouldn't have to pay anything until BeeWee got paid.

After cashing BeeWee's check, paying on the home loan if it was due, and paying whatever utility bills were due, they went to the market to "settle up" with the grocer and get more groceries every payday. Then, they stopped at the Chinese restaurant on 35th Street and ordered beef chop suey with steamed rice to take out, or they drove to Tegg's Log Cabin Barbecue at Ward's Corner, and Grandma went into order barbecues to take out. Ward's Corner seemed to be a long distance away because the speed limit was only twenty-five miles per hour. They took the food home, and Grandma made a pot of coffee to go with it. The takeout food was a treat we all looked forward to once every two weeks on BeeWee's payday.

Payday Agony

Although we always ended up having a treat at the end of BeeWee's paydays, BeeWee lost his temper with Grandma almost every payday morning. He thought she was trying to do too many things in the house before they left to cash his check and pay bills. He was worried about getting home late and being late for work.

He gave no thought to paying some of the bills the next day. It was important for him to be at work on time and to pay his bills on time. Waiting until the next day after payday to pay a bill would mean to him that he was paying the bill late.

It was important to Grandma to cook for her family, clean up afterward, and to keep a spotlessly clean house and clean clothes. She worked continually to please everyone in the family, which BeeWee didn't mind her doing except on payday mornings.

One payday morning, he called her a scrubwoman, and I'll always remember the hurt look in her eyes.

Another payday morning, he rushed her until she ran to the car and forgot about the string with strips of white cloth that BeeWee had tied between two sticks of wood to keep the birds from eating the grass seed he'd planted. She tripped over it and fell on her knees in the dirt, tearing the knees of her only pair of hose. I'll always remember the same hurt look in her eyes as he flew into a rage and yelled at her.

Flying into a rage is never becoming. It distorts a person's face and makes the person on the receiving end very sad.

Those who observe a loved one being treated in a demeaning manner are put in an unusual position. I loved both of them, even though I was with Grandma more and became closer to her. I loved BeeWee, too, because I thought he loved me and allowed me to live with them.

It made me sad. It made me want to tell him I hated him, but I didn't think I could say that and expect him to overlook it. I wouldn't blame him if he told me I'd have to leave his house. Instead, I instinctively became even closer to Grandma and slightly distant from BeeWee. I don't think he knew it because I kept it inside.

I still loved him; I just didn't like him yelling at my grandmother. She didn't deserve it.

Shopping, Buses, Streetcars, and a Switching

One day, Mama said I was outgrowing some of my clothes, and she needed to take me downtown to buy a few new things. The next day, we left Grandma's after lunch and walked a block and a half to the bus stop, which was on the corner of 35th Street and Colley Avenue, in front of a drugstore. Although it was a cold February day, I was comfortable in my legging set, which consisted of a tan woolen coat, leggings, and a hat.

We waited about five minutes for the bus to come to drive us downtown. When the bus stopped, the driver opened the door. Mama told me to step up, and she put the fare in the slot at the top of a small, clear glass box. The driver was friendly, asking us how we were and commenting on how it was a nice, sunny day. There were only a few people on the bus, so we had our choice of almost any seat. A block before our stop, Mama let me reach up and pull the cord that made a sound to let the driver know we wanted to get off at the next stop.

When we got off the bus, I noticed there were tracks in the middle of Granby Street. "Look, Mama! Railroad tracks!"

"They look like railroad tracks, but they're not. They're streetcar tracks."

"Grandma said BeeWee used to work on a streetcar."

"That's right, but we have buses now," said Mama.

"Aren't there any streetcars left?" I wondered.

"Some streetcars are still running, but they'll eventually be replaced by buses."

Mama took me to the Cinderella Shop and picked out some clothes for me. Then I stood beside her at a table of girls' white cotton underwear while she looked for my size. When she picked up an undershirt and turned to hold it in front of me to see if it was big enough, I was gone. She walked around the small shop to look for me, and as she neared the front door, she saw through the wide plate glass store window that I was outside in the street. She set down the things she was planning to purchase for me and ran outside to get me. Luckily for me, it was a side street that had little traffic.

Mama grabbed my hand and pulled me along with her.

"I don't know how you could do that to me. You had me scared to death. After the way you've behaved, I shouldn't buy you anything, but I'd be cutting off my nose to spite my face if I didn't buy the clothes we came for. As soon as I get you home, you're getting a switching, young lady," she said.

My mother's chilliness toward me matched the chilly, late afternoon air. She said nothing to me on the bus ride home and pulled the cord herself when the bus was a block from the 35th and Colley stop.

When we got to Grandma's house, and Grandma opened the door, Mama set her pocketbook and the bag of clothes on the sofa and headed for the back door. I knew she was going outside to get a long, fresh switch, just as she'd said she was going to do.

I took off my coat and hat and looked out the back kitchen window. I saw Mama break off a long twig from the wild cherry tree near the corner of the house. She carefully removed each leaf from the twig because it was the small, raised places where the leaves had been pulled off that caused a switching to break the skin and hurt.

Grandma looked out and saw what Mama was doing, too. "What did you do to make your mother so mad?" She wanted to know as I sat on the chair. She helped me take off my leggings.

"While Mama was in the store, picking out clothes for me, I left the store and went out in the street," I confessed.

"Oh, my Lord, have mercy! That was a dangerous thing to do. You could have been hit by a car, or someone could have taken you off, and we'd never see you again. No wonder she's mad."

Mama came up behind me and grabbed me by my left arm to hold me still as she switched my bare legs, but I tried to pull away. "Don't pull away from me, or I'll switch you harder," Mama warned.

The switching stung my legs and brought tears to my eyes, but I really started blubbering when I realized I'd ruined what started out to be such a nice day for Mama and me.

Grandma intervened by saying, "Florencie, don't you think that's enough?"

Mama stopped and said, "Those stripes on your legs are to remind you not to leave my side when we're in a store together and not to go in the street again."

The 'stripes' on my legs were the red scratches left by the switching.

"Spare the rod and spoil the child," said Mama.

That's how parents believed in disciplining their children. They learned it from their own parents and said it helped them to learn to behave.

New Beginnings

By March, there were signs of spring, such as the little pale-yellow daffodils that seemed to poke through the still-cold ground in Grandma's front yard overnight.

Grandma said spring was like a new beginning for flowers that had been dormant all winter.

"My mother planted those daffodil bulbs when she first bought the house, and they bloomed the next spring. Ever since then, they've been the first sign of spring in this yard," said Grandma.

Spring was like a new beginning for me, too, because I was beginning to appreciate the beauty of nature.

My birthday was coming soon. My mother said, "Shirley, I'd like to have a birthday party for you, but you don't have any friends."

I hadn't met any children because there weren't any children living on the street, so she didn't think I had any friends to invite.

"I have friends," I said. "I have Paulette, Gina, Arlene, Mattie, and Camille."

"They're your Aunt Nita's friends," Mama reminded me.

"They're my friends, too. They talk to me every time they call Aunt Nita."

Mama mentioned it to Aunt Nita, and she said it was all right to invite them, that those who didn't have to work would probably come.

On March 17th, BeeWee and Grandma took Mama and me to Mrs. Urquart's Bakery on Colley Avenue to pick up a round, white-iced, devil's food layer cake that had dark green writing and two shamrocks in icing in the center. Mama read the words: 'Happy 4th Birthday, Shirley.' She said the shamrocks stood for St. Patrick's Day.

When we came home from the bakery, Mama and Grandma put an ivory-colored lace tablecloth on the big round oak dining room table. Then Mama set the cake on a clear, cut glass cake stand that Grandma said had belonged to her mother. Mama opened packages of pink and white "Happy Birthday" paper plates and napkins. She placed them on the table. Then, Grandma set one of her mother's green glass punch cups at each place. Mama set a silver-plated fork at each place. Then, she opened a bag of little white cups and put two of them in each place. She put mints in one cup and peanuts in the other.

Excitement built up inside me until I thought I would burst, but that feeling was soon replaced by the feeling that Aunt Nita's friends probably weren't going to show up for a four-year-old child's birthday party. Aunt Nita had already said some of them couldn't come because they had to work. Camille and Gina had to work, but Paulette, Arlene, and Mattie came.

We stood around the dining room table while Mama lit the candles on the cake. She said I should make a wish, take a deep breath, and try to blow out all the candles so my wish would come true. I began worrying that I wouldn't be able to blow out all the candles with everyone watching me, but I tried with all my might and blew them out.

Mama sliced cake for everyone, and Grandma opened pints of Sealtest vanilla ice cream, cut it into slices, and put a slice on each plate beside the slice of white-frosted devil's food cake. Then Mama poured ginger ale into the punch cups.

Everyone agreed that the cake was the freshest we had ever had and that all the other refreshments went perfectly with the cake.

Then we sat in the living room, and they watched me open my presents. My family and Aunt Nita's friends gave me some nice gifts, such as a pair of soft cotton, red and white pinstriped pajamas from Paulette.

Everyone sat around talking for a while. Then Aunt Nita and her friends got ready to leave. They said they had a good time and thanked me for inviting them. I thanked them for coming and for giving me the gifts, as Mama, Grandma, and Aunt Nita had already told me to do, and we said goodbye.

When they left, and Grandma closed and locked the door behind them, I walked into the living room, let myself fall back on the sofa, and screamed.

"What in the world is the matter with you?" asked Mama.

"I'm so happy I can hardly stand it," I answered.

Grandma and Mama laughed.

"I think we can say that the party was a success," said Grandma beaming.

Mama agreed.

BeeWee's Trick, Chicken Pox, and My Tricycle

One morning when I went downstairs to eat breakfast, BeeWee said, "Sugie, there's a white string hanging down below the hem of your dress."

If a white string was hanging below the hem of a woman's or a girl's dress, it usually meant that the string was hanging from her slip because most women and girls wore white slips under their dresses and skirts. Slips worn by little girls were called underskirts. No woman or girl wanted to think her underwear was showing, even if it was just a string hanging from the bottom of her slip. If someone said your slip was showing or a string was hanging, you looked down immediately and tried to do something about it, such as leaving the room to look for a safety pin or a pair of scissors. It was a combination of wanting to be modest and neatly dressed.

When I looked down, BeeWee hollered, "April Fool!"

Realizing he had tricked me, I blurted out, "BeeWee!"

He threw his head back and laughed, seeming to take great pleasure in playing an April Fools' trick on me.

Grandma said, "Don't worry, honey. It's April Fools' Day, and BeeWee catches all of us with that same trick every year."

One morning in May, I woke up itching. I scratched the itchy places and didn't think much about it until I noticed two flat, pink dots near my waist. I showed them to Mama and Grandma. Grandma told Mama to call Dr. Kight, our family doctor. He said he'd stop by the house and take a look at me on the way home from his office that afternoon. Grandma said he was the doctor who delivered me to the hospital.

Dr. Kight appeared to be about the age of Grandma or BeeWee. He came up to the bedroom, wearing a brown suit and carrying a black leather doctor's kit. It took him about two minutes to look at the dots and say I had chicken pox, which meant I could expect to get many more spots and have a lot more itching.

The doctor also said I'd have to stay in the house for two weeks. He said if any adults in the family hadn't had chicken pox, I should be kept away from them. He said although it was a contagious childhood disease, it could adversely affect adults who'd never had it. Since BeeWee and Daddy didn't think they'd had chicken pox, I had to stay away from them.

That night, when Grandma told BeeWee I had chicken pox and had to stay in the house for two weeks, he said he was going to try to adjust my tricycle the next morning so I could ride it in the house every afternoon. He said he'd put wooden blocks on the pedals, lower the seat and the handlebars as low as they'd go, and we'd see if I'd grown enough to ride it.

I could hardly wait to go downstairs after BeeWee finished adjusting it. I saw it in the dining room, with the wooden blocks on the pedals.

"Can I try it out?" I asked Mama and Grandma, who were watching me.

"Go ahead," said Mama.

I sat on the tricycle, held on to the handlebars, extended my legs so my feet would reach the wooden blocks, and started pedaling. I rode around and around in the house for about five minutes. I was so excited I didn't want to stop to eat lunch, but Mama said Grandma was trying to keep the food warm for me and wanted me to eat before it got cold.

"Tell BeeWee I said, 'thank you for fixing my tricycle."

"I'll be sure to tell him when he comes home tonight," said Grandma.

It was fun having the tricycle to ride every afternoon. It made the days of being covered with itchy spots and having to stay in bed every morning much easier to endure.

I sat up in bed each day until BeeWee went to work. Grandma cooked my breakfast, and Mama brought it to the bed. I colored in my coloring book. Mama bought me some Old Maid cards and taught me how to play the game. She read to me from a little Whitman book, *A Child's Garden of Verses*, by Robert Louis Stevenson, and it became one of my favorites.

As soon as BeeWee left for work, I went downstairs and ate lunch. Mama ran my bath water. I'd take my bath, rub on some Johnson's baby powder, and put on clean pajamas and socks since I was just staying in the house. I got a lot of use out of the pajamas that Paulette gave me for my birthday. I didn't take a nap since I'd been sitting in bed all morning. I went back downstairs and rode my tricycle in my pajamas, socks, and bedroom slippers.

It must have been hard for Aunt Nita to have to sleep with a kid who was covered with itchy spots. It's a good thing she, Mama, and Grandma had already had chicken pox.

After I scratched until I put a small but fairly deep scratch on my face, Mama cut my fingernails as short as she could. She said if she didn't cut them, I'd have a face full of scratches that would leave scars. Since I'd stopped biting my nails, she'd started cutting them about once a week, but I didn't like getting my nails cut. I liked it even less now that I already felt miserable from all the itching.

I could hardly wait to be able to go downstairs every morning and to go outside again because Mama said I could start riding my tricycle on the sidewalk.

It was lucky for me that after all the scratching I did, I was left with only one small scar on my face.

The Bully

I liked riding my tricycle on the sidewalk. I was allowed to ride as far as the driveway of the house next door and to the front of the apartment building on the other side of Grandma's house. It was so nice to be outside in the sunshine, breathing fresh air again.

When a boy with short blond hair, who looked to be about my age and size, came out of the house next door and said his name was Darrell, I thought he was being friendly. Then, before I could tell him my name, he stepped in front of my tricycle, reached out and grabbed the middle of the handlebars, and gave them a little twist. "I could easily turn over your trike," he said, with a mean look on his face.

"Mama, Grandma!" I yelled as loudly as I could.

He removed his hands, ran to his house, and went back inside.

I rode to Grandma's as fast as I could, got off my tricycle, and ran to the door as Mama and Grandma, who thought they'd heard me, were opening it. Of course, there was no sign of Darrell by then.

Grandma and Mama told me a story about a little boy who cried wolf, and I didn't understand how that had anything to do with what happened to me. Mama said if there was a boy next door and he was bothering me, I should stay away from the front of his house.

I did as she suggested the next day, and the same thing happened again, this time near Grandma's driveway. When I hollered for Mama and Grandma, Darrell ran into his house again, but this time they said they were watching and saw him. They apologized for not believing me the first time, but they said they didn't know a little boy lived there. He must have moved in during the time I had to stay in the house.

"Mama, will you tell him to leave me alone?"

Then Mama surprised me by saying, "No. You'll have to tell him yourself."

"But I can't. I'm too scared. I'm afraid he'll hurt me," I insisted.

After that, each time that Mama asked me if I wanted to ride my tricycle outside, I told her, "No. I'd rather ride in the house."

Grandma's living room and dining room were spacious, and the hall, which extended from the front door to the kitchen, was wide, so I had plenty of room to ride.

Mama and Grandma turned the knob on the little brown Emerson radio on the kitchen table to soap operas every weekday afternoon.

Starting with *Ma Perkins*, there was a soap opera every fifteen minutes until the news came on around six o'clock. Some of the titles were *When a Girl Marries*, *Portia Faces Life*, *Young Widow Brown*, *Backstage Wife*, *Stella Dallas*, and *Lorenzo Jones*. I remembered the names of the soap operas because I liked to listen to the way they came on. The announcer was always a man with an eloquent voice. He said something like, "Portia Faces Life. When we left you yesterday, Portia was trying to decide…what will her decision be…? Stay tuned to find out, but first, a message from our sponsor."

Of course, the sponsor was the soap company, and the messages were the commercials, such as "Duz does everything," "Rinso white, Rinso bright," and "Ivory soap, ninety-nine and forty-four one-hundredths percent pure."

I rode my tricycle from room to room, up and down the hall, singing the soap jingles, but I tried to make it back to the kitchen to hear the announcer sign off.

He said, "Be sure to tune in tomorrow to find out if Portia.…"

I didn't know what any of the stories were about because I didn't listen to them.

During the week that I rode my tricycle in the house, I began to stop feeling sorry for myself because Mama hadn't told Darrell to leave me alone.

I felt bad because I'd let Darrell bully me, and I hadn't defended myself. When I yelled for Mama and Grandma, Darrell knew I was scared, which I was. Somehow, I got up the nerve to try to handle it myself, but I don't think I would have if Darrell had been older and larger. I didn't know what I'd do, but I knew I had to do something because I wanted to ride my tricycle on the sidewalk again.

The next day, I asked Mama to set my tricycle on the sidewalk so I could ride. I deliberately rode as far as Darrell's driveway, hoping he'd see me.

When he came out of his house, I was madder than I was scared because I thought he was about to taunt me again.

I still didn't know what I'd do. I just knew I'd had enough, and I wasn't going to take it anymore.

Then he threatened me the same way he'd done before, and I heard myself say, "If you don't move your hands and get out of my way, I'll get off my tricycle and hit you as hard as I can."

Darrell looked astonished and said, "Can you come over to my house in the morning?"

Darrell's House and the Ice Man

I told Mama that Darrell invited me to his house, and she said I could go.

The next morning, I went to his house, and he came to the door as if he'd been watching for me. "I forgot to ask you your name," he admitted.

"My name is Shirley."

"Come in. I want you to meet my mother and my sister. My daddy's not here. He's away on a ship in the Navy."

I followed him upstairs and stopped behind him at the bathroom door. His mother was kneeling over the bathtub, scrubbing clothes on a washboard.

"Mama, this is Shirley."

"Hello, Shirley." She smiled after she stood up and turned toward us. She was tall, slim, and young, with shoulder-length, wavy auburn hair. She dried her hands on the bottom of a white apron that was tied in a bow at the back of her waist. She then lifted a baby from a metal stroller.

"This is Darrell's sister, Brenda. She's nine months old," she told me while holding the baby on her hip. The baby was wearing a white cloth diaper, pinned with a large, silver-colored safety pin on each side.

Then we heard a man's voice coming from the direction of the screen door downstairs. "Ice man!" he shouted.

"Oh. The ice man's here. I have to go downstairs to let him in," she excused herself, and we all went downstairs to the door.

"Do you want your usual twenty-five pounds of ice today?" he asked through the screen door.

"Yes. That'll be fine," Darrell's mother replied.

The iceman walked to the orange truck parked at the curb, slipped his hands into heavy-looking, rough leather gloves, picked up huge tongs, and extracted a big block of ice from blocks of ice that were piled up from the middle to the back of the truck.

"Can we have a piece of that ice?" Darrell pointed to the slivers of ice near the edge of the truck bed.

The man nodded to indicate that it was all right.

"Go ahead and take one, but don't get one that's too big, or it'll freeze your hands," Darrell warned, picking up a medium-sized sliver for himself.

I picked up a sliver a little smaller than his, and we walked to a narrow strip of grass beside his driveway. The ice in my hand felt cold. It was a warm, sunny day, so we stood in the shade under a pretty tree, so our ice wouldn't melt. "This is a powder puff tree. See all the pink powder puffs on it?" Darrell pointed out.

"It's pretty," I said. "Where's the man putting all that ice?"

"He's putting it in the ice box to keep the food cold. Don't you have an ice box in your house?"

"No. My grandma has a refrigerator to keep the food cold. She says I can't keep opening and closing the door, or the food will spoil."

"That's what my mother tells me about the icebox. She says it makes the ice melt faster, too."

"This ice tastes good. It's so clear, not cloudy like ice cubes," I told Darrell.

"Ice cubes? What are they?"

I explained, "They're little blocks of ice that Grandma makes by putting water in two metal trays in the frozen part of the refrigerator. After the water stays in there for a long time, it turns to ice."

"I've never had ice cubes."

"It's just as well. Grandma says ice cubes aren't good to eat because they have a refrigerator taste."

"Then, what do you do with them?" he wondered.

"My mother puts ice cubes in glasses and then pours in the warm tea that Grandma makes every morning when the weather's warm. The ice makes the tea cold, and you get iced tea."

"That doesn't sound very good. Do you have to drink that?"

"Yes, but what makes it good is that I put a lot of sugar in the tea and stir it with a long iced tea spoon. Then, I squeeze in lemon juice and stir the tea some more."

"First you make it sweet, then you make it sour?" he was curious.

"You just squeeze in a little lemon juice, not enough to make it sour. It's good."

Mama called me in for lunch a few minutes before we were going to eat because she and Grandma wanted to know if I'd had a good time at Darrell's house and to find out what we'd done.

I told them about my morning and told Grandma about Darrell's mother using a washboard. "Grandma, you should get a washboard so you can scrub the clothes on the board instead of having to scrub them with your hands."

"Thank you for thinking about me, honey. I know my hands stay red and rough from keeping them in water, scrubbing all the time, but I've tried using a washboard, and it almost kills my back to lean over the tub," said Grandma wearily.

"So, you like Darrell now?" asked Mama, changing the subject.

"I liked him today," I said cautiously. "I didn't know he could act so nice."

"I'm glad you're getting along well together now. You should ask him to play in the back yard with you sometime," Mama proposed.

Since Darrell had bullied me at that time, I never really thought that we would be friends. However, he did end up being a great playmate for me; he fulfilled the tomboy side of me that the girls in the neighborhood couldn't fulfill.

Grandma's Kitchen

Just before lunch, the house always had the wonderful smell of whatever Grandma was cooking.

The kitchen was next to the dining room, but there was no doorway between the two rooms. The kitchen doorway led to the hall, so when Grandma was serving a meal, she had to take everything through the back hallway to the doorway leading to the dining room. It was inconvenient and unusual because there was a door leading from the dining room to the back porch. The big oak buffet took up nearly the entire back dining room wall and blocked the door.

Grandma may not have used the dining room for everyday meals anyway because even though she put in long hours of hard work in the kitchen, she said it was her favorite room in the house. The family spent much more time sitting on hard wooden chairs around the kitchen table, talking with Grandma, and listening to the radio than sitting on the soft living room chairs and sofa, but I don't think any of us paid much attention to the fact that the kitchen chairs were hard. We just wanted to be with Grandma.

Our lunch was actually our dinner because BeeWee worked the three to eleven shift, and Aunt Nita usually ate out with her friends at supper time. Daddy picked up Mama about six o'clock, so Grandma and I were the only ones at home for supper. We had a bowl of Campbell's soup with all the fresh white bread and butter we wanted. There were several flavors of Campbell's soup. I liked Chicken Noodle, Vegetable, and Bean with Bacon the best. Grandma's favorites were Chicken Gumbo, Chicken Rice, and Vegetable Beef.

Grandma always gave me a choice of two soups. She said, "Do you want noodles or gumbo soup for your supper tonight?"

By the time we ate supper around six o'clock, Grandma had been working for at least twelve hours.

Grandma listened to the news every time it came on the radio, so the news was always on at suppertime. It only lasted for fifteen minutes. Then some soft music came on, which we hardly listened to because we were talking. We could carry on a conversation about almost anything.

It was still spring, and the evening air was chilly, so we'd usually stay in the kitchen after supper and listen to the radio programs we both liked. Grandma's favorite was *Jack Benny*, which was the most popular radio show in the country. Jack Benny could really make us laugh. You knew nearly everyone in the country who didn't have to work at night would be watching the show. He was a very funny comedian, who supposedly played the part of himself, but it was in name only. His real wife, Mary Livingston, played the part of his wife on the show, and actors played the roles of his employees, Dennis and Rochester. He pretended to be a cheapskate and a terrible violinist who could only play the beginning of one song, *Love in Bloom*. He was so cheap that he had a pay phone in his living room. Grandma laughed a lot when *Jack Benny* was on. I liked to see her laugh because she was usually very serious.

I enjoyed all the weeknight programs that we listened to, but I especially liked *Fibber McGee and Molly* because Fibber McGee had a junky closet he would open at some point on every show, causing everything in it to come clattering to the floor. It took a long time for all the junk to fall, as his wife Molly, who hadn't wanted him to open the closet door in the first place, kept yelling, 'Oh, no!' I always thought that was hilarious.

Daily Rituals

The nine o'clock gun is a cannon at the Norfolk Naval Shipyard in Portsmouth, Virginia, which is across the Elizabeth River from Norfolk, Virginia. Traditionally, the cannon had gone off every night at nine. I soon realized the nine o'clock gun was the signal for Grandma to get ready to take me upstairs to bed.

After putting on my pajamas, I knelt beside the bed and waited for Grandma to kneel beside me so we could say our prayers. We started by saying, "Now I lay me down to sleep…" Next, we asked God to bless each person in our family as we named each one, and we asked Him to bless us. Finally, we said, "Amen."

I climbed across the bed to my side and lay on my back, waiting for Grandma to get in bed.

She wound the Baby Ben clock and set the alarm to be sure she would wake up at eleven, so she could be downstairs to open the doors for Aunt Nita and BeeWee when they came home. Then she lay down beside me. Every night she lay on her back for about a minute and then said, "It hurts me to lie on my back. I've got to turn over on my side." She turned over on her right side, with her back to me. I turned in the same direction, snuggled as close to her as I could get, put my arm around her waist, and fell asleep.

When I woke up the next morning, Aunt Nita had gone to work, and Grandma was propping the pillows behind my back so I could sit up and drink my coffee.

She said it would help me to get my eyes open.

"Grandma, I wish you had someone to bring you coffee to the bed. How do you get your eyes open?"

"Don't worry about me, honey," Grandma explained her routine. "I splash cold water on my face, and I make a pot of coffee as soon as I go downstairs every morning. I'm sitting at the kitchen table, drinking my first cup of coffee while you're still sleeping."

"But you have to make it yourself, and you don't have anyone to take it to you when you're still in bed," I noticed.

"That's all right, honey. I don't mind."

"I've never seen you eat breakfast, Grandma. When do you eat your breakfast?"

Grandma explained that she had her first cup of coffee to warm up. After she built a fire in the coal stove, she had her second cup of coffee with a slice of fresh white bread and butter and a bowl of Cream of Wheat with a little butter in it. She made enough Cream of Wheat for BeeWee to have a bowl of it when he ate breakfast. She kept it warm, and when he came downstairs, she soft-fried an egg to put in the center of it. He liked it, with a slice of fresh white bread, butter, and apple butter. Grandma mentioned she didn't like to eat eggs, but she liked cooking them for us.

Mama only had a cup of coffee; she'd already had breakfast with Daddy.

I noticed that BeeWee drank his coffee by pouring a small amount into his saucer. He waited a minute for it to cool, and then he sipped it from the saucer.

One morning after he'd gone out in the back yard, I said, "Mama, I want to start drinking my coffee the way BeeWee drinks his."

"You may as well forget about that because you're not going to do it," Mama declared.

"Why won't you let me do it?"

"Because it's bad manners to drink out of a saucer."

"But BeeWee does it."

"BeeWee pours his coffee in his saucer to cool it because he thinks drinking hot coffee and eating hot food causes cancer."

Grandma interjected, "He worries about drinking hot coffee, but he smokes two packs of Camel cigarettes a day. I think the cigarettes are bad for him. It seems to me that he coughs every time he smokes one."

Mama chimed in, "Bill smokes two packs of Lucky Strikes a day. He falls asleep in the living room chair with a cigarette in his mouth every night. When he snores, the cigarette falls out on his shirt and burns a hole in it. When it burns through to his skin, he wakes up."

Sometimes I saw Daddy wearing a light blue sport shirt with a little round hole that was brown around the edges. The hole was near his left pocket, and I saw his white undershirt through it. Now I knew it must be a cigarette burn.

"That's dangerous!" Grandma exclaimed. "The cigarette could fall down on the chair cushion and start a fire. Can't you watch him and take the cigarette out of his mouth before it falls out?"

Mama sighed. "I try, but if he wakes up and catches me taking his cigarette, he gets mad."

"Well, if it were me, I'd rather for him to be mad than to risk starting a fire."

Mama got up and pushed her chair under the table. "That's easier said than done."

Great Day in the Morning

"Can I go in the back yard?" I asked as I did every morning after breakfast.

"May I go in the back yard," corrected Aunt Nita on one of her rare mornings at home.

"Aunt Nita, why do you have to ask to go in the back yard?"

"I don't have to ask. I'm trying to teach you to say, 'may I' instead of 'can I'," she clarified.

"Oh."

"You can go outside as soon as you brush your teeth and let me plait your hair," said Mama.

I had long, straight-as-a-stick, dark blonde hair that I wore down when the weather was cold, but when it started getting warmer, Mama parted my hair in the middle and plaited each side, which was the same as braiding.

As soon as Mama finished fixing my hair, I went into the back yard. It was a beautiful, warm, sunny morning. I looked for BeeWee to see what he was doing, but he wasn't in the back yard or in the woodshed. He was in the front yard, bending over some pretty burgundy and white flowers, so I walked over to watch him.

"Well, it's a great day in the morning. Look who's here. Hello there, Sugie," he called out.

"Hello, BeeWee. What're you doing?"

"I'm pulling weeds from around my favorite flowers – Sweet Williams. Remember when I planted them?"

"I don't remember any pretty flowers like these."

"That's because they grew from the seeds I planted last year."

"I remember when you planted the seeds." I saw that BeeWee didn't have to take the cigarette he was smoking out of his mouth to talk. I also noticed that he seemed to cough even more than last year.

"There's no wonder you like them so much. They're pretty, and they smell good."

"I guess that's why I like them," he said with a twinkle in his eye.

"Where did you get the seeds?"

"I bought them from the store. One day I'll show you where I got them," he offered. "You know, it's a funny thing. Remember when I put up this white picket fence last year because your grandma was afraid a coal truck would back into the house?"

"I remember."

"Now she's worried that a coal truck will back into the fence." BeeWee chuckled, straightened up from his bent-over position, tossed what was left of his cigarette on the sidewalk, and ground out the remaining fire in it with the sole of his scuffed brown work shoe. "Well, I've got some work to do in the woodshed now."

I followed him to the woodshed to see what he was going to do. While he was unlocking the door, I started looking around and noticed something over the door and asked about it. BeeWee said it was a horseshoe he'd nailed there for good luck.

Then, to the right of the door, I saw the most amazing tree trunk. It was shaped like the back and neck of a horse. The back part was growing next to the woodshed, and the neck part was leading to the woodshed roof. The bark covering the trunk was smooth and gray. "What kind of tree is that BeeWee?"

"It's not really a tree. It's a wisteria vine that your great-grandmother planted so long ago that it's gotten a big, strong trunk and vines on it and spread out all over the place," he explained. He walked into the woodshed, and I climbed on the "horse's back" part of the trunk, stood up, and pulled myself up the "horse's neck" by holding onto a strong, hanging vine. I sat on the roof with my feet and legs dangling over the edge.

Then I looked up and thought I'd never seen anything so beautiful. The wisteria was like a canopy over the woodshed and half of the yard. Purple flowers hung like clusters of grapes. Green leaves surrounded the purple flowers with a density that allowed only a few patches of bright blue sky to peek in.

It was so beautiful and peaceful up there; I thought it was like Heaven. Anyway, it made me feel closer to God and Heaven. It was a good place to think.

I thought about how much I loved my family, but I didn't think I fit in. Mama and Daddy moved a lot and never had room for me. When they moved into the apartment, I didn't live with them long before they took me back to stay with Grandma.

Daddy's car was designed for two people, and he hardly noticed me. BeeWee thought he was too young to be a grandfather, but I could understand that. When I was born, his two daughters were still teenagers, fifteen and nineteen years old, and he was in his forties. I didn't think it was right for Aunt Nita to have to share her new bed with me. I didn't know if she stayed out with her friends all the time because she was that happy-go-lucky or if she just tried to spend as little time at home as possible. Even though I loved Grandma, and I knew she loved me, she told Mama she would have to come to take care of me every day. I could understand that, too, because Grandma had already raised two daughters of her own.

Grandma and BeeWee were kind and loving toward me, but I didn't know how long I would be staying with them. I was supposed to be there because roach powder was put down in Mama's and Daddy's apartment, but how long would that last? I never knew when they were going to say it was time for me to go back to live with them. I'd gotten so accustomed to my grandparents that I would like to live with them, but no one ever said I was living there. They said I was 'staying' there. Maybe they were just putting up with me until Mama and Daddy took me back to their apartment. Since I didn't 'live' with them and didn't 'live' with my parents, I didn't seem to have a place anywhere.

If Mama and Daddy came one day and said they were ready to take me to live with them, I knew I'd miss being with Grandma the way I missed her when I lived with Mama and Daddy. I'd miss hearing her call me, honey. I loved her so much because I knew she loved me all the time, almost unconditionally. She cared about my well-being, bringing me coffee to bed every morning, buying little Whitman books and reading them to me, carrying on conversations with me as though we were equals, listening to radio programs with me, laughing with me, working so hard for her family, telling me about her mother, and dozens of other things. I'd miss everything about her.

I would miss the way BeeWee called me Sugie, sat in his chair at the kitchen table and lifted me up on his knee, put his arm around me, nuzzled my cheek with his chin, and handed me a shiny half-dollar every payday, letting me follow him in the yard and watch what he did, carrying me upstairs when I fell asleep in the car late at night.

I would miss BeeWee because I loved him, too, except when he was mean to Grandma. Like when he said mean things to her on paydays when he was ready to go out, but she still had some chores to finish before they could leave. On days like that, I couldn't help hating him for a while.

I would miss Aunt Nita sitting beside me in the living room chair every Sunday evening, reading the Sunday funnies to me. Whenever I woke up when she came home at night, we would take turns scratching each other's backs. I'd miss that, too. She let me talk to her friends because she knew I didn't have any, she let me watch her sew when she made the coat for my doll, she bought riding breeches for my birthday, and she never complained about my sleeping in her bed.

Grandma and BeeWee took me to Sunday school every Sunday and went to their own Sunday school classes. I liked learning about God.

I liked kneeling by the bed and praying with Grandma every night. She had great faith in God, and I admired that. She taught me to have the same faith in God that she had, and I'm thankful for that.

Sitting on the edge of the woodshed that beautiful morning, under the canopy of purple wisteria, with patches of blue sky peeking through, I felt as though I was one with the world as if I'd been lifted to Heaven long enough to feel God's presence in my life more than ever. It was as though

He was telling me to have faith in Him, and He would see me through. He would do what He knew was best for me in my life.

It felt like God was saying, "Don't worry. Trust in me, have faith in me, and I will see you through."

I hoped and prayed that I would be able to live with Grandma and Mama would come to take care of me every weekday, as she had been doing. Then, knowing that God had been with me so far in my life, I prayed that He would always be with me and with my family.

In His own way, God let me know that everything would be all right because I wasn't worried anymore. My life was in God's hands.

I climbed down the trunk of the wisteria and walked to the woodshed door in time to see BeeWee putting the finishing touches on something white with red feathers that he was making at his workbench. He said it was a fishing lure.

He hung it on a line that stretched from one end of his workbench to the other and turned out the light. "What do you say we go in and get ready for lunch, Sugie?"

"I think that's a good idea, BeeWee."

When we got halfway across the yard, the wonderful smell of fried pork chops was pushing its way through the back kitchen window screen.

BeeWee washed his hands at the sink and said he was going upstairs to take his nap. He took a nap every day, either before or after lunch, depending on what we were doing. In an hour, Grandma sent Mama upstairs to tell him it was time to get up. On weekends, when Mama wasn't there, Grandma went upstairs to wake him.

He came to the table dressed in his railroad clothes.

Grandma walked to the stove, picked up a long fork, and lifted the sizzling pork chops from the frying pan to the white platter trimmed with bluebirds. When she put the platter on the table and sat down, we said grace, and everyone began serving themselves except me.

Mama put a pork chop on my plate and cut it into small pieces. Then, she put a spoonful of pork chop-flavored pork and beans and a spoonful of lettuce and tomato salad on my plate. I always liked having a slice of bread and butter with this meal.

BeeWee finished eating, stood up, pulled out his railroad watch, and looked at the time the way he always did. After checking the time, he said, "It's almost two o'clock, time for me to go to work. Do you have my sandwiches ready, Florence?"

"They're right here, Clarence," she said, handing him the same almost worn-out brown paper lunch bag that he seemed to take his lunch in every day. It made me wonder how long someone could use a brown paper bag before it fell apart.

"Did you put two bean sandwiches in here for me?" he asked, holding up the bag.

He said something about the sandwiches every day, too.

"You know I always do," she said, smiling.

BeeWee kissed Grandma on the forehead, walked to the back door, put on his cap, and told Grandma he'd be home a few minutes after eleven.

Mama and Grandma said they didn't know how BeeWee could eat two bean sandwiches for his supper every night and not want a new bag for his lunch until the old one was completely worn out.

"Doesn't he take anything to drink?" I asked.

"He says he only wants water, and he can get it at work," Grandma explained as she sat down.

"You look worried, Mama. What's the matter?" Mama said to Grandma.

Grandma shook her head. "Well, after listening to the news today, I'm mighty afraid we're going to have war." Grandma almost always said that after listening to the news.

"But President Roosevelt says he doesn't want our country to go to war," Mama reminded her.

"I know he says that in every one of his 'Fireside Chats,' but he's doing more all the time to get ready," worried Grandma. "He says he doesn't want war, and I know he means it in his heart, but I think it's going to get to the point where the poor man doesn't have a choice."

After hearing them talk about it so much, I finally had to ask, "What is war?"

"You and Grandma can talk about that tonight. Right now, we have to go upstairs so you can take your bath and your nap."

A Typical Summer Afternoon at Grandma's House

Mama ran water in the tub for my bath. It was a white porcelain tub on curved legs. I liked the way it sat beside the open window because I could look through the screen and see the top of the pretty, pink-flowered tree beside Grandma's driveway. Mama said it was a crepe myrtle tree that my great-grandmother had planted.

I liked taking my bath at Grandma's when the weather was warm. I didn't have to hurry because it wasn't cold in the room; I liked the way I could feel the fresh air coming through the screen.

I had time to observe what the room actually looked like. It had medium blue wooden wainscoting and chair rails around the lower part of the walls. The small, wooden, mirrored medicine cabinet was also painted medium blue. The top of the walls, the ceiling, the door, and the bottom of the tub were painted ivory.

While I was washing with Cashmere Bouquet soap and a washcloth, Mama pulled a small wooden, ivory-painted Windsor chair closer to the tub and sat reading a love story from her *Modern Romance* magazine. I knew my bath would last as long as it took her to read one of the stories. I got to stay in the tub longer if she was reading a longer story. Then, the water got cool, and my fingers and toes were a little shriveled by the time I got out of the tub.

She stood up, put down the magazine, grabbed a towel from the rack, and handed it to me to dry myself. She dried the middle of my back, which I had a hard time reaching. Then, she said, "Hold out your hands."

I knew to cup my hands because she was going to shake Johnson's Baby Powder from a tall can into my hands, so I could rub it on my body to smell nice. Then, I put on the clean white underwear that she held out and ran into Grandma's and BeeWee's room to take my nap on their bed. They had a dark-colored metal bed and dark oak furniture.

It was relaxing to lie on my back on the soft, mauve-colored chenille bedspread, with a soft, feather pillow under my head, and look around the room. I took in the tall wardrobe with the mirrored doors, the chest of drawers, the dresser and mirror, the open, screened windows, the dark green window shades pulled halfway down the window, and the ivory-colored lace curtains. Then, I got sleepier and sleepier and drifted off to sleep.

Grandma said she and BeeWee were never satisfied with the shades and the curtains in their room. She didn't like the window shades that were dark green on the inside of the room and ivory on the other side. He liked them because they helped to darken the room in the afternoon when he took his nap. BeeWee thought the lace curtains looked too feminine for a bedroom where a man slept, but they compromised and kept both.

After my nap, I dressed in the clean clothes Mama had set out for me, put on my sandals, and went downstairs.

She set my tricycle on the sidewalk, and I rode until I heard the sounds of the hucksters headed our way. They always yelled, "Can-ta-loupe!"

Then, I heard the clop, clop of the horseshoes on the asphalt as the horse slowly trotted up the street. It was a brown workhorse, pulling the dark green wooden wagon with big round wheels that had tan-colored wooden spokes. Poles extended a few feet above the wagon to hold up a dark green canvas canopy to shade the men and the produce in the wagon. There was no shade for the horse.

The hucksters shouted until the first housewife in her plain cotton housedress came outside, clutching a little change purse, to buy a small amount of fruit or vegetables. After they stopped near the curb, a few more ladies, wearing their plain cotton housedresses and clutching their small change purses, approached the wagon. Each lady carried her own container for whatever she was buying.

The hucksters wore wide-brimmed straw hats and clothes that were faded to the point of being colorless. One man sat on a seat at the front of the wagon, holding the horse's reins, and the other man stood on a step at the back, holding onto a pole. He would step down to select what each lady wanted, weigh the fruit or vegetables, and state the price. The lady would open her change purse, take out a few coins and hand them to the man. Then he would empty her purchase from the scale to her container.

Grandma and the other ladies usually bought only a few vegetables, never any fruit. I wondered who bought the watermelon, cantaloupe, and peaches. Sometimes Grandma said, "I think I'll buy a few snaps." This meant she was going to buy green beans. She called them snaps because the ends had to be snapped off before they were cooked.

The only time Grandma sat on the front porch during the day was when she snapped the green beans or shelled the butterbeans she'd just bought. If she bought butterbeans, she sat on the porch and shelled them. It hurt Grandma's fingers to open the tough green shells, so she only bought a few once in a while.

Grandma enjoyed the porch since Aunt Nita had paid for BeeWee to buy the paint to give the floor and the steps a fresh coat of light gray paint. Aunt Nita had also bought a good-looking maroon and white glider with maroon cushions and dark green and white striped canvas awnings to shade the porch from the glare of the sun during the day and the streetlight at night.

Gliders and awnings were fashionable, but BeeWee wouldn't have been able to afford them.

Sometimes Grandma said, "I think I'll buy a couple of ears of corn to cut off the cob and cook with the butterbeans."

When her fingers were too sore to shell butterbeans, she bought several ears of corn, boiled them, cut the corn from the cob, and fried it with butter in the small iron frying pan. She wouldn't shuck the corn on the porch, though. She said she'd shuck it in the kitchen to keep the corn silk from getting on the new glider or the porch floor.

Grandma never gave special names to anything she cooked. She called succotash "corn and butterbeans." We didn't care what she called it; we just knew whatever she cooked was good.

Not long after the hucksters left, I started listening for the ringing of the popsicle man's bell. While I waited for him, I rode my tricycle and tried to decide which flavor I wanted. Would I get my favorite, a banana popsicle, or my second favorite, an orange popsicle?

When I heard his bell, I ran to the screen door and yelled, "The popsicle man's coming! Hurry! He's almost here!"

Mama had already said she'd give me the money for a popsicle, but she wanted to watch me while I stood at the curb to buy it. She and Grandma always referred to the popsicle man as the ice cream man and suggested that I buy a cup of ice cream, but this was my only chance to get a popsicle.

I bought my popsicle and stood on the grass in front of Grandma's house to eat it. I wasn't allowed to sit on the steps when I started eating it and then move to the grass anymore. Grandma said she was afraid it would start to melt, drip on the steps, and draw ants. When I finished eating it, I had to put the wet sticks in the wrapper, call Mama to the door, and hand her the wrapper to throw away. Then I had to go in the house to wash my sticky hands with Ivory soap and water at the kitchen sink. I didn't mind washing my hands because I didn't like for them to be sticky, either. I certainly didn't want to get the handlebars or the bell on my tricycle sticky.

A Summer Evening at Grandma's House

Since the awnings shaded the front porch from the glare of the streetlight, Grandma and I started sitting out there after supper every evening. She sat in the high-back dark green rocker near the front door, and I sat in the low-backed green rocker on the other side of the porch. We talked about almost everything.

We never sat on the glider at night because it was lower than the rocking chairs, and we couldn't see well over the railings to know who was walking by or what was going on.

Neighbors were outside sitting on their porches, walking to the mailbox at the corner, or walking to one of the two drugstores at the corner of 35th Street and Colley Avenue. Some of the neighbors stayed inside and listened to their radios, with the windows raised to try to get a little breeze, if one existed. I sometimes heard parts of radio programs and laughter coming from the second-floor apartment next door. It wasn't because they were loud; it was because their windows were raised.

I liked rocking in the low-backed rocking chair, but Grandma sat still in her chair. "Why don't you rock, Grandma? It's fun."

"I'm glad you're enjoying it, but rocking makes me feel sick. You rock all you want to rock, but I'm content to sit still and relax," she explained.

Little bugs would light up with a yellow light as they slowly flew through the darkness of the summer night. Grandma said they were called lightning bugs and that Mama and Aunt Nita used to catch them and put them in a jar.

"What did they do with them?"

"They'd see how many they could catch and watch them light up in the jar all evening. Before they came in for the night, they'd let them go."

"Can I catch lightning bugs one night?"

"We'll see. Sometimes BeeWee keeps a clean mayonnaise jar on a shelf in the woodshed in case we need it for something. You can ask him tomorrow if he has one. If he doesn't, you'll have to wait until I use all the mayonnaise in the jar in the refrigerator, then I'll wash it for you. BeeWee will punch holes in the lid for you with an ice pick."

"Why do holes have to be punched in the lid?"

"So, the lightning bugs will have air. All living things need to have air, or they'll die," Grandma explained.

The next morning, BeeWee found a jar on the woodshed shelf and punched holes in the lid for me.

That evening, while Grandma sat on the porch, I set the jar on the steps and followed lightning bugs around the front yard, cupping them in my hands and putting them in the jar. Sometimes a lightning bug that I already had in the jar would fly out while I was trying to put in a new one. Catching lightning bugs was fun, so, for a while, I did it almost every summer evening.

Some evenings Grandma and I walked to the drugstore to get an ice cream cone. The drugstores usually had chocolate, strawberry, and vanilla ice cream. Grandma usually got vanilla, but sometimes she got strawberry. I liked all three flavors and spent the time we were walking to the drugstore trying to decide which one I'd order when we got there. We ate our ice cream cones as we slowly walked back to Grandma's house.

When we got in the house, we walked back to the kitchen to wash our sticky hands and drink a small glass of water. Grandma thought we should always drink water after eating ice cream.

Rocking and talking with Grandma on the front porch, catching lightning bugs, or walking to the drugstore with Grandma to get ice cream cones were all enjoyable things to do, but some summer evenings were not only not enjoyable; they were scary.

At the first sound of thunder, Grandma started raising the awnings. Then, I held the door open for her to take in the glider cushions. I dreaded the thunderstorms. Grandma and I sat quietly on the sofa, side-by-side, in the dark, with all the windows and doors closed. She made sure the doors and windows were shut, so there would be no drafts.

The storms usually came in the evenings, after several days of extremely hot weather, so the house was already hot. The window shades at all the windows were always raised halfway up, and Grandma didn't pull them down just because we had a storm.

It poured down rain, the thunder ranged from low rumblings to startling crashes, and lightning flashed brightly outside every window. The lace curtains at the windows did nothing to block the view of the sharp lightning. I closed my eyes so I wouldn't have to look at the lightning, but I'm sure I saw some of the brighter flashes through my eyelids. Every storm seemed to go on for the entire evening. Grandma and I were so hot we began to sweat, but we never went upstairs to go to bed until the storm was over because it would have seemed worse upstairs. We wouldn't have been able to go to sleep anyway, with the windows closed and the noise of the loud thunder.

It was a relief when the storm finally ended, and we could go upstairs, open the front bedroom windows, and lie on the bed. After such a severe storm, one would think the weather would be cooler, at least for the rest of the evening, but it was as hot and humid as ever.

It was hard to get comfortable enough to fall asleep on hot, humid nights. I liked sleeping with the top sheet over me in the summer, but sometimes Grandma had to take it off the bed when there wasn't the slightest breeze stirring, and we started sweating. Then Grandma said we could sleep with our heads at the foot of the bed, but that didn't help me to feel a bit cooler.

BeeWee had an oscillating fan on his dresser, which turned from side to side and kept him comfortable all night. Grandma didn't like the fan at all and said the air blowing on her made her bones ache.

Sometimes I was still awake when Aunt Nita came home. "Hi, Aunt Nita," I said when she walked into the room.

"You're still awake? I see you're sleeping at the foot of the bed, so I know you must be hot." She got ready for bed by the light from the streetlight, just as I did. She slipped out of her clothes and into her pajamas without exposing any of her underwear or skin. I don't know how she did it. Then, she stood in front of the dresser mirror and rolled up her hair with bobby pins. She would comb her hair, pull out a small section, and then wrap it around her finger. She would hold the curl flat to her head with one hand, use her other hand to get a bobby pin, use her front teeth to open it up, and then she would secure the curl in place. She would do this with all of her hair, and she did it remarkably fast. When she got in bed, she said, "I'll scratch your back if you'll scratch mine."

I rolled over on my side, and she scratched my back first. Then I scratched her back. We took turns scratching each other's backs until we fell asleep.

To this day, I lovingly think about those warm summer nights when I felt so close to Aunt Nita and Grandma.

The New Car

One morning Aunt Nita had the day off from work and ate breakfast with us. There was always a small, chrome, two-slice, two-door toaster on the kitchen table, but I'd never seen anyone use it. Aunt Nita sat behind the table, opened each door, and put in a slice of bread. Then she extended the black and white cloth cord that was barely long enough to reach the outlet on the wall by the back window and plugged it in. She opened a toaster door several times to see if the bread had been toasted yet. Then, she took out the toast, set it on her plate, buttered it, and cut each slice in half. Grandma brought her a cup of coffee, which she drank with a little pure cream that she poured from a small white pitcher.

After breakfast, Aunt Nita told BeeWee she thought it would be a good idea for him to get a new car.

BeeWee said, "Why do you think I need a new car? My De Soto has a lot of life left in it yet."

"First of all, the old cars have looked old-fashioned ever since the 1941 models came out. The 1941 cars are modern," Aunt Nita persuaded. "Daddy, the automobile manufacturers are saying that if we have a war, they'll turn their factories into defense plants and not make any cars until the war is over. Your car has life left in it now, but what if the war goes on for a long time and your car doesn't hold out? How would you get to work?"

"You make a good point, Juanita, but the fact is, I can't afford to buy a new car. That's why I've never had one before."

"Daddy, the cost of a new Chevrolet is reasonable, and you can even trade in your old car and get a good allowance on a new one. You don't have to pay for the new car all at once; you can make a payment each month until the car is paid off."

"I don't believe in that. If something happened to me and I couldn't work, I wouldn't be able to make the payments, and they'd take the car back. Then I wouldn't have any car at all."

"Let's go in the living room. Little pitchers have big ears," said Aunt Nita, glancing at me.

"Grandma, what does 'little pitchers have big ears' mean?" I asked after they left the room.

Grandma laughed. "It means that Juanita wants to talk to BeeWee without anyone listening."

In a few minutes, BeeWee and Aunt Nita came back to the kitchen and told Grandma they were going to the Chevrolet dealer to look at new cars.

We wondered if they would come home with a new car. In fact, Grandma, Mama, and I left the kitchen and went to sit on the front porch, which we never did during the morning. We didn't want to miss seeing them pull into the driveway in a new car if they bought one.

When we saw them coming down the street in the old De Soto, we scurried to the front door and hurried into the house, hoping they hadn't seen us.

"Why were all of you running in the house?" asked Aunt Nita, as if she didn't know.

"I guess curiosity kills the cat," said Grandma, laughing.

Mama and I had tried to keep a straight face, but when Grandma laughed, we burst out laughing, too.

When they walked into the house, they said they had something to tell us; but we all had to sit down in the living room to hear it. As soon as we sat down, they told us they'd ordered a new 1941 Chevrolet in black, and it would be delivered to the dealer in a few weeks. The dealer would call when it came in. We were all happy about it.

BeeWee said, "I'm still trying to get used to the idea of having a brand-new car, but it's not here yet, so I don't want to count my chickens before they hatch."

In a few weeks, the dealer called, and Aunt Nita and BeeWee went to pick up the car. We sat on the porch again, excited to know they would soon come home with the new car. When they pulled into the driveway later in the morning, we were surprised that BeeWee wasn't driving a black 1941 Chevrolet.

He was driving a navy blue 1941 Chevrolet.

They said the manufacturer was out of black Chevrolets and sent the navy blue one to see if they would like to have it instead. The dealer said they could either take the navy blue one or put in another order for a black one. He said there was no guarantee any more Chevrolets of any color would be made, and they already had a customer who wanted a blue one, so the salesman couldn't hold it for them.

BeeWee and Aunt Nita knew they could miss out on getting any new car if they waited because auto manufacturing plants were likely to become defense plants any day.

We all liked the color, though. I liked navy blue better than black. Grandma, Mama, and I could hardly wait to sit in the new car. It was more compact than the De Soto, but it had room for just as many people to sit, three in the front and three in the back. I liked the nice new car smell.

It had four doors and a heater. There was a clock, a cigarette lighter, and a glove compartment. There was also room on the dashboard for a radio if they ever wanted to have one installed, which BeeWee said he wouldn't listen to if he had it.

I'm so glad Aunt Nita and BeeWee decided to buy a new car. I like the way they planned ahead and talked it over so BeeWee would have transportation during the war. They were being prepared like President Roosevelt, which made us all feel ready in case of war.

Riding Downtown at Night

The week after Aunt Nita and BeeWee got the new car, she had a day off and drove the car. She drove it in the morning and came home in time to take BeeWee to work, so she could drive the car in the afternoon and the early evening. She said she'd pick up BeeWee when he got off from work at eleven o'clock that night.

After spending time with her friends, Aunt Nita picked up Grandma and me after supper to drive us downtown to see the lights and the people. Grandma was looking forward to buying some hot roasted peanuts from the Planter's Peanuts store. She sat in the front seat with Aunt Nita, and I sat in the back seat.

Downtown Norfolk was bright and colorful at night, with all the lights on the movie marquees and in the store windows. The speed limit was twenty-five miles per hour, but people drove about ten or fifteen miles per hour so they could watch people walking on the sidewalk and window shop from their cars.

My favorite lights were on the tall Loews Theater sign over the marquee. It wasn't colorful, but it was eye-catching the way a lot of white light bulbs moved around the edges of the sign, stopped for a few seconds, and moved around again.

After we drove to the end of Granby Street, Aunt Nita made a right turn and drove through a side street to Boush Street. She drove on Boush and made a right turn to drive by the telephone company to show us where she entered the building to go to work. She pulled over to the curb, so we could look across the street and see the uniformed guard standing on the other side of the safety glass-topped double doors. She said each employee had to have a telephone company identification card to show him to be allowed to enter. The long-distance telephone operators were all women, and the telephone repairmen were all men, as their titles indicated.

Aunt Nita then drove back down Granby Street and stopped in front of the Planter's Peanuts store, where Mr. Peanut was walking around the outside. There were meters on both sides of the street where people could park for a nickel, but those parking spaces were all taken. Aunt Nita didn't want to park anyway.

She let Grandma out of the car to go to the Planter's Peanut store. Then, she drove around the block several times until Grandma came out of the store with a white bag in her hand and a big smile on her face. Grandma was happy because she'd bought a two-pound, twenty-five-cent bag of hot roasted peanuts in the shell.

As much as she liked those peanuts, she wouldn't eat even one of them until we were back at her house and she was sitting down at the kitchen table. She said she didn't want to mess up the new car with peanut shells. Aunt Nita sat in the living room and played records until it was time to leave to pick up BeeWee. I listened to the records with her.

The Scary Ride

Just before it was time for Aunt Nita to leave to pick up BeeWee, Grandma said it was too dangerous for her to drive there by herself late at night, so we were going with her.

It was ten-thirty when we got in the car, so it had gotten damp outside. Grandma sat with Aunt Nita in the front seat, and I sat in the back seat, just as we had earlier in the evening. As Aunt Nita drove, she passed by Robbins' Confectionary and her good friend Camille's house, which she pointed out to us. It was a two-story white house that was similar to Grandma's house.

When we reached a certain point down the road, there were no more houses, just a small store here and there that had dark windows because it was closed for the night. The old, dim streetlights were spaced farther apart, and there was only darkness on the road between them, except for the car's headlights.

"Check your doors to be sure they're locked," cautioned Grandma.

As we neared the end of the road, Aunt Nita had to drive very slowly and roll down her window to give a left-hand turn signal. She had to roll the window all the way down because she had to stick her arm straight out the window.

"Don't waste any time pulling in your arm and rolling up the window in case someone's standing there, waiting to grab your arm when you slow down," said Grandma.

It was easy for me to see why Grandma didn't want Aunt Nita to drive there by herself. The speed limit was only twenty-five miles per hour. At the end of the road, there was the Elizabeth River. The railroad yard had a tall, barbed wire fence on the left. The driver had to come to almost a complete stop or risk losing control of the car and having it slip off the road into the water. There was no room to turn around if you changed your mind about driving down the dark road. The only lights were the car's headlights and the headlights of an occasional car coming from the opposite direction.

I was getting more and more scared, but I didn't say anything. Then, on the right side of the road, I saw a dim light on an old telephone pole, open gates, and a tiny, weathered shack. A man who appeared to be about BeeWee's age, but was shorter and heavier, stepped out of the shack. My heart started pounding in my chest. He was wearing baggy dark pants, a dark jacket, and a dark hat, all of which seemed to be old, faded, and nearly worn out. I almost screamed when he walked toward the car.

When he stopped by Aunt Nita's door, I tried to scream, but no sound came out, as though I was having a nightmare.

Aunt Nita told him who she was. He looked up BeeWee's name and license plate number. He said he knew her daddy, and it was all right for her to go to pick him up. When she closed the window, I asked who he was, and she said he was the watchman. "He's only supposed to allow railroad employees, or a family member of an employee, to go through the gates."

So, I was all that scared for nothing.

Aunt Nita made several left turns, driving over railroad tracks, past docks with ships beside them, trains, and pier cars like BeeWee's. There was a strong odor of coal dust mixed with salt water and creosote pilings.

After driving past all of that in near darkness, we came to a gravel parking lot with a lot of cars and saw a large, two-story brick building with lights in all the windows in the background.

Grandma said BeeWee was in that building, taking a shower to wash off all the coal dust before he came home. Some men came from the building in their railroad clothes, got in their cars, and drove away. Some carried black lunch boxes. BeeWee came out carrying nothing. He kept his Zane Gray western novel and a worn brown paper bag in the big pockets of his denim jacket.

He sat beside me in the back seat, and I fell asleep on the way to Grandma's. I woke up a little when we stopped in the driveway, but when BeeWee picked me up in his arms, I kept my eyes closed and enjoyed being carried upstairs and put on Aunt Nita's bed. Then, he went downstairs to drink his two bottles of Rupert beer.

Grandma came upstairs to help me put on my pajamas, but I was too sleepy, so instead, she just took off her dress and put on her pastel-striped seersucker robe. Aunt Nita came upstairs, put on her pajamas without showing any of her body, and started rolling her hair on bobby pins. I fell asleep before she picked up the second bobby pin.

What began as a scary ride for me turned out to be a pleasant experience. I was able to see where BeeWee worked, loading coal from his pier car onto ships that carried it around the world.

Lynnhaven

BeeWee was beginning to talk about his vacation, which he said was coming up soon. He said Grandma, Mama, Aunt Nita, and I were going to go to Lynnhaven for the day the way we did last year. I looked forward to going back to the beach.

Grandma started talking about the food we'd take with us.

Aunt Nita said she'd arrange her work schedule so she could go with us.

The day before the trip, we went to the grocery store to buy a loaf of fresh white Nolde's bread, thinly sliced boiled ham, American cheese, Kraft mayonnaise, soft drinks, and snack cakes.

I spent time trying to decide whether to take a Seven Up, an Orange Crush, a Grapette, or a Dr. Pepper. I liked all of them, but the Grapette was smaller, so I eliminated that as a possibility and tried to decide on one of the other three. I finally chose the Orange Crush.

When it came to choosing the snack cake, I was pretty sure I'd get the round devil's food cake filled with soft white cream because it was my favorite, although I thought of getting the package of orange frosted yellow cupcakes because there were two of them. Then, I decided on the devil's food cake because I thought I'd be sorry if I didn't.

Grandma, Mama, and Aunt Nita wanted Coke, which Grandma still called Coca-Cola, even though almost everyone said "Coke."

Soon, we were happily getting ready to go to the beach. Mama bought me a metal sieve for sifting sand. A sieve was a round piece of metal with screen wire in the middle. The fine sand would go through the screen into the bucket, and any rocks would remain in the sieve.

On the day we were to go, Grandma made the sandwiches, and BeeWee went to get a bucket of minnows from the creek. I went with him to watch, and Mama came along to watch me.

BeeWee tied a rope around the handle of a galvanized bucket and lowered it into the creek. He pulled it up and poured out about three-fourths of the water. The tiny fish swam in the water that was left. "I've got what I need. Let's go."

We went back to the house and put all our stuff in the car. Grandma was worried that the bucket would turn over and the water would spill into the new car, but BeeWee assured her that it wouldn't happen. "No water ever spilled in the DeSoto, did it?"

Grandma hesitated. "Well, I don't know. I guess I didn't think about it until we got the new car."

"Take my word for it. No water's going to spill in the car trunk," BeeWee assured her.

We put our things in the car, BeeWee backed out of the driveway, and we were on our way. I sat on the front seat, between him and Grandma, so I'd have a good view of the sand dunes and the Lynnhaven River from the bridge.

The speed limit was still twenty-five miles per hour, but it was more than worth the long drive to spend the day at the beach while BeeWee fished from the bridge. The windows in the car were all rolled down, so we were comfortable all the way. I was thrilled to see the tall sand dunes again and the incredible view of the river from the top of the bridge. Just smelling the salty air was exhilarating.

BeeWee found a good parking spot on the road just past the bridge. He parked the car, got his fishing gear together, Grandma handed him his lunch bag, and he headed toward the bridge. Since he always ate pork and bean sandwiches for his lunch every day, he broke the habit and ate a ham and cheese sandwich like the rest of us when we went to Lynnhaven. His fishing clothes had not changed since last year. They were the same clothes he wore when he worked around the house.

Grandma and BeeWee decided on how we'd meet at the car when it was time to go home. Grandma knew how much it meant to BeeWee to fish as long as he could. If the fish were biting, it meant BeeWee could catch more fish for all of us. BeeWee knew Grandma couldn't take but so much of the hot sun without getting a headache. Grandma liked Lynnhaven because she could sit under the shady trestle if she started to feel a headache coming on. She didn't want to sit in the shade until she had to because she knew Aunt Nita and Mama would want to get some sun. She also knew they would move under the trestle if she moved so we could all be together.

They agreed that Mama would walk to the bridge to tell BeeWee when we were ready, and then we'd all meet at the car to go home.

Grandma, Aunt Nita, Mama, and I got our things together and headed for the beach. They wore the same things they wore last year, and I wore a new sun suit because I outgrew the one I wore last year. I could still wear my cotton sun hat. Since my white rubber beach shoes stretched, I could wear those, too. I carried my sand bucket, shovel, and the new sieve, which I was excited about using.

They spread out the same old large, worn blanket near the trestle in case we had to move under it, and they'd brought plenty of reading material, as usual. Grandma brought the *Sunday Mirror*, which was a weekly newspaper, and *Life*, a weekly magazine that had a lot of pictures of events that had taken place during the past week. Aunt Nita brought movie magazines, *Photoplay* and *Modern Screen*, and Mama brought a love story magazine, *True Confessions*. I didn't take books to the beach.

Mama handed me my sieve, and I began playing in the sand by putting my sieve over the sand bucket and shoveling sand into it. When the bucket was filled with sand, I emptied it and emptied the rocks from the sieve. Then I started over.

Grandma exclaimed, "I don't know about anyone else, but I'm hungry!"

Aunt Nita laughed. "Mama, you always say that as soon as we get to Lynnhaven."

"She sure does," Mama added.

Grandma started laughing, too. "I can't help it. The salt air makes me hungry. What time is it, Juanita?"

"It's eleven-thirty."

"Well, no wonder I'm hungry; it's almost lunch time. Let's eat at twelve o'clock," Grandma suggested.

"That'll give me time to take Shirley to the water's edge," said Mama, standing up. "Anyone want to come? Nita? How about you, Mama? You used to swim. Don't you want to swim?"

"I just want to read and get some sun. I don't want to go in the water," Aunt Nita told her as she was getting her movie magazine out of her bag.

Grandma shook her head. "Remember what I told you last year? My swimming days are over."

"I know, but you used to like to swim," Mama reminded her.

"I did like to swim. I liked to crab, too, when I was a young girl, and we lived near the water. I just don't want to do it anymore."

"All right, but come down if you change your mind." Mama took me by the hand, and we walked along the water's edge. She said I could take off my rubber shoes, and she'd hold them.

The firmly packed wet sand felt cool to my feet as they squished into the sand.

Suddenly, Mama stopped. "Look at the sand behind you. You've left footprints in the sand." I looked back and was surprised to see all the little footprints I'd made and the larger prints made by Mama's feet.

"Will my footprints stay here in the sand forever?"

"They'll stay until someone else comes along and steps on them, or the waves wash over them."

I was a little disappointed to learn they wouldn't last. Mama told me to step into the water, and I did, but it was cold. She said it would feel warmer to me after I got used to it. I did get used to it and had fun walking in and out of the water and kicking at it with my feet to make it splash.

Mama said it was time to eat lunch, so I put on my rubber shoes again, and we headed back to where Grandma and Aunt Nita were sitting.

It was a happy time for all of us. The weather was sunny and warm, but there was a light breeze. The sand under the spread felt warm. We watched waves wash in and out on the shore and inhaled the salty air as we ate our lunch.

After eating lunch, Grandma, Mama, and Aunt Nita read and talked. I played with my sand bucket and sieve again and listened to them talk about what they were reading. There was no talk about war, only talk about happy things, like movies and movie stars.

Grandma said she was starting to get a headache, so we all moved over and sat on the sand under the trestle. It did feel cooler under there in the shade.

I asked about the scent that was starting to mix with the salt air. I liked it, so I wanted to know what it was.

Grandma said, "It's coming from the creosote in the pilings under the trestle. They put creosote in the pilings to preserve the wood."

"What is a trestle?" I had never heard them use that word before.

Aunt Nita explained, "It's something that a train runs on."

I looked up to see if I could see the train tracks, and they seemed very close to where we were sitting. "Is a train going to run over our heads?"

Aunt Nita reassured me, "You don't have to worry. The train doesn't run on this trestle anymore."

"Why doesn't it?"

"I guess they just don't need it here," Aunt Nita surmised.

"I'm glad the trestle is here so Grandma can have a place to sit under to get out of the sun, and I like sitting under it."

After a while, Grandma called out, "Is everybody ready to go?"

We knew that meant that Grandma was ready, so we started picking up our things and heading for the car. Mama went to get BeeWee.

He said he'd caught a few fish, but not nearly as many as he'd hoped to catch. "It's just enough for a good meal for all of us."

We passed the sand dunes again on the way home.

"It would be fun to climb up to the top of a sand dune and roll down," I hinted.

"You'll have to do that next time, honey. I still have a headache, and I need to go straight home and take two Bayer aspirins."

By the time we got home, Grandma had headed for the front door, unlocked it, walked back to the kitchen, took her aspirins, and went upstairs to lie down.

We took things from the car and put them away. Mama and Aunt Nita went up to Aunt Nita's room to change from their bathing suits to their clothes. Then we sat in the living room. Everyone was quiet, partly from being tired and partly because we were sorry that Grandma wasn't feeling well, and we were trying not to disturb her.

After about an hour, she came downstairs wearing the seersucker robe over her white slip and said she was feeling better, but she didn't feel well enough to clean fish and fry them for supper. She said we'd have to have soup with bread and butter because that was all she felt like fixing.

When Grandma walked to the kitchen, I told Mama I was very worried about her. Since I'd never seen her like that before, I thought something was terribly wrong.

"Don't worry about Grandma. She'll be fine. Sitting in the sun at the beach has always given her a headache. The next time we go to Lynnhaven, she should sit under the trestle as soon as we get there instead of waiting until she gets a headache."

We went to Lynnhaven two more times while BeeWee was on his vacation. We stayed longer, and he caught a lot of fish, including what he said were good-sized flounder, which he always hoped to catch at Lynnhaven. Grandma sat under the trestle the entire time we were there and didn't have a headache, so I got to climb to the top of a sand dune and roll down on the way home. Mama went to the top with me, but she walked down sideways and slowly, so she wouldn't tumble down. When we got home, Grandma cleaned some of the fish and fried them for BeeWee, Aunt Nita, and me for supper.

She invited Mama and Daddy to stay and eat, but Daddy said he needed to go home, take a shower, and change clothes. Then, they'd eat out.

The next time we went to Lynnhaven, it was cloudy all the way there, and a misty rain began as we were taking our things from the car.

"If it's all the same with you, I say we just stay in the car while your daddy fishes. We can't get any sun anyway," Grandma offered.

We didn't mind staying in the car. The view was beautiful, and we all liked to watch the rain. BeeWee put on the black rubber rain slicker that he kept in the trunk of the car and headed for the bridge with his fishing gear.

It began raining harder, but we still had a good time eating, talking, and reading. I should say they read, and I looked at the pictures in all their magazines and newspapers. I wanted to learn to read someday because those magazines and newspapers looked interesting, and I was impressed with the way they could read them.

My Summer Friend Visits Her Grandparents

After supper, Grandma, BeeWee, Aunt Nita, and I were sitting on the porch. It was a rare occasion when anyone other than Grandma and I sat there at night unless BeeWee was on vacation and he was watching a thunder and lightning storm.

A large car pulled up in front of the apartment house. A dark-haired woman and a little girl went inside. When they came back out to get the luggage, I thought that it was Janet.

I didn't think Janet's mother would want to come back to Norfolk after what happened to us last summer when that man stopped his car at the curb and called us to come over.

They went inside and didn't come back out that night, but when I went outside the next morning, Janet came over. We were happy to see each other. We sat on Grandma's steps and walked up and down on the sidewalk. I let Janet pretend to be a mother with my mother's dress, my carriage, my doll, and Mama's old pocketbook because I knew she wouldn't have those things at her grandparents' house. Grandma let me wear one of her old house dresses to pretend I was the grandmother that the mother and baby were visiting.

It was so much fun that we played again during the week. In the afternoon, we walked up and down, sat on the steps and talked, waited for the popsicle man, and ate popsicles. We stood on the grass to eat them.

I missed Janet when she went back to Pennsylvania. She said she'd miss me, too. Janet was the kind of friend I always wanted to see every summer. Her mother had to drive from Pennsylvania, which Grandma and Mama said was a long drive. When each summer came, Grandma and I sat on the front porch, and I'd wait for Janet to come again. She came for two or three more summers, but then the war put a stop to that because of the gas rationing.

Aunt Nita Plays Her Records

We ate the delicious fried flounder that BeeWee had caught at Lynnhaven, and Grandma had cleaned, breaded, and fried golden brown. Afterward, BeeWee and I sat in the living room and listened to records that Aunt Nita played on the Victrola phonograph. The records were as big around as dinner plates and just as thick, but they were flat, with a small hole in the center. She placed the record on a turntable, lifted a piece with a small, short needle underneath, and carefully placed it on the record to avoid scratching it. She said the phonograph needle could easily scratch the record, and the records could chip and break easily, so I wasn't allowed to touch the records or the phonograph, which I never did.

Aunt Nita played one of her newest records; *I Don't Want to Set the World on Fire (I Just Want to Start a Flame in Your Heart)*, by a group of men called The Ink Spots, who harmonized well together. I thought that was the longest song title I'd ever heard.

BeeWee liked train songs, so she played two records about trains that she'd bought especially for him. One was *The Wabash Cannonball*; the other was *The Orange Blossom Special.*

Mama and Daddy stopped by after supper to listen to Aunt Nita's records and to talk since BeeWee was on vacation and Aunt Nita was there. Mama was about twenty-three, and Daddy was about twenty-seven at that time.

Grandma finished washing dishes and came into the room, so Aunt Nita played *You Are My Sunshine* by Bing Crosby.

When it was time for me to go to bed, Mama took me upstairs to see that I put on my pajamas and got in bed. I liked lying in bed, listening to Aunt Nita's records and their talking and laughter. I couldn't make out what they were saying; I just liked the happy sound of the family being together. Then I thought about our three wonderful days at Lynnhaven this year. BeeWee said we'd go back again next July when he had his vacation, and I was already looking forward to it.

In the meantime, he said he was planning to paint in the morning, and I was planning to watch him.

BeeWee Paints the House

Although BeeWee liked to fish, most of his vacation days were taken up with painting. This time, he was painting the house on the apartment building side. He propped a long ladder against the house and painted as many mornings as he could. He took pride in painting the house that he owned.

I watched BeeWee climb to the top of the ladder holding his gallon bucket of paint and a wide brush in one hand and holding on to the ladder with the other. A paint rag was sticking out of the pocket of his old navy-blue pants. He wore the same old white shirt and scuffed brown work shoes that he always wore when he was working around the house or fishing.

He got so far up that I had to crane my neck to see him.

When he started painting, I could see that the new coat of paint was making a big difference. The new white paint looked much brighter than the old white paint on the house, especially on the parts where BeeWee had already scraped off loose paint.

Grandma and Mama came out of the house and told me that I had to move in case BeeWee fell or dropped something. By then, the back of my neck was starting to hurt from holding my head back so far to see BeeWee. "I know. I'll go upstairs and watch BeeWee through the side bedroom window."

"You certainly will not," said Mama. "You'll make BeeWee fall off the ladder because he'll be looking at you instead of paying attention to what he's doing. When he's finished painting for the day, you can go outside and see what he's done." I looked forward to seeing BeeWee's daily progress.

One morning, when it was raining, BeeWee said he was going to paint some of the woodwork downstairs in the house since he couldn't paint outside. Grandma spread old newspapers on the floor. He painted the doorway between the hall and the living room and then moved his paint bucket to the living room mantle. He'd already put one coat of paint over the aluminum paint, but he wasn't satisfied with the way it looked. "It doesn't have a finished look. It'll look much better if I give it another coat of paint."

Grandma came into the room and spread old newspapers on the floor around the mantle, and took everything off of it again.

I watched him off and on all morning until he stopped painting, put the lid on the can of paint, and took it to the woodshed. He cleaned his brush with turpentine and wiped his hands with a cloth. Then he went into the kitchen and washed his hands with soap and water at the sink.

We enjoyed a round steak ground patty meal. Round steak ground patties were like hamburger patties without the bun. It was a typical meal for us, fried in a large black cast iron skillet in hot, sizzling Fluffo shortening with lots of onions chopped into bite-sized pieces and cooked until soft and golden brown. Afterward, BeeWee said he was going upstairs to take a nap.

I was sitting on the sofa in the living room, waiting for him to come back, when my head started to hurt. My head was feeling worse and worse when Grandma came from the kitchen to check on me to be sure I was still in the house. By then, my head had started to throb, and I was holding my hand to my forehead.

"What's the matter, honey? You look as though you're not feeling well."

"Grandma, my head hurts," I practically moaned.

"You haven't fallen and hurt your head, have you?"

"No. I've just been watching BeeWee paint."

"That explains it. You have a headache from the paint. The oil paint he uses has strong fumes. I'm going to raise the window to give you some air and let some of those fumes get out." She raised it as high as it would go.

Back then, the oil-based paint had strong fumes that could easily give you a headache. Grandma's remedy would always do the trick.

"You stay right here. I'm going to dissolve half a Bayer aspirin in some water and bring it back for you to take. That's what I used to do for your mother and Juanita when they had headaches."

Grandma brought two little glasses, one with the aspirin dissolved in water and a second glass with plain water for me to drink afterward. "Now, this is going to have a little bit of a bitter taste, but you need to take all of it to get rid of your headache. Aspirin helps me when I have a headache." She sat beside me on the sofa, holding the glass of water while I took the aspirin. Then, she switched glasses with me so I could drink the plain water. "Good! That wasn't so bad, was it?"

I slowly shook my head from side to side to show her that I was saying 'no' because, by now, my head hurt too badly for me to speak.

"I'm going upstairs to get a pillow to put under your head so you can lie down. I'll be right back." Grandma came back with the pillow, placed it at one end of the sofa, and told me to lie down. She sat on the edge of the sofa and gently rubbed my forehead with Spirits of Camphor. I liked the way it smelled, and it made my forehead feel cool. "Let me rub some on your temples, too. This always makes me feel better when I have a headache."

Then, she took off my shoes and set them on the floor beside the sofa. "Now, it'll take a few minutes for the aspirin to take effect, so you just close your eyes, lie here on your back as still as you can, and try to fall asleep." I did what Grandma said, and I soon fell asleep. When I woke up, my headache was gone.

Grandma knew just what to do. She not only knew to give me half an aspirin, but she did everything she could to make me comfortable while the aspirin was taking effect.

I loved Spirits of Camphor. I wish they still had it. It would really allow you to relax and feel better. Today when I get a headache, I take an Anacin, which has aspirin in it, and have a Coca-Cola to relax. I often think back to Grandma's headache remedy, which is the best ingredient of all, her love.

Grandma, BeeWee, and a Squirrel Get Ready for Fall and Winter

One day in September, Grandma and BeeWee were busily working on the front porch. It was beginning to feel a little cool in the early mornings, so the sunshine felt good on my face, arms, and legs as I sat on the edge of the porch, with my feet, still in sandals, on the steps. I'd turn to watch them for a while and then turn to watch a squirrel scurrying around on the ground under the tall oak tree that grew between the sidewalk and the curb. I asked BeeWee why he took the screens out of the living room windows.

"I'm storing them for the winter," he said as he lifted the heavy wooden frames, one at a time, and took them to the garage.

I knew what Grandma was getting ready to do. She had the hose in her left hand and a sudsy brush with stiff bristles in her right hand. Her galvanized scrub bucket was beside her. She was going to scrub the front of the house. I'd seen her do it before to wash off the fine, black coal dust that settled on the whiteboards.

There was a train track about a block away. We couldn't see it from the house because of a bend in the road, but we could certainly see the black dust from the steam engines that the wind deposited on the boards.

Grandma scrubbed as high as she could reach, so the front of the house was clean up to that height.

After scrubbing some of the boards, she turned the hose on them, and the sudsy, dirty water trickled down each board until it reached the porch next to the house, and she hosed it off so that it ran, under the white porch railings on the sides of the porch and onto the ground.

BeeWee came back and told Grandma he'd finished taking all the screens out of the downstairs windows and put them in the garage. "If you want me to clean the outside of the living room windows, you need to hurry and finish your scrubbing. By the time I finish smoking this cigarette, you'd better be finished, or I won't have time to help you." He put the cigarette between his lips and struck a match.

While he was smoking, I showed him the squirrel.

BeeWee watched it for a while and chuckled. "It looks like that squirrel's getting ready for winter, too. It's gathering acorns to store for the winter."

Grandma finished scrubbing, so BeeWee tossed his cigarette butt on the sidewalk, ground it out with his shoe sole, climbed the porch steps, and walked over to the windows. He cleaned the outside panes while Grandma went into the house and cleaned the inside panes. They rubbed Bon Ami on the panes first. Then, they wiped it off with a clean cloth. Grandma saved socks that were too worn out to be darned to use for cleaning cloths.

Grandma said she could never get all the smudges off the windows unless they cleaned them that way.

The next day, Grandma told me we were going downtown to a department store called Ames and Brownley to look at a fur coat that Nita was thinking of buying for the winter. "I don't know why in the world she wants a fur coat, but I promised her I'd look at it," confided Grandma as we walked to the bus stop. "I wouldn't wear a fur coat if somebody gave it to me."

We stood under the awning of the corner drugstore, waiting for the bus. Grandma saw it coming and said it looked crowded. We stood in the aisle at first. Then I noticed that the long seat at the back of the bus was empty.

"Look, Grandma. We can sit on that long seat at the back."

"No, honey. We need to save that one for other people who might have to sit there."

"But, Grandma, nobody's back there."

A man got up and gave us his seat, which was on the aisle. Grandma held me on her lap.

"I can't talk about the back seat now. I'll explain it later," she whispered in my ear.

At some of the stops, I noticed that women carrying large shopping bags got on, paid their fare, walked directly to the back of the bus, and sat on the long back seat.

"Grandma, are they the people we were saving the seats for?"

"Yes, but I can't explain it now," Grandma whispered in my ear again.

I can remember that I didn't want to let that go. I wanted to know. It didn't make sense to me that they couldn't just sit anywhere on the bus. I was insistent and would ask her about it later that night.

The Bus Accident

The bus driver was getting ready to make a wide left turn at Colley Avenue and Olney Road to proceed downtown. I liked that turn because it meant we were almost there. Then, instead of turning left, he veered right.

There was a Chinese laundry on the corner. I knew Chinese people owned it because I once asked Mama about the pretty writing on their signs, and she said it was Chinese. When the weather was warmer, they left the front door open, and I saw that it was a laundry. Today, the front door was closed because of the cooler weather.

The bus crashed right into the Chinese laundry's front door! When the driver slammed on the brakes, Grandma, I, and some other people sitting in the aisle seats were thrust forward to the floor. I was thrown in the aisle, and Grandma was thrown to her knees on the floor behind me. Neither of us was hurt, but Grandma's hose were torn at the knees. Her black skirt barely covered the torn hose.

The police came to investigate, but I don't know why the bus driver couldn't complete the left turn. I don't think anyone on the bus or in the laundry was hurt because the driver had slowed down to make the turn. I knew Grandma was nervous, though, because she was sniffing.

A different bus driver in another bus came for us and drove us the rest of the way downtown. As we got on the other bus and sat down, Grandma said, "I know it'll make us late, but I can't help it. As soon as the bus lets us off downtown, I go into Jimmie Barnes' Drugstore to get a small Coca-Cola with ammonia to settle my nerves. What kind of drink do you want, honey?"

"I want a small cherry smash."

The ammonia in Grandma's Coca-Cola was Spirits of Ammonia. Most of the drugstores kept a bottle of it behind the soda fountain and put some in a Coca-Cola when a nervous customer ordered it.

We finished our drinks and walked a short distance to the Ames and Brownley department store, where Aunt Nita was waiting inside the front door for us.

The Fur Coat

Grandma didn't mention the bus accident, and Aunt Nita didn't say anything about our being late.

We walked up the main aisle to the back of the store, where the elevator was. Aunt Nita pushed a button on the wall, and the elevator soon came down from upstairs and stopped. The door opened, we waited for some people to get off, and an elevator operator dressed in a gray uniform said, "Watch your step, please."

We stepped up a little to get on because the elevator hadn't stopped, even with the floor.

"What floor, please?" she asked.

Aunt Nita gave her the number of the floor, and soon we arrived upstairs in the fur department. Aunt Nita led us toward the back wall, where there was a glass showcase filled with fur coats hanging on thick wooden hangers.

A saleslady opened one of the sliding glass doors and took out the coat Aunt Nita wanted Grandma to see.

"Mama, I want you and Shirley to sit down while I try on the coat in the dressing room. When I come out wearing it, I'll turn around so you can see it from all angles. Then, I want you to tell me what you honestly think of it."

When Aunt Nita went to try on the coat, I wondered if Grandma would tell her what she'd told me about fur coats.

Aunt Nita walked out of the dressing room and turned slowly so we could see the coat. I thought the coat was beautiful, and Aunt Nita looked wonderful in it, but I didn't say anything. I knew she only wanted to hear what Grandma thought of it, and I was waiting to hear what Grandma would say.

The saleslady stood by and said, "This is a full-length mink-dyed muskrat coat. They're very popular now, and the prices are lower at this time of the year than if you wait until winter to buy one. We'll even store it for you at no extra charge until you're ready to pick it up."

"What do you think, Mama?" asked Aunt Nita eagerly.

"I think it's beautiful. You look like a model!" Grandma exclaimed.

"Then I want to get it."

"It's your money, Juanita. If you want the coat, you should buy it," reassured Grandma.

"I want it, so I'm going to go ahead and buy it. What happened to your hose, Mama? I just noticed they're torn."

"Oh, it's nothing to worry about."

"As soon as I make arrangements to buy the coat, we'll go downstairs, and I'll buy you a new pair of hose."

"No, you're not. I wouldn't hear of it." That was a typical thing Grandma would say.

When we left the store, Aunt Nita offered to buy us something at Jimmie Barnes' drugstore, but Grandma thanked her and said we'd already been there, it was getting late, and she wanted to go home.

Aunt Nita said she was meeting her friends to eat and go to a movie. Then she thanked Grandma for coming to look at the coat.

I don't think Grandma ever told Aunt Nita or anyone else about the bus accident. If there was a picture of it or an article in the newspaper, Grandma never mentioned it. I often think back to that day, so long ago, when Grandma and Aunt Nita smoothly handled the situation, and were able to avoid spoiling our pleasant afternoon.

I Don't Understand Why Some People Have to Sit at the Back of the Bus

When we got home, we had chicken noodle soup for supper. Then, I reminded Grandma about her promise to explain to me about the seat at the back of the bus.

"Well, it's a long story, honey. Are you sure you want to hear it?"

"Yes. I want to hear it, Grandma."

"Maybe I shouldn't tell you. You might be too young to understand."

"I'll understand it."

Grandma laughed. "But you haven't heard it yet, so you don't know if you'll understand. I don't understand it myself." I thought, for some reason, Grandma was trying to get out of telling me, so I was more anxious than ever to hear her explanation.

"Do you still want me to tell you about the people on the bus, honey?"

"Please tell me, Grandma."

"The people who walk to the wide seat at the back of the bus are required to sit there." Grandma had tears in her eyes as she explained, "The women who walked to the back seat had worked hard all day and should be allowed to sit in the first empty seat they came to, not the last one. It isn't the bus drivers or policemen who make them sit at the back. It's the men who make the laws who do it. I'd like to see the laws changed, so everyone would have equal rights. Always remember the golden rule: treat others as you would have them treat you."

I thought about it more when I went to bed that night. Grandma was right. I was too young to understand because I didn't know why some people were allowed to make laws that hurt other people.

Getting Ready for the Holidays

By October, BeeWee was standing on his tall stepladder, taking down all the curtains in the living room, dining room and back hall. There were three windows in the living room, two in the dining room, and one in the back hall. There were two lace curtain panels at each window.

Mama got the curtain stretcher out of the hall closet and set up the stretcher in the dining room. It was a large, natural wood, adjustable frame that had spikes that looked like short needles. When she finished adjusting it, the frame stood up on straight wooden legs, and the whole contraption was taller than Mama, who was five feet four inches tall.

As Grandma washed, rinsed, and starched each curtain, she would wring it out and hand it to Mama to put on the stretcher.

For two days, Grandma washed, and starched curtains and Mama put them on the stretcher.

Grandma had quite a job, standing at the sink, washing one panel at a time in sudsy water, and rinsing it several times. She'd wring out as much water as she could from the panel to prepare it for starching. Then, she would dip the curtain panel in a dishpan of starch that she had mixed carefully to ensure that once the curtain was dry, it would have just the right amount of stiffness but not too much.

"If I make the starch too thick, the curtains are like stiff boards, and if I don't make it thick enough, the curtains become as limp as dishrags before we can do them again," Grandma explained.

Mama read a love story magazine while she waited for the first panel, but once she put down the magazine and picked up the first panel, she was busy for two days. She had a tedious task before her, but she kept putting the curtains on the stretcher, yelling 'ouch' each time she jabbed her finger on a spike.

I watched Grandma for a while and then went to the dining room to watch Mama.

"Mama, why do you have to put the curtains on the stretcher instead of hanging them on the clothesline to dry?" I asked.

"The curtains have to hang straight at the windows. If they dry on the line, they won't hang straight."

At least she didn't have to wait for each panel to dry. She could put one on top of another, and they'd still dry because the lace material allowed the air to circulate.

On the third day, Mama removed the curtains from the stretcher, one at a time, and handed them to BeeWee, who stood on the ladder by the windows to slip them on the rods and put the rods back in their brackets.

When the curtains were back at the windows, Mama and Grandma adjusted them and complimented each other on how nice they looked.

"Florencie, you sure know how to stretch curtains. They're perfect, just as straight as they can be."

"Mama, they look nice because you put just the right amount of starch in them."

Grandma smiled. "It's a relief off my mind to know the windows are all done for the holidays."

"I know. The holidays are right around the corner," Mama added.

I think starching and stretching curtains was one of the most time-consuming and tedious processes I've ever seen. Taking down the curtains and hanging them back was no easy task either. I am glad I've never had to do it.

Thanksgiving Dinner

It wasn't long before Grandma was preparing for Thanksgiving. On the day before, she washed a big turkey, put it in a black enamel pan with a matching cover, and set it in the preheated oven to roast.

While the turkey was roasting, she started cutting up the celery and onions that would later go in the dressing, saving some of the celery for eating raw.

"Do you want to taste something good? Try this. It's a celery heart." She held it out for me.

I chomped on it. "It's good!"

"It's from the center of the celery. I think it's the best part for eating raw."

"I like the way it's crunchy, too."

She washed and dried a large, heavy white platter covered with red flowers. It had a gold band around the edge.

"That's a pretty dish, Grandma."

"I always put the turkey on it. It belonged to Mama. She always cooked Thanksgiving dinner on this same stove and put the turkey on this same platter. I make my dressing the way she made hers, too."

"Is that the good stuff we had with the turkey and cranberry sauce last year?"

"That's it. I'm glad you liked it and remembered it."

"It was delicious!"

Grandma smiled. She liked it when someone complimented her cooking.

She stayed up late, taking up the cooked turkey, waiting for it to cool, and adjusting the shelves in the small refrigerator to make room for it. No one knew exactly how late she stayed up because we had all gone to bed.

The wonderful aroma of roasted turkey filled the house as did the love of the one who was preparing the Thanksgiving dinner for us.

The next day, when Grandma, BeeWee, Mama, Daddy, Aunt Nita, and I were all eating Thanksgiving dinner at the dining room table, Aunt Nita probably described the meal better than anyone by saying it was scrumptious. Besides the turkey, dressing, and cranberry sauce, Grandma had prepared baked whole sweet potatoes and collard greens.

When Grandma set the plate of hot rolls on the table, she cheerfully said, "I bought a dozen rolls, and the bakery gave me a baker's dozen."

"Grandma, what is a baker's dozen?"

"Well, there are twelve rolls in a dozen. If the bakery puts an extra roll in the bag, you have thirteen rolls, and that's called a baker's dozen."

"They must really like you to give you a free roll, Grandma."

"Oh, I don't know about that. They probably give all their customers a baker's dozen."

Halfway through the meal, Grandma let us know, "There's Nolde's pound cake for anyone who wants a slice after dinner."

I liked having the whole family together, sitting around the dining room table, and eating the wonderful food so lovingly prepared by my grandmother. I thought it was a glorious occasion, made special by my grandmother.

Aunt Nita's Date

The night after Thanksgiving, Aunt Nita had a date with a young man who had been a school chum of hers in high school. He was attending the Merchant Marine Academy and was at home for the Thanksgiving weekend.

She'd gotten her new fur coat out of storage and was planning to wear it for the first time.

Grandma and I sat on the sofa, waiting for Aunt Nita to come downstairs so we could see how she looked to go out on her date. We heard her coming down the steps, and a light scent of perfume filled the air as she walked into the room.

Grandma exclaimed, "Juanita, you look like a million dollars."

Aunt Nita always looked good and smelled good, but tonight she looked even better. She was wearing a pink angora sweater that brought out the beauty of her long dark brown, softly curled hair, dark brown eyes, and perfectly shaped red lips.

There was a knock at the door, and Grandma went to open it. A young man, who looked dashing in his uniform, walked into the living room, holding his hat in his hand.

"Hi, Russell. You can put your hat on the table." Aunt Nita gestured with her hand toward the pretty, new, scallop-edged corner table she'd bought. It was dark walnut, much larger and taller than an end table, and it had six legs. She sat down on one end of the sofa, and Russell sat on the other end. Grandma and I just stood there in the middle of the room, looking at them. She knew the young man and knew his family from the neighborhood.

"It certainly is nice to see you again, Russell. How do you like your school?" asked Grandma.

"Oh, very much, thank you, Mrs. Daugherty."

Then, Aunt Nita looked at me. "This is my niece, Shirley. She's Florencie's daughter."

"Hello, Shirley. Nice to meet you. Would you like to try on my hat?"

I was delighted and didn't hesitate to say, "Yes."

He walked to the table, picked up his hat, and put it on my head. Then, he sat back on the sofa, close to Aunt Nita this time. They laughed at the way the hat was too big for me and almost covered my eyes.

Then, Grandma said, "Well, it's time for us to go upstairs now."

"It is?" I was completely taken aback.

"Yes, it is, honey. Give the young man his hat."

Russell stood up from the sofa with Nita and said, "We have to go, too. We're going to a movie, and we don't want to be late."

"Let me get my coat." Aunt Nita walked to the dining room, picked up her coat from the chair she had draped it over earlier, and brought it on her arm into the living room.

The young man took the coat and held it while she slipped her arms into it. "You have a beautiful coat."

Aunt Nita smiled. "Thank you." Then, they left for the movies, and Grandma closed the door behind them.

"Grandma, why do we have to go upstairs when the nine o'clock gun hasn't gone off yet?"

"Oh, I just said that because I was trying to think of an excuse for us to leave the room so they wouldn't waste time with us and make themselves late for the movie.".

"Is he Aunt Nita's boyfriend?"

Grandma laughed. "Aunt Nita says he's just a friend, but I don't know."

The next day, Aunt Nita gave the angora sweater to Mama. "Florencie, you can have this sweater. I'm never wearing it again. I was never so embarrassed as I was when we said goodnight, and I saw that the sweater had shed all over the front of Russell's jacket."

Mama smiled. "I'll be happy to take it. I won't mind if it sheds a little."

Aunt Nita and Russell wrote to each other, but she insisted to Mama and Grandma they were just friends.

Mama was happy to be given a new sweater, and she could hardly wait to wear it. The next time she went to a barn dance with Daddy, she wore the sweater and said she liked it, but she couldn't wear it again, either, because Daddy said it made him sneeze all night.

I thought the sweater was beautiful, so I asked Mama to save it for me until I grew big enough to wear it.

Mama and Grandma laughed, and Grandma said, "That will be a long time."

"I'll save it for you, but don't be surprised if the moths get to it before you do," added Mama. She and Grandma laughed again.

Years later, I begged Mama to let me try it on one day, even before I had gotten big enough to wear it. When I tried it on, it turned out that it made me feel so itchy that all I wanted to do was take it off. Looking back, I guess I was allergic to the angora sweater, too.

Christmas is in the Air

When Grandma, BeeWee, and I went to Robbins' Confectionary on the Sunday after Thanksgiving, they were displaying Christmas cards and tree decorations on the counters and shelves. Grandma was saying there was a feeling of Christmas in the air. Mama saw in the newspapers that they had started printing a countdown of the number of shopping days left until Christmas. Orr's Seed Company was advertising in the newspaper that they were going to begin selling Christmas trees on their lot on December 10th.

Grandma and Mama were busy talking about the color of the Christmas lights Mama would put in the front living room windows this year.

Grandma explained to her, "Your daddy has always wanted to have all blue lights, but I think it would make me feel too sad to have all blue lights."

"We've always had a combination of two or three colors, and the windows have looked pretty and cheerful."

"They certainly have, Florencie. So, I think we should continue with our tradition."

Mama wasn't ready to make a decision yet. "I guess we could have blue and white since Daddy likes blue."

"That would be pretty, but the red and blue that we've had so often is pretty, too. I'll leave it up to you, though. You always have the window lights looking nice."

Although blue was one of my favorite colors, I agreed with Mama and Grandma that the traditional multi-colored lights were the best. I loved the idea that when our family came home from work, our house would look so cheerful at Christmastime.

Sunday, December 7, 1941

On Sunday, December 7th, people were already talking about Christmas, planning for it, and beginning to shop for cards and presents.

In a few more days, people would begin buying Christmas trees and putting them up in their houses. Christmas cards would start arriving in the mail.

Grandma, BeeWee, and I went to Sunday school at Park Place Methodist Church, which was on the corner of 34th Street and Colonial Avenue. The big brick building covered the corners of 34th and 35th Streets and a whole block of Colonial Avenue.

BeeWee dropped off Grandma and me on the 35th street side of the building at the door leading to our Sunday school classes. Then, he went to park the car and go to the men's class. Grandma took me by the hand to my class, gave me a dime for the offering plate, and then went to the ladies' class.

I liked my class. The teacher was nice. She gave us our Sunday school papers that had the lesson for the week, and she read the lesson to us as we listened and tried to follow the words with our eyes since we were all too young to read. I learned a lot about God and Jesus as we sat in those small, light blue chairs around light blue tables.

At the end of the lesson, she gave each of us a colored star for attending. I licked the star and stuck it inside the back cover of the booklet where we kept our weekly papers. Our papers were fastened in our booklets with brass brads, which she unfastened each week to add our new papers. Our names were on the front cover of our booklets, which we took home with us every week.

When Sunday school was over, Grandma came to my class to get me. BeeWee pulled the car around to pick us up where he had dropped us off.

Then, he drove directly to Robbins' Confectionary.

Grandma said BeeWee didn't drink beer on Sundays because Methodists were supposed to abstain from drinking, but he went to the confectionary to work behind the beer counter for Miss Ginnie, so she could attend her church. He took off his suit jacket and hung it on the store's hat rack with his hat. Then, he rolled up his sleeves and opened bottles of beer for anyone who came to the counter to buy one while the store owner filled in for Miss Ginnie at the soda fountain.

Grandma and I sat in the booth closest to the penny candy counter, which was next to the soda fountain. She got her usual small Coca-Cola, and I had a small cherry smash.

I left the table to look at the comic books to try to decide which one to buy. I liked *Bugs Bunny*, *Tom and Jerry*, *Little Lulu*, *Mickey Mouse*, *Donald Duck*, and others, so it was a difficult decision to make. If I got the *Bugs Bunny* comic book, Elmer Fudd would be in it, and I liked him. On the other hand, if I got the *Mickey Mouse* comic book, Minnie Mouse and Goofy would be in it, and I liked them.

I decided to get the *Mickey Mouse* comic book, and I took it to the booth to Grandma, so she could pay for it before we left. Then I sat down across from Grandma, sipped my cherry smash, and looked toward the glass showcase, where the penny candy was. I tried to make up my mind which pieces I wanted, so I could tell Miss Ginnie as soon as she came in from church.

Miss Ginnie was a nice lady who might have been about BeeWee's age because she had gray hair. She pulled her hair back into a large gray bun on the back of her head. She was tall and always wore a brown cardigan sweater over a gray uniform. She wore no makeup.

I liked hard candy or Mary Janes because if I let them melt in my mouth instead of chewing them, they'd last all afternoon. I might even have two or three pieces left for the evening.

She finally came in, and when she saw me standing at the counter, she got out a little paper bag and held it open, waiting for me to tell her what I wanted. I decided on Mary Janes, ribbon candy, and cut rock candy. Then I didn't have anything chocolate, and I wanted something chocolate, too. I asked Miss Ginnie to put back the cut rock candy and give me

Tootsie Rolls instead. They were chewy, but I didn't have to chew them, so they'd last longer.

Grandma pulled out her little black change purse and gave me the money to pay for the comic book and candy. BeeWee unrolled his shirt sleeves, buttoned them, put on his jacket, and lifted his hat from the rack. The three of us walked back to the car together.

As soon as we got home, Grandma and I went upstairs and changed our clothes. Then, Grandma went to the kitchen to start cooking our Sunday dinner of fried chicken, creamed potatoes, and butter beans.

BeeWee stayed upstairs to take a nap. He was so used to working around the house that he hardly knew what to do with himself on Sunday afternoons because he didn't believe in working on the Sabbath Day. I thought he worked behind the beer counter at Robbins' Confectionary, but I'd heard Grandma say that BeeWee didn't consider it worked when he took Miss Ginnie's place, selling beer so she could go to church. He didn't get paid for it, so he thought he was doing a good thing. I thought he was doing a good thing, too. It would be a shame if a nice lady like Miss Ginnie couldn't go to church on Sunday.

I sat in the living room, looking at my Sunday school booklet and my new comic book. I knew I couldn't read, but I already knew the story in that day's Sunday school paper. I was just going through it again in my mind.

There was always a picture in the paper that showed a scene from the story, and I'd look at the picture again and again and wonder what it must have been like to have lived in those times. I imagined it would have been wonderful to see Jesus, to hear Him speak, and to know Him.

I could practically figure out the stories in the comic books because there were so many pictures.

By the time Grandma said our dinner was ready, I'd smelled the mouth-watering aroma of fried chicken for about an hour, and I was hungry. She woke up BeeWee, and we ate another delicious meal together.

After we finished eating, BeeWee said he was going upstairs to finish his nap. Grandma cleared the table, washed and dried dishes, and put them away. Then, she sat in her place at the kitchen table and read the Sunday newspaper. The house was quiet on Sunday afternoons because Grandma didn't turn on the radio, and Mama wasn't there to carry on a conversation with her.

I looked forward to listening to my favorite radio program, *The Shadow*, but it didn't come on until five-thirty, which was much later in the afternoon. I looked at all of the papers in my Sunday school booklet and thought of the stories again. Then, I admired my attendance stars inside the back cover. I got out all of my comic books and looked at each of them again.

If it wasn't so cold outside, I'd ride my tricycle on the sidewalk. I decided to ride it in the house for a while. I wondered what Mama and Daddy were doing, what Darrell was doing at his house, and I thought it would soon be time for my program because the sunlight was not as bright in the room.

Grandma brought in the radio, set it on the end table beside the chair, and plugged it in.

I turned to the station that broadcast *The Shadow* and thoroughly enjoyed the program. I liked everything about it, from the eerie music to the Shadow's eerie laugh. I loved it when the main character, Lamont Cranston, became the Shadow and surprised the crooks.

"Who's there?" they asked.

"It's the Shadow," said Lamont Cranston.

Then when the crooks asked the Shadow how he knew what they'd done and how to find them, Lamont Cranston said, "The Shadow knows," and laughed his eerie laugh.

I liked his girlfriend, Margo Lane, too. I thought she had a pretty name.

The moment the show was over, Grandma came to take the radio back to the kitchen to listen to the news. It was dusk, so Grandma pulled the chain in the brass floor lamp beside the chair to turn on the seven-and-a-half-watt light bulb.

There was nothing for me to do until Aunt Nita came home and read the Sunday funnies to me. I knew she'd be home soon, so I sat in the chair and looked toward the front windows to watch for her and to watch for it to become dark enough outside for the streetlight to come on.

Then, I stood on the radiator by the side living room window, pulled back one side of the lace curtain and the shade enough to look up at the sky to see if I could see the evening star. If I saw it, I'd make a wish.

I'd just sat down on the chair when Grandma came into the room, obviously distressed, and exclaimed, "The Japanese have bombed Pearl Harbor! They just announced it on the news."

That was the first time I'd heard of Pearl Harbor.

Grandma briefly explained to me that bombing meant blowing up something. I understood that from watching one cartoon character hand another character a bomb with a lighted fuse and run away as the bomb exploded and charred the bomb holder black.

In a cartoon, the character who'd just been blown up appeared in the next scene, seeking revenge, but I knew that in real life, the character would have been killed.

Grandma said the bombs were dropped from airplanes onto our Navy's ships, and it was a very serious thing. Some ships were sunk, and others were seriously damaged.

Many of our Navy men were killed.

I knew Japan was a country. I'd seen a lot of things in the dime stores with printing underneath that said: "made in Japan." When I asked Mama what the words said and why so many things were marked that way, she read the words to me and said Japan was the country that made them.

From what Grandma told me about Pearl Harbor, I could easily picture ships docked in a harbor because I was used to seeing ships docked at the piers when we went to pick up BeeWee from work.

The worst part, the part that I could actually understand best, was hearing about who was on the ships. It was sailors, maybe some of the same sailors, who were once stationed at the Norfolk Naval Base. I'd seen sailors in Norfolk for as long as I could remember.

While Grandma was calling Mama to find out if she'd heard the news, I thought back to the times when BeeWee gave rides to sailors.

Some Sunday afternoons, when the weather wasn't so cold, BeeWee took Grandma and me for a ride as far as the Naval Base's main gate, then turned the car around and drove us back home. BeeWee thought if he saw some sailors waiting for a bus, that it was his patriotic duty to give them a ride downtown. He stopped and offered them a ride. They piled into the car, and he drove them downtown. Sometimes Grandma had to sit in the middle and hold me on her lap because the back seat wouldn't hold all of them.

Grandma didn't like for BeeWee to pick up strangers, even if they were young men in Navy uniforms, but BeeWee said he did it to make them feel that someone in the city cared about them. Before the bombing of Pearl Harbor, many of the citizens of Norfolk ignored sailors.

I liked for BeeWee to pick up sailors because I liked riding downtown. They were all very nice; they talked with BeeWee about where they were from and thanked him for the ride.

Eventually, he picked up a group of sailors who were different from the rest. They used vulgar language when they were talking with each other. When we finally arrived downtown, and they got out of the car, Grandma was upset. "I'm so sorry you had to hear that kind of talk, honey. You won't hear it again, though. You and I just won't go for a Sunday drive anymore. Clarence, you can give rides to all the sailors you want by yourself from now on."

BeeWee surprised both of us by saying, "My days of giving rides to sailors are over. I'll find another way to do my patriotic duty."

"Grandma, why were they so different from the other sailors?"

"Honey, in all walks of life, there are good and bad people. There are plenty of good sailors in the navy. We've met a lot of them who are good, but that last group was bad. It's a shame they give a bad name to the rest of them."

I felt sad for the sailors at Pearl Harbor and wondered if any of the ones BeeWee had given rides to were there.

I thought about what would happen next. Would we still eat supper? Would Aunt Nita be able to come home? If so, would she still read the Sunday funnies to me? Would the planes that dropped bombs on Pearl Harbor fly over Norfolk and drop bombs on us, too?

When BeeWee came downstairs, Grandma told him the news, and he just shook his head from side to side.

Grandma said she'd warmed the leftovers from lunch for our supper, but BeeWee said he wasn't hungry. He never ate supper on Sunday night. I didn't know if he had no appetite, if he wanted to leave more for us, or if he missed having the bean sandwiches that he always took to work for his supper.

When Aunt Nita came home, she said she'd heard the news, and they'd been busier than ever at the telephone company. We sat side-by-side on the sofa as she read the Sunday funnies to me. She was always dressed in pretty clothes, had her brunette hair softly curled, wore Max Factor makeup, and smelled of Tweed or Bond Street cologne.

I liked the way the funnies were in color and were longer than they were during the week. *Blondie* was one of my favorites. I thought her husband Dagwood was funny, and his hair was combed in a funny way. *Henry* was a good one, too. He was a funny, bald-headed boy.

When Aunt Nita finished reading, she told Grandma that she was going out with her friends.

"Juanita, maybe you'd better stay in. At a time like this, you never know what's going to happen next."

"Mama, whatever happens, will happen, whether I'm at home or somewhere else."

"All right, but be careful."

"Don't worry. I will, Mama."

Grandma and I ate supper. She washed and dried the few supper dishes, then put them on the shelf. She took the radio into the living room, and we listened to *Henry Aldrich* and *The Great Gildersleeve*. Henry Aldrich was a teen-aged boy. At the beginning of each program, his mother called out, "Henry? Henry Aldrich!" He said, "Coming, Mother." The Great Gildersleeve was a middle-aged man who had a very funny voice and a funny way of laughing.

I was halfway listening to the programs and halfway wondering what would happen next.

That night I had a hard time going to sleep because I was thinking about what had happened and feeling sorry for the sailors. If I fell asleep, would I wake up the next morning? Or would enemy planes drop bombs on us while we were sleeping?

I listened for enemy planes until I finally fell asleep.

December 8, 1941

When I awoke the next morning, I opened my eyes slowly because I didn't know what I'd see. Had we been bombed in the night, and I'd see everything around me in complete shambles? Was my family still alive?

When my eyes were fully open, I saw that nothing had changed. Grandma soon came into the room and told me to sit up while she propped the pillow behind my back and said she'd bring my coffee, as she always did.

Grandma brought the cup of coffee and waited for me to drink it so she could take the cup downstairs. She didn't say anything about Pearl Harbor being bombed, so I was hoping I'd just had a bad dream.

I dressed and went downstairs to eat breakfast. BeeWee had finished his breakfast and was getting ready to go to the woodshed to clean and oil his rod and reel to prepare to go rock fishing when he got off from work.

Grandma and Mama said they thought it was too cold for him to go fishing.

BeeWee insisted, "I'll be wearing my union suit and my railroad jacket and cap, so I'll be all right. It'll be worth being cold to catch a couple of good-sized rock fish. That would be some good eating."

A union suit is another name for long underwear, so I did not believe that BeeWee would be warm enough, but he went anyway.

The morning newspaper was on the kitchen table at Grandma's place. She didn't usually keep the paper on the table at breakfast time. There was a tall, bold black headline that I couldn't read. Even if I could have read it, the headline was upside down from where I was sitting at BeeWee's place. Grandma always had me sit there when BeeWee wasn't at the table.

I didn't have to read it to know that it wasn't just a bad dream because Grandma started talking about it. She said the newspaper reported it was a surprise attack on Sunday morning in Hawaii that sank some of our ships and killed and wounded our men. President Roosevelt was going to ask Congress to declare war on Japan today.

Around noon, Grandma tuned to the news, and we heard that Congress had voted to declare war on Japan. We also heard that a lot of young men across the country were enlisting in the various branches of the service.

Three days later, we heard on the news that Germany and Italy had declared war on the United States.

Congress then had no choice but to declare war on those two countries. Although President Roosevelt wanted to keep our country out of war, he was forced to enter it after we were bombed by Japan. All the times that Grandma had said she was afraid we were going to war, she was right.

When President Roosevelt said in his "Fireside Chats" that he didn't want war, but we would prepare in case we were put in a position where we had no choice, he was right to do that. It was terrible to think we were at war, but good to know that our country had been preparing for it.

It was hard for me to believe our country was at war with three countries on two continents.

All the young men who lived on our block enlisted in the service. Grandma and the rest of the neighbors always referred to them as boys, just as they referred to their daughters and their neighbors' daughters as girls, even after they were married and had a child.

Our country was referring to them as young men who would report for training and eventually be sent overseas. Had it not been for the bombing of Pearl Harbor, they probably would have been at home, looking forward to celebrating the holidays with their families.

Getting Ready for Christmas

The day after BeeWee's payday, we went to buy the Christmas tree. It was a freezing cold day, cold enough for me to wear my tan woolen coat, hat, and legging set. The Christmas tree lot was filled with rows and rows of trees of all heights and sizes.

BeeWee told the salesman he wanted at least a ten-foot-tall tree, so the man led us to the rows of taller trees, taking out one at a time to spin it slowly so BeeWee could see if it was full enough. After choosing the tree, BeeWee and the man tied the cord around the branches, lifted the tree to the top of the car, and secured it with BeeWee's rope.

Back at Grandma's house, BeeWee got his hammer and some long nails from his toolbox at the bottom of the kitchen cabinet. I watched him position the holes in the tree stand over the small holes that were already in the floor, and I asked him why they were there.

"Those nail holes go back a long way to when your mother and Juanita were no older than you are now. I've always put the tree in this corner, so I wouldn't end up with nail holes all over the room."

For a few moments, I felt as though I was back in the time when Mama and Aunt Nita were little girls. I'd seen the picture of them sitting in a pony cart when they were about my age. They were wearing pretty, long-sleeved, light-colored dresses and had bobbed hair. Mama's hair was light, and Aunt Nita's was dark, the same as it was now. I could picture those two little girls standing in the same corner, watching their daddy.

Then, he started hammering, and the loud sound brought me back to the present. "That ought to do it," he said after driving in the long nails. He went to get the tree, and Grandma stood on the porch to hold the screen door open. When he set the tree in the stand, it was a little taller than the ten-foot ceiling, so he took out his pocketknife and cut a few inches from the top.

Grandma went upstairs and came back with a shoebox full of colored bulbs and several strands of lights.

BeeWee asked, "What do you think about having all blue lights this year?"

"I feel blue enough because we're at war, Clarence. I need to see something colorful and cheerful."

"Well, I guess I'll never have my way about the blue lights." He screwed in one bulb of each color, and then he repeated the process until each little socket contained a bulb. He plugged each strand of light into an electrical outlet. "I have to test each strand to be sure it'll light up. If one bulb has burned out, the whole strand won't light up. It's easier to find the bad bulb before I put the lights on the tree."

"BeeWee, if all the lights are out, how can you tell which one is burned out?"

He chuckled. "That's a good question, Sugie. If you look carefully at each bulb, you'll see that one of them has a brownish spot on it. That's the one that's burned out." He arranged the lights on the branches. Then, he turned them on and stood back to see if he'd arranged them uniformly over the tree. "That ought to do it. Now you and your Aunt Nita can decorate the tree when she comes home from work."

I was really excited when BeeWee said I could help Aunt Nita to decorate the tree. When Aunt Nita came home, Grandma went upstairs and came back with one of the two drawers from the bottom of the big wardrobe in the back bedroom.

"Juanita, you already know this, but I'm saying it for Shirley's benefit. The tree ornaments are in this drawer. Each one is wrapped in tissue paper because they're old and fragile. That means they'll break easily if you hold them too tight or drop them on the floor."

As Aunt Nita and I unwrapped all of the ornaments, I was in awe of the shiny colors, designs, shapes, and sizes. Some were long like icicles. Others were shaped like children's toys, such as blocks or dolls. There were round ornaments of all sizes and colors. I marveled over each ornament I unwrapped. Aunt Nita said they had belonged to her grandmother, who was my great-grandmother and Grandma's mother.

Aunt Nita stood on a kitchen chair to put the white star on the tree first. She had to be sure the white bulb at the top of the tree was behind the white, translucent plastic star, so the star would look bright. Then, she asked me to hand her one small ornament at a time to put on the top branches. She stood on the floor and reached up to put ornaments on the middle branches.

"Aunt Nita, I thought I was going to decorate the tree, too."

"Who said that, Shirley?"

"BeeWee."

"Oh, all right. You can put ornaments on the lower branches that you can reach, and you can help me put on the tinsel."

We finished putting on the ornaments, and Aunt Nita took a long, flat box from the drawer and opened it. She pulled out shiny, silver-colored strands that were about as long as BeeWee's foot-long ruler and showed me how to hang them by demonstrating on the top branches. "The tinsel is supposed to look like icicles on the tree."

We finished decorating the tree, Aunt Nita turned off the lights in the living room, and we stood back to look at it. It looked so beautiful that I lay back on the sofa, with my head on the arm, and gazed at it. The lighted star at the top of the tree looked heavenly.

Aunt Nita went to the kitchen to get Grandma so she could see the tree.

As Grandma walked into the living room, she marveled, "I've never seen a tree look prettier. You certainly did a nice job of decorating it."

The next day Mama and Grandma decided to put red, white, and blue lights in the windows.

Mama sat on the sofa with the shoe box of colored Christmas bulbs, now about one-third full, and two long, ivory-colored, plastic candlestick window light sets that had electrical cords. There were ten candlesticks on each light set. Each one was cylindrical in shape, like candles. The tops had small round openings, or sockets, where the bulbs were screwed in. The two candlesticks in the center were the tallest. The four candlesticks on each side gradually tapered off in height until they were short on each end. Grandma was right about Mama knowing how to make the window lights look pretty.

She arranged the bulbs in a pattern, putting two white bulbs in the center and alternating red and blue lights on each side. Then, she screwed in the bulbs in the other light set in the same pattern. She set the light sets on the two front living room windowsills, making sure they were centered. Then, she arranged the lace curtains so they were back in place.

When she was ready to plug in the lights, Mama asked Grandma to come into the living room to see if she was satisfied with the color pattern.

"I think they'll look fine," Grandma said as she followed Mama into the living room.

Mama pulled the sofa away from the windows enough to reach the electrical outlets and plugged in the lights.

I thought they looked beautiful through the lace curtains.

"Florencie, you've done it again! You've come up with just the right colors. I think the two white lights on the top make it look better than ever," Grandma exclaimed.

Then, we went on the front porch to see how the lights looked from the outside of the windows and came into the house shivering from being in the cold air without our coats. A lot of work had gone into making those two front living room windows look beautiful for Christmas.

Was it worth it? Absolutely. When a family works together to keep traditions, it is a loving way to live.

Going Downtown to See Santa Claus

One afternoon Mama took me downtown to see Santa Claus, who was in the window of a large department store that I hadn't seen before because it was farther downtown than Granby Street, where most of the stores were.

We arrived downtown and walked the short distance to the department store.

There he was. Santa was big, and he was sitting on a wide, high back chair in the corner window of the store, saying, "Ho, ho, ho."

Other children were standing there, holding their mothers' hands, just as I was.

After we watched Santa for a few minutes, I began worrying about getting back to Grandma's house in time to hear Santa's radio program that was broadcast from the North Pole, so we crossed the street to wait for a bus.

The bus that drove us back wasn't crowded. Mama said the sailors wouldn't be on the bus because they'd stay downtown all evening, and the people who worked downtown and rode the bus home hadn't gotten off from work yet. Some people who worked downtown had cars, but they left them parked at home and rode the bus to and from work because there weren't enough parking spaces downtown. I liked being able to sit down while the bus was moving.

We got back in plenty of time for me to hear Santa Claus. Daddy picked up Mama, and Grandma and I ate our soup before the program started. It came on with *Jingle Bells* playing. Then Santa started talking to the boys and girls. He said we could write letters to him addressed to the North Pole, but I couldn't write yet.

As I listened to more Santa Claus programs, I enjoyed listening to him read the letters from boys and girls who could write. His radio program was only on for about fifteen minutes each weekday, around supper time. He always called out the names of children whose homes he planned to visit on Christmas Eve. He said for us to listen for our names but not to be disappointed if we didn't hear them because he'd still be paying a visit to all of us anyway. I listened carefully for my name each time, but I didn't hear it until one of his last programs before Christmas.

Grandma told me Santa fell down the chimney and broke some of her toys and that he brought her a pair of shoes with pointed toes that caused her feet to hurt. She also said he left switches and ashes for bad children.

"Do you think he'll bring me switches and ashes, Grandma?"

"Not if you're a good girl."

"Do you think I've been good enough not to get switches and ashes?"

"Well, Santa will have to decide that according to whether he thinks you've been good all year, not just if you've been good in the weeks before Christmas."

I thought Grandma was joking about Santa falling down the chimney and breaking some of her toys, and bringing her shoes that hurt her feet because she was laughing.

He called out my name on the radio, so I knew he planned to bring me something. I just wanted to see Santa when he came, with his reindeer pulling his sleigh full of toys.

By Christmas Eve night, Grandma was making the same preparations for the Christmas dinner that she'd made for Thanksgiving. The turkey, roasting in the oven, already smelled good.

Sometimes I left the kitchen to look at the Christmas tree in the living room or to look through the front door glass to try to see if Santa was flying over the rooftops on his sleigh, pulled by his reindeer. I stood at the front door and looked as hard as I could, but I never saw Santa and his reindeer.

My favorite Christmas song at the time was *Up on a Housetop*, which I heard on the radio almost every night. I didn't know most of the words, but I liked to sing what I did know, which was, "Up on a housetop, click, click, click, down through the chimney comes good Saint Nick."

Aunt Nita came home and said, "I've always heard Santa won't come and leave you anything as long as you're awake."

"I'd better go upstairs to bed and go to sleep. Goodnight, Grandma. Goodnight, Aunt Nita."

Grandma took me upstairs and lay beside me until I fell asleep, wondering if Santa would come at all, or if he'd come and leave switches and ashes, or if he'd leave broken toys and shoes with pointed toes.

I suddenly thought he might not know I was here. He might think I lived with Mama and Daddy, and they didn't have a chimney. I drifted off to sleep, deciding I'd much rather for him to bring me broken toys, or even switches and ashes, than not to come. If he didn't come at all, I wouldn't know why. Maybe he may have thought I'd been too bad during the year, or maybe he just didn't like me.

Christmas of 1941

I woke up the next morning when Grandma came in the room to tell me I could go downstairs in my robe and slippers. I put on my long, rose-colored chenille robe with matching slippers and followed Grandma downstairs. BeeWee was sitting in the high-back chair in the corner. When I looked toward the Christmas tree, I saw that Santa had come. There was a child's maple table and chair set beside the tree and some boxes underneath.

I was so happy and excited that I started trembling.

There was a square box with a cellophane center, and I saw a tea set with little green glass dishes, cups, saucers, and a teapot. There were little metal knives, forks, and spoons. I'd use those to set my table. I saw a pretty doll baby through the cellophane top of a rectangular-shaped box.

BeeWee showed me my stocking that was nailed to the mantle. It was actually a new, white work sock that was bulging with bumps of various shapes and sizes. The 'bumps' turned out to be a shiny red apple, a bright orange tangerine, a banana, and some English walnuts. At the very bottom, there was something wrapped in a small square of waxed paper. I opened it and saw hard Christmas candy that was broken into small pieces. "Grandma, Santa must have fallen down the chimney again because my candy is broken."

Grandma and BeeWee laughed.

"Well, honey, I'm glad your candy is in small pieces. I've never liked big pieces of hard candy since your mother got a jawbreaker caught in her throat in Woolworth's five and ten cent store. She lost her breath and sank to the floor. I had to reach my finger down her throat and pull out the candy. My fingernail scratched her throat, and she ended up having an abscessed throat and missing a semester of school."

I was sorry Mama and Grandma had to go through that, but I didn't like jawbreakers anyway because they were too big and round.

Grandma said she was going to cook breakfast, and we'd eat. I had to get dressed in case someone came; then, I could go back into the living room to play with my things.

After breakfast, I opened the box containing my tea set and carefully placed the dishes on the table. I opened the box with my doll and cradled her in my arms. BeeWee had that little twinkle in the corner of his eye as he sat in the living room chair and watched me enjoy seeing my things for the first time.

Eventually, Grandma came from the kitchen, where she'd been washing breakfast dishes and preparing dinner, to remind me I needed to get dressed in case somebody came.

BeeWee said sadly, "I thought Florencie would be here first thing this morning. She should have been here. When is she coming?"

"I don't know, Clarence." Grandma sighed.

Grandma put out my clothes and shoes for me, and I got dressed. She combed my hair, and we went downstairs.

We had soup for lunch, and then I played a waitress. I was the customer, telling the waitress what I wanted. Then I was the waitress, taking the order, serving it, and pretending to collect the money for the meal.

By the early afternoon, BeeWee was near tears because the day was going by, and Mama hadn't come.

"Clarence, why don't you take a nap? You haven't had a nap all day. By the time you wake up, Florencie will probably be here. You know everybody's coming for the Christmas dinner."

After BeeWee went upstairs, Grandma shook her head. "Don't worry about BeeWee. He's depressed, but he'll get over it when your mama and daddy and Juanita come."

"What does 'depressed' mean, Grandma?"

"It means he feels sad."

"Why?"

"He thinks your mother should be here on Christmas morning, and he starts feeling sad when she doesn't come."

"Oh." I went back to playing waitress.

Mama and Daddy eventually came in the late afternoon, Aunt Nita got off from work and came home, and BeeWee woke up and came downstairs. Grandma put the food on the dining room table and called us to eat.

The food was as delicious as it had been on Thanksgiving. We had all the same things except there was not only a Nolde's pound cake for dessert, but there was a fruit cake, too. It had pecan halves, candied cherries, and candied pineapple on the top.

By the time we finished eating all the good food Grandma had cooked, we said we didn't know if we had room for cake, but we all managed to eat a small slice of one or the other of the cakes. I had fruit cake for the first time, and I really liked it.

Grandma put the leftovers away and washed the mountain of dirty dishes while the other adults sat in the living room and talked. As usual, BeeWee and Daddy smoked cigarettes and talked shop, which meant they were talking about their work on the railroad. Whenever they got together, Mama and Aunt Nita always talked about clothes, movies, and people they both knew. I played on the rug with my new Tiddley Winks game and listened to their conversations for a while, and then I went to the kitchen to talk with Grandma.

Grandma finally got to the point where she had put everything away and washed a few dishes. Then, she came into the living room for the family to exchange presents.

Grandma and BeeWee gave Mama, Aunt Nita, and me a locket from Frank Ford's jewelry store. Theirs was a large gold heart on a black velvet ribbon chain. Their lockets opened so they could put in a little picture. Mama said she was going to put in her favorite baby picture of me. My locket had a small gold heart on a short, gold chain. Grandma and BeeWee said I could wear it to Sunday school and take it off afterward, so the chain wouldn't get broken.

Grandma received a new white slip and a box of three pairs of Hanes hose. BeeWee received a carton of cigarettes from Mama and Daddy, and a smoking stand for the living room from Aunt Nita. Cigarette companies sold special holiday cartons that were popular gifts for smokers.

Grandma said we were blessed to have such a nice Christmas because so many families didn't have their boys with them this year because of the war. Those families included all of Grandma's neighbors who had boys who were old enough to enlist in the service.

I guess my family and everyone else in the country knew the holidays were the calm before the storm. We couldn't be at war with three countries and expect everything to go on as it had before.

Part II – 1942

New Year's Resolutions and Prayers

Aunt Nita let me know we'd make New Year's resolutions when she got home from work on New Year's Day. I didn't know what that meant, but she said she would explain it when she got here.

While I ate breakfast that morning, Grandma told me she read in the paper that President Roosevelt proclaimed New Year's Day as a National Day of Prayer. Grandma and I knelt beside the bed and prayed together every night. After the Pearl Harbor attack, we included prayers for our country, our servicemen, and our president. We were already praying for everyone in the world because Grandma said countries were at war and children in some parts of the world were starving. I felt sorry for them.

From the time I heard about the bombing of our ships at Pearl Harbor, I was always afraid the United States would be bombed. When I heard a plane fly over or saw one in the sky, I always prayed that it wasn't an enemy plane about to drop bombs on us. There were searchlights trained on the evening sky every night to spot enemy planes if they flew over.

When Aunt Nita came home, we sat side-by-side on the sofa, and she explained that we made New Year's resolutions to try to improve ourselves. "Shirley, can you think of something you'd like to do better this year than you did last year?"

"I want to stay with Mama when we go shopping, not leave the store, and not go out in the street again."

"Those are good resolutions. I'll write them down now; then, I have to get ready to go out."

I always wished that Nita and I could spend more time together.

The Soldier

I was disappointed that Aunt Nita didn't spend more time with me, but I was happy when she said she had a date with a soldier who would be here in an hour. I could hardly wait to see him in his uniform.

She met a lot of young servicemen because they filled every bus, taxicab, and streetcars that were still running. When they were not on duty, they headed for downtown Norfolk. We all liked to go downtown. It was the place to go because almost everything was there. You didn't even have to drive. There were buses to take you there from anywhere in Norfolk. For example, there were three large first-run movie theaters on Granby Street and four theaters on side streets with lower-priced admissions because they didn't show first-run movies. All kinds of restaurants, large department stores, drugstores, specialty shops, and dime stores were downtown. You could find almost anything you wanted. There was even a large city market for those who wanted to buy fresh fruit, vegetables, flowers, and eggs. There were even lunch counters, where you could sit and eat homemade soup and drink iced tea or have a sandwich and coffee.

Aunt Nita went upstairs to get ready for her date, and I ran to the kitchen to tell Grandma about it.

"Grandma, I wonder what a soldier's uniform looks like."

"I wonder why Juanita didn't tell me someone was coming over."

"I was going to tell you, but somebody beat me to it," said Aunt Nita as she walked into the room.

"How in the world did you meet a soldier?" exclaimed Grandma.

"Oh, Mama, busloads of soldiers have started coming downtown because they're stationed way out in the boondocks, where there's nothing to do."

"Well, I'll be. I didn't know that. Don't you want me to fix you something to eat before you go out?"

"No. Thanks anyway, but we're eating out." She smiled.

Grandma turned toward me. "I guess we should go ahead and eat our supper before he comes, honey."

"Don't worry. He won't be here long."

"Aren't you going to wear your fur coat, Aunt Nita?"

"No. It's just a casual date. We're double dating with Paulette and another soldier. We're going to get cheeseburgers and shakes and go to a movie."

When the soldier came in, he put his hat on the table and sat on the sofa. Aunt Nita introduced us, and he let me wear his hat, just as other young men had done. The only difference was that the soldier's uniform and hat were khaki.

After they left, I just had to be silly. "You know what, Grandma? I think soldiers' uniforms are cute."

She laughed.

Our city was called a navy town because the Norfolk Naval Base was one of the largest naval bases, maybe the largest in the world.

The same families had lived in the same houses and apartments and had known each other for years. My mother and Aunt Nita were actually the third generation of a family who had lived in the same house since my great-grandmother had bought the house when Grandma and her sisters were teenagers. Although I was the fourth generation to live in the house, I was the only child who lived on the block. Some of Mama's and Aunt Nita's neighborhood friends were single and working; others had married and moved away or were in the service.

Before Pearl Harbor was bombed and the United States entered World War II, sailors were practically ignored by many Norfolk citizens because they thought if their daughters dated sailors, the sailor would soon be transferred to another port and break their daughters' hearts when they left.

Their attitudes might have changed when their sons, grandsons, brothers, nephews, and neighbors enlisted in the service after the bombing of Pearl Harbor. Their young men were stationed in other cities, states, and countries, which enabled many Norfolk citizens to empathize with the sailors here. They were welcomed by USO's and churches, and local residents. As a child, seeing them all over the city made me feel better protected.

Aunt Nita's Mail

Aunt Nita enjoyed writing letters to the servicemen she knew, and they wrote to her, even before the war, but she never shared the letters with us. She only showed us the stationary she bought, with the funny cartoons around the edges.

Mr. Watson, the mailman, came about the same time each day. Since he was very nice and friendly, Grandma, Mama, and I went to the door to speak to him and get the mail. He always handed it to me, and I gave it to Grandma, who sorted it between hers, BeeWee's, and Aunt Nita's mail while Mama and I watched. Then she put Aunt Nita's mail on the top shelf of the living room mantle.

One of the envelopes had the letters S.W.A.K. printed on the flap of the envelope. I wondered what the letters meant, but before I could ask, I heard Mama say to Grandma, "That one must like her a lot to write 'sealed with a kiss' on the envelope."

"That doesn't mean a thing, Florencie. He probably writes to a lot of girls and puts it on every envelope."

Mama laughed. "Nita sure gets a lot of mail these days."

"I know! I never thought I'd see more letters for Juanita than bills for your daddy."

They both laughed, obviously enjoying seeing Aunt Nita get so many letters.

Grandma, Mama, and I were anxious for Aunt Nita to mention receiving the letters and to tell us something about the letter writers. I wondered if some of the letters were from the young men who had let me wear their hats.

From what I heard Grandma and Mama say, I thought they would like to know if she cared more for one young man than the others or if one young man cared more for her than the others.

Nita definitely wasn't the type of girl to share any of her business with the family. Then, I had what I thought would be a good idea. I thought if I looked at Aunt Nita's letters, I'd find out the information we wanted to know. I even thought that Mama and Grandma would be pleased with me if I could find out something to tell them.

If I could see the word 'love' in a letter, I'd know the young man who wrote it was the one who cared the most for Aunt Nita. It was ridiculous reasoning because the only names I could read were Grandma, BeeWee, Mama, Daddy, Aunt Nita, Shirley, and Grandma's sisters, Mary, Grace, and Sadie. If I saw the word 'love,' I wouldn't be able to read the name of the person who wrote it, but I hadn't thought that far ahead.

Grandma always shared her letters from her sister, Mary, in Tampa, Florida, and her sister, Grace, in Annapolis, Maryland. After she read a letter, she handed it to Mama to read and then let me look at it. That's how I recognized the names. Her sister Sadie lived in Norfolk, so she didn't write letters to Grandma, but she sent a Christmas card every year.

One night, when I was in bed and still awake but with my eyes closed, Aunt Nita came into her room, sat on the vanity bench at her dressing table, turned on one of the pretty little dressing table lamps, and read her mail. When she finished reading it, she put the letters in the top right dressing table drawer.

The next afternoon, while Grandma and Mama listened to soap operas, I tiptoed upstairs, opened Aunt Nita's right dressing table drawer, and saw a stack of letters. I picked up the letter on the top of the stack, took it out of the envelope, and searched it for the word 'love.' It was there, near the end of the letter, but I was disappointed because I couldn't read the name of the person who signed it.

When I heard someone coming up the steps, I threw the letter and envelope in the drawer as quickly as I could, closed it, and hurried from the room.

Mama and I met in the hall as she reached the top of the stairs and turned left.

"What are you doing up here?" demanded Mama.

"Nothing."

"Why did you come upstairs?"

"To go to the bathroom," I lied.

"You're not getting into Nita's things, are you?"

"No," I clung to the lie.

"Go on to the bathroom, then. I'll wait for you," she replied suspiciously.

I went into the bathroom, hooked the door, stood for a minute, flushed the toilet so Mama would hear it, and washed my hands. I thought I was fooling her. She gave me a look when I came out of the bathroom that practically told me she didn't believe me. I knew, too late, it was wrong for me to open Aunt Nita's drawer and look at her letter, but I'd already done it.

I tried to convince myself that Aunt Nita wouldn't mind because she knew I couldn't read, but I knew I shouldn't have gone into her room except to sleep and to dress. I also felt terrible about lying. It was the first time I'd told a lie, so I had no idea how terrible it would make me feel. I should have felt guilty enough to confess, but I decided to try to get by with it.

That night when Aunt Nita came home and opened her drawer, she said, "Shirley, you've been in my drawer, looking at my letters, haven't you?"

I pretended to be asleep. I didn't want to admit what I'd done because I was afraid she'd tell Mama, and I'd get a switching.

"I can tell you were bothering my letters because I always keep them in the envelopes, and this letter is not in the envelope. You stay out of my mail. It's very bad to read someone else's mail. I know you hear me, so don't expect me to scratch your back anymore until you admit what you did."

Now I felt worse than ever. If Grandma asked me, I'd tell her the truth, but she didn't ask. She just said, "They say curiosity kills the cat."

The next morning, after breakfast, I went upstairs with Mama to brush my teeth. It was darker in the hall because Aunt Nita's door was closed. That was unusual because the door was always open during the day.

I knew why it was closed, and I thought it was probably locked, too. Mama or Grandma had to have done it because Aunt Nita had gone to work before I woke up. She might have asked them to close her door, though.

As soon as Mama and I went downstairs to the kitchen, I told Mama I was sorry for looking at Aunt Nita's letter and for not admitting it to her right away.

Mama walked to the Hoosier cabinet, stood on her tiptoes, and pulled down a switch.

I started crying, and Grandma intervened, "Florencie, the child's never done anything like this before; she said she's sorry, and she told you she wouldn't do it again. Can't you forgive her just this one time?"

"I'll let it go this one time, but don't expect to get away with anything like this again, young lady."

After Mama left, I thanked Grandma for saving me from a switching. I told her I was going to apologize to Aunt Nita when she came home.

"I'm just glad to see that you have a conscience, honey."

"What's that?"

"A conscience is something like a little voice inside that tells us right from wrong. If you do something wrong to someone and it bothers you, then you have a conscience. It will play on your mind and make you feel bad until you admit you did wrong and apologize for it. If you do something wrong to someone and it doesn't bother you, then you don't have a conscience."

I apologized to Aunt Nita that night. She thanked me for the apology and forgave me. The terrible feeling in my stomach went away.

"Let's scratch backs," Aunt Nita suggested.

I was happy to hear those words again.

The next day I noticed her bedroom door was left open.

Going to the Movies with Grandma

Grandma started taking me to see a movie about once every week or two. We walked to the Rosna, which was a nice neighborhood theater on 35th Street, about three or four blocks from Grandma's house. We both liked the same kinds of movies, especially musicals. Some of those were in technicolor.

Besides seeing the movie, we saw a newsreel and three cartoons. I liked the movies, and I thought the cartoons were funny, but for some reason, I never laughed out loud at them the way some people in the theater did.

Grandma liked the newsreels because they were a review of the week's news. There was news of happenings in sports, entertainment, and other areas of interest, especially the war. I was surprised that reporters and photographers went all the way to Germany and to the other war zones. I'll never forget seeing the picture of the horrible Adolf Hitler standing on his balcony to review the Nazi army as they marched on the street below him. They wore high, black leather boots, carried long guns, and had a quick, high-stepping march that scared me.

I was afraid of Hitler because I knew he was the meanest man in the world. He had declared war on us and was our enemy. I heard on the news and saw in the newspapers, *Life* magazine, and in the newsreels that he was invading other countries and ordering atrocious things to be done to Jewish people, even in his own country. German people who were not Nazis lived in fear of him. I wondered how long it would be until his Nazi army invaded our country and did the same atrocious things to us.

It was dark when Grandma and I came out of the theater, and we had those three or four blocks to walk home. There were houses all along the way, but most of the windows were dark. One house had a large, wooded lot beside it. Grandma didn't want to walk past it after dark because she said she was afraid someone might hide there and jump out at us.

Just before we got to that house, Grandma and I crossed the street and walked on the wide, grass-covered median that separated one side of the street from the other in that block. When we reached the end of the median, I liked to stop and look up at the stars because there was an unobstructed view of the night sky. Grandma was anxious to get home before anything happened to us. I guess I was, too, but I still wanted to gaze at the sky. I was in awe of how there were so many stars and how they did seem to twinkle like diamonds high up in the sky, as someone wrote in the rhyme *Twinkle, Twinkle Little Star*.

Signs of the Times

We were sorry to hear there was a sugar shortage. Grocery stores had to start rationing their customers, and everyone in the country had to cut down on the amount of sugar they used. Grandma never bought a lot of sugar anyway. She always bought the smallest bag, so it didn't affect us much. We were just afraid the shortage would become worse until there was no sugar at all. We'd miss sweetening our coffee and iced tea.

For some reason, Mama and Daddy weren't satisfied with the apartment, so they moved again. This time they moved to a white, second-floor duplex on a corner, where they had more rooms than they'd had in the apartment. There were outside stairs on the back of the house that led to the second floor, where there was a small porch with a swing. Behind the swing, there was a window. The back door was to the right of the swing and the window.

I liked their new place, mostly because of the swing and the fact that there was a huge fig bush in the back yard that was said to bear lots of figs every summer.

Because of the war, they had difficulty getting a telephone installed. No one could have a new telephone installed unless the War Production Board determined it was absolutely necessary. Daddy explained the railroad needed to contact him to let him know what time to report to work when he was on the extra board.

The railroad put Daddy's name on the extra board when a coal strike was over. Then he couldn't work as an auto mechanic because he had to stay at home in case the railroad called. When they called, he had to be available to go to work at any time of the day. Being on the extra board was good because he received credit for every day that he worked, which added to his seniority. The drawback was that he might not receive enough work to earn full-time pay for a while until enough coal was mined to send to the railroads again.

Daddy eventually got the telephone before he was put on the extra board.

BeeWee wasn't laid off during coal strikes because he had seniority, which meant he had worked there for a long time.

President Roosevelt told John L. Lewis, the leader of the mine workers, that during the war, he didn't want any delays in mining coal because it could result in America's defeat.

The labor unions agreed there would be no strikes. President Roosevelt was given the authority to take charge of the coal industry if there was another strike. Work was stopped in some mines anyway, but President Roosevelt appealed to the coal miners to go back to work for the good of their country.

He said he would try to help the miners and all workers in the country by controlling prices. He would control rent and lower the prices of necessities if they rose too high. We were happy to hear there would be price controls because Grandma had already noticed that prices had gone up on some groceries, especially meats, or as Grandma put it, "The price of meats has gone sky high."

Grandma read in the newspaper there were now twice as many long-distance calls as there had been in the past year. Men who enlisted in the service, those who were drafted, and those taking defense jobs in other parts of the country made a lot of telephone calls to their family members and friends they had left behind.

Aunt Nita said they stayed busy at the telephone company, but she was used to being busy because she worked during the day when all the businesses were making their calls.

Just as Aunt Nita had heard from the Chevrolet salesman when she talked BeeWee into trading his old De Soto for the 1941 Chevrolet, the automobile manufacturers stopped making cars and became defense plants. They were now making airplanes and other equipment for the war.

BeeWee and Aunt Nita said they were glad they got the new car when they did.

We heard on the news that record numbers of married women, who had traditionally stayed at home to cook and care for their families, were now filling jobs that had been held by men who enlisted or were drafted.

They discovered they could do jobs that previously had been done only by men. A lot of those jobs were in defense plants. The women worked on assembly lines, making airplanes and all the essential supplies for the war.

Before December 7, 1941, those women probably would never have dreamed they'd ever make planes, ships, and tanks.

There were ration coupons for almost everything, including meats, sugar, and gasoline. Mama stood in the long lines to get the ration coupon books for each member of the family.

People had ration coupon books because the government required them to limit the number of certain items that people could buy. Everyone in the family had a ration book. You had to take your ration book to the store. The coupon book and the money would be handed to the cashier, who would tear out the coupons for the items being purchased. If you didn't have your coupon book, then you couldn't buy the item. Some things like produce and unsliced bread didn't require coupons.

We were lucky that we lived near the Eastern Shore, where vegetables were grown, so there were plenty of vegetables year-round.

Slicing Bread and Rolling Cigarettes

Soon there was no more sliced bread. It only came in whole, unsliced loaves.

When I asked Grandma about it, she said, "That's all right. I have a bread knife, and I'm used to slicing pork and bean sandwiches in half every day."

When we had a slice of bread with a meal or a bowl of soup, Grandma could easily slice bread from the whole loaf because it didn't have to be any particular size, but she found that slicing bread for sandwiches wasn't as easy as cutting a sandwich in half. The bread had a soft crust and had to be mashed flat every time a piece of bread was sliced. It seemed to be impossible for her to cut two pieces of bread the same size. We laughed until our sides hurt every time Grandma made a sandwich because one slice of bread was thin and lopsided, and the other slice was thick and lopsided. Even BeeWee laughed when he saw his funny-looking bean sandwiches.

There might have been whole loaves of hard-crusted, coarse bread that would have been easy to slice, but Grandma liked Nolde's freshest soft white bread. The rest of the family liked it, too.

Mama remarked that she couldn't understand why Grandma had such a hard time slicing the bread evenly.

One day, Grandma became a bit exasperated and announced that she'd turn over slicing bread for sandwiches to Mama.

Mama was happy to try her hand at it, and BeeWee said, "I don't care how the bread looks as long as it holds my sandwiches together. Maybe you can slice the bread, so my sandwiches won't fall apart when I'm trying to eat my supper."

We laughed just as much at Mama's bread-slicing as we did at Grandma's.

"I thought it would be easy, but slicing two pieces of bread the same size is not as easy as it looks," Mama admitted.

"I'll bet I could do it," I blurted out.

"No, honey. I don't want you cutting your hand."

"Please, Grandma. I know I can do it."

"Let her try it, Mama, so she can see for herself. I'll watch her with the knife. If she can slice bread better than we can, then she can slice all the bread for sandwiches from now on."

"Go to the sink and wash your hands good with soap and water and dry them," Grandma told me.

I did as she said and then stood beside what was left of the loaf of bread.

"Now, be careful with this knife, honey. Don't get your fingers in the way, or you'll cut yourself."

I carefully cut two slices of bread from the loaf, but my bread slicing was worse than theirs. I couldn't even cut complete slices. They didn't laugh at me, though. "You were right. It's not as easy as it looks."

I wondered how long we'd have to slice our own bread. Since none of us could slice it well enough to make a good sandwich, I hoped, for BeeWee's sake, that the stores would have sliced bread again soon. I wouldn't want to try to eat a bean sandwich that was falling apart. The only time the rest of us ate sandwiches was when we went to Lynnhaven, and we couldn't do that until gas rationing and the ban on pleasure driving was over.

Since BeeWee didn't give rides to sailors anymore, he said he was looking for another way to do his patriotic duty, and he found it.

One morning after breakfast, Grandma cleared his dishes away, and he set out a little white cloth bag with a yellow drawstring and a little stack of small, thin pieces of paper.

"What are you going to do, BeeWee?"

"I'm going to roll my own cigarettes because cigarettes might become scarce. If I roll my own, I'll be sure not to run out of them, and there'll be more for the troops." He set a wrapper on the table, opened the little bag, shook some tobacco on the paper, and rolled it. He licked one edge of the paper and pressed it against the side of the freshly rolled cigarette to seal it. Then, he put it between his lips, struck a match to light it, and began smoking. When he started coughing, he took it from his mouth just before it fell apart.

After he stopped coughing, he put the cigarette back in his mouth. It hung from his lips in a flimsy, bent way that made him look like a bum who was smoking cigarette butts. We doubled over with laughter.

BeeWee walked into the living room and looked at his reflection in the mirror over the mantle to see what was so funny about the homemade cigarette in his mouth. Then, he turned around and said, "I don't see anything wrong with it."

We burst out laughing again, and I thought I saw a twinkle in the corner of his eye.

BeeWee was not the type of person who would pay money for something and not use it, so he rolled all of the cigarettes he smoked in the house until he used up the tobacco and the wrappers.

When I asked him if he was going to buy more, he explained, "Well, it takes up time, and so far, there doesn't seem to be a shortage. We might not even have one."

BeeWee could be funny without meaning to be and had a good sense of humor about it.

The War Effort

Everyone pitched in to help with the war effort. People saved everything from scrap metal and old rubber tires to soap scraps because everything was needed. There were scrap metal drives to collect all the old metal everyone could find. People cleaned out their woodsheds and garages, looking for broken metal yard tools, old hubcaps, and old metal toys. Rubber drives rounded up the worn-out automobile and bike tires, inner tubes, and garden hoses.

The 'bars' of soap that BeeWee made from soap scraps were too soft. They were all right for washing hands but terrible for taking baths because they'd fall apart in the warm bath water. We solved the problem by using only store-bought bars of soap for baths and using homemade soap for washing our hands.

Some people had victory gardens in their yards. They grew their own vegetables, but fresh vegetables were plentiful in Virginia because there were so many farms. Growing their own vegetables was a bit more economical, though, and it assured their families of having plenty to eat.

Fresh fruit and vegetables were so plentiful we didn't need ration coupons for them because Virginia and many other states had plenty of farmland and farmers who had the skill to raise abundant crops.

I wanted to plant a victory garden of my own, so BeeWee helped me to plant potato "eyes." For a while, I was excited to think I was growing potatoes for the family. I could hardly wait to go out and look at them each morning. Green plants grew, and they got leaves and beetles on them, but no potatoes. I figured out later that potatoes grow in the ground, but I didn't know at the time; I guess I should have asked BeeWee.

Luckily, everyone could buy all the potatoes they wanted. Grandma said nothing was cheaper than potatoes and onions.

President Roosevelt encouraged people to have some meatless meals, which was easy for us because we already had two meatless meals a day. Even before the war started, we also had a meatless day once or twice every two weeks. On a day or two before BeeWee's payday,

Grandma always made delicious potato soup that we ate with bread and butter.

On payday, Grandma and BeeWee bought enough potatoes and onions to last for two weeks, and Grandma called the market to order a stick of butter and a loaf of bread a couple of days before the next payday. She used part of the butter to flavor the soup and saved the rest for us to spread on our bread. We enjoyed the soup as much as we enjoyed all of Grandma's good cooking. She had the knack for being able to make something delicious out of very few ingredients.

Citizens who could make out without a car did their part to help the war effort by parking their cars in their back yards or in their garages. They said they were leaving them there until the war was over.

Lost and Found

For my fifth birthday, Grandma, Mama, BeeWee, and I had devil's food birthday cake with white frosting, vanilla ice cream slices, ginger ale, peanuts, and butter mints, the same as we had last year.

I didn't invite Aunt Nita's friends this year. I was old enough by now to realize that even though they were friendly to me on the telephone, they were Aunt Nita's friends, not mine. In fact, I was embarrassed when I thought back about inviting them the year before.

I received nice gifts from my family, including a gold signet ring from Grandma and BeeWee. They explained they didn't have it engraved with my initial because they weren't sure it would fit me. The ring was a little loose on my pinky finger and too small for the finger next to it.

Grandma, Mama, and BeeWee decided I would wear the ring on my pinky finger, but I needed to be careful with it because it was a little loose. Grandma and BeeWee said they would take it to have my initial engraved on it on BeeWee's next payday when they would have the money for the engraving and be dressed to go downtown to the Frank Ford jewelry store.

A few days later, Aunt Nita was reading the Sunday funnies to me when she suddenly stopped. "Where's your ring?"

When I saw that it wasn't on my finger, I knew I had lost it because I never took it off. I looked for it on the living room floor, under the sofa cushions, and under the chair I had sat in for part of the afternoon. Although I rode my tricycle in front of the house, I couldn't look for my ring outside because it was already dark.

Worrying about my ring kept me awake for a long time after I went to bed. I was trying to retrace my steps in my mind, but there were so many places I could have lost it. Maybe it was in the car, Sunday school, the confectionary, almost anywhere in the house, in the front of the house, or even down the drain when I washed my hands.

I was going to look for it outside the next morning, but I woke up later than usual. I got dressed and ate breakfast late. Now I could do more for myself, like combing my hair, but Mama said I missed the hair on the back of my head. I stood in the middle of the living room while she combed the back of my hair, and there was a knock at the door.

Mama went to the door, and I heard her say, "I never thought we'd see that little ring again."

I rushed to the door and saw a little girl standing there.

Mama told me, "This little girl found your ring."

When Mama showed me the ring, I saw it was bent too badly for me to slip it back on my finger.

"Maybe BeeWee can straighten it out for you," she suggested.

The little girl looked like my exact opposite. She was short and pudgy, and I was tall and slim. She had short, dark brown, curly hair, and I had long, straight, dark blonde hair. She had dark brown eyes and freckles. I had blue eyes and no freckles.

Mama brought my coat, and I went outside on the porch.

"My name is Shirley. What's your name?"

"My name's Crissy." She walked me over to where she'd found the ring. It was surprising how quiet she was after she was able to knock on the door and talk to Mama about the ring.

"Where do you live?" I asked.

She stood on the sidewalk and pointed to a house that was at the end of the block.

That was the house with the mean, barking dog that caused me to run to Grandma's when I saw it coming from half a block away. It was small, dark brown, and ferocious. It barked and growled at everyone. "I'm scared of your dog."

"Princie won't hurt you, Shirley."

"How do I know he won't hurt me when he's running toward me, growling and barking?"

"He hardly ever bites anyone."

That didn't make me feel any more comfortable about Princie.

I liked Crissy, though. She started coming to my house every day. We played Mother and Child on Grandma's front porch. We wore our mothers' old dresses and high-heeled shoes and played with their old pocketbooks. Both of us loved our doll babies and enjoyed dressing them and taking them for rides in their carriages.

I'd never had a girlfriend, except my summer friend from Pennsylvania, and I don't think Crissy had either, so we enjoyed playing together. When Mama called me in to eat lunch and take my bath and nap, she told Crissy she should go home and come back when she saw me outside later in the afternoon.

As much as I liked playing Mother and Child with Crissy, I missed watching BeeWee work in the yard and in the woodshed. I also missed climbing up the wisteria vine to the woodshed roof and exploring the back yard by myself.

To look at the back yard; no one would ever know how many interesting things were there. That's why I liked to explore. There was always something interesting to see or to do. I thought Crissy would like to explore, too, but she said she wasn't allowed to go into anyone's back yard.

I'll always remember my friend Crissy. Playing with her was a pleasure because she was so nice and thoughtful.

Going Out with Mama and Daddy

One night when Daddy got off from work, he and Mama took me to a restaurant to eat with them. We rode in Daddy's black Pontiac coupe. A coupe was a small car that had only a front seat. Mama sat in the middle, but there wasn't as much room as there was when I sat in the middle on the front seat of BeeWee's and Aunt Nita's Chevrolet.

The restaurant where we ate had blue and white checked oilcloth tablecloths, even on the tables of the booths. There was a counter with lighted glass blocks underneath and stools with shiny chrome legs and blue padded seats. There were jukeboxes on the counter. The booths had them, too. We sat in a booth because it was more comfortable, with its lower, padded seats and high backs.

The waitress came and took our order, and then Mama asked Daddy for some money for me to play the jukebox. Mama told me I could play a song, but since I couldn't read many words, she wanted to know what song I'd like to hear, and she'd show me where it was on the jukebox.

"I'd like to hear *When You Wish upon a Star.*"

She checked all the songs listed, and that title wasn't there. "*You are My Sunshine* is on here. You like that. Why don't you play it?" she suggested.

"I like it, but I don't want to hear it right now." I didn't want Mama to know, but we'd only been out for a few minutes, and I already missed Grandma. I'd think about the times when we were so glad to see each other, and she called me her little sunshine, so that song always reminded me of her. I didn't want to start crying in the restaurant.

Mama mentioned a couple of songs, but they were hillbilly songs that I didn't like. Then, she said there were some older songs called old standards that she always liked. She thought I might like to hear the one called *Stardust* because it was a pretty song. I could tell by the expression on Daddy's face that he'd heard all he wanted to hear about my choosing a song, so I hurried and told her to play that one.

"You put the money in the slot and press the button beside the song," Mama showed me, pointing to *Stardust*.

That was fun to do, but I didn't hear the song until songs that were selected by other restaurant patrons before me had played.

I don't remember what meals we ordered, but I remember the waitress bringing coffee to Mama and Daddy and iced tea for me. There was a basket of small corn bread muffins wrapped in a blue and white checked cloth. I'd never had those, and they were really good with butter on them.

As usual, Mama ate only half of her food, so they switched plates. Daddy ate the rest of the food on her plate.

Then, someone started singing, "And now the purple dust of twilight time…" which Mama said was the beginning of Stardust. I'd never heard such a beautiful expression in a song, so I mentally added it to my list of favorites.

After supper, we went to the Visulite Theater on Colonial Avenue to see a Tarzan movie, which I sat down and watched with rapt attention.

Playing Tarzan

I'd already told Crissy that I wanted to stay in my back yard the next morning. The first thing I wanted to do was to climb up the wisteria vine and sit on the woodshed roof. While I sat there, I got the idea to stand up, hold on to a vine, yell like Tarzan, and swing to the ground, the way I'd seen Tarzan swing from vines in the jungle.

After doing it a few times, I heard someone shout, "What're you doing?"

The voice came from Darrell's yard, and there he was, standing as high up on his wire fence as he could climb, holding on, with his face pressed against the wire so he could see into Grandma's back yard.

Darrell lived next door, but Grandma's house had a side yard and a driveway that separated the two houses, so he was still pretty far away.

"Have you ever seen a Tarzan movie?" I yelled.

"Sure. My daddy took me to see one once before his ship had to go to sea," he shouted back.

"I just saw one last night, and I'm playing Tarzan. Do you want to play?"

"I'll ask my mother if I can come over." In about a minute, he was running into the yard, and we took turns being Tarzan. "I've got a good idea, Shirley. Why don't you play Jane, and I'll be Tarzan."

I shook my head. "That wouldn't be fun because Jane doesn't yell the way Tarzan does."

"But Tarzan is a man, and you're a girl."

"I don't care. We're just play-acting, so I can be anyone I want to be."

Darrell and I played Tarzan the next day, but then I told him I wanted to play Mother and Child with Crissy the following morning.

He seemed disappointed, so I asked him if he wanted to play Mother and Child with us and be the daddy, but he said he didn't want to. I wasn't surprised that he didn't want to play with doll babies.

The Day I Got Stuck on the Fence

One day Crissy came over, and we walked to the backyard, where I showed her the wisteria vine and asked her if she'd like to climb up and sit on the woodshed roof. She shook her head from side to side to let me know she didn't want to do it.

As we walked, I tried to think of something we could do that Crissy would like, or she probably wouldn't want to come in the back yard again. When we came to the fence on the apartment side of Grandma's house, I suggested, "I know what we can do, Crissy. We can climb over the fence."

The tall wire fence enclosed the back yard on the apartment side of the house as far as the back edge of the house. The white picket fence that BeeWee made enclosed the side of the house from the back edge to the front sidewalk. The same kind of wire fence enclosed the back of the yard, behind the woodshed and the garage. At certain times during warm weather, a honeysuckle vine grew on the fence at the back of the yard and filled the air with its fragrant yellow flowers. It was the nicest scent.

I was disappointed when Crissy shook her head from side to side, but I still wanted to climb over the fence.

"It's easy. Watch me." I started climbing the fence as Crissy watched. I got to the top and climbed over to the other side.

When I couldn't talk Crissy into climbing over the fence, I started climbing back over to Grandma's yard, but when I got to the top and stepped over, I slipped. I started to fall headfirst to the ground, but my dress got caught on the fence, and I was suddenly hanging upside down.

I couldn't see if Crissy was still there, but in case she was, I decided to say, "Crissy, go get Mama."

It was embarrassing to know my dress was over my head and my underpants were showing. I hoped Darrell couldn't see me from his yard.

Then I heard Grandma exclaim, "Oh, my Lord, have mercy!"

Mama tried to remove my dress from the wire.

"Hurry, Florencie. The blood is rushing to the child's head."

"I'll have to unbutton the dress and slip you out of it, Shirley."

"Then I'll be out in the yard in just my underpants, Mama!"

"You'll just have to put up with it because I don't want to tear the dress."

Grandma told me she'd go inside and hold the back-porch door open so I could run in. As soon as they got me out of the dress, I saw Crissy standing there. I wanted to thank her, but I had to run before anyone saw me. I didn't mind if Crissy saw me because, somehow, I knew she wasn't the kind of person who would laugh at me.

Grandma explained that Crissy had knocked on the front door and told them I was stuck on the fence. We were all impressed with the way Crissy returned my ring and went to get Mama and Grandma when I was hanging by my dress on the fence. She was a good friend.

After standing at the fence, fiddling with the dress for a long time, Mama worked it from the wire without tearing it. I wondered if she'd be mad at me, but she just told me not to climb the fence anymore.

Crissy didn't want to come in the back yard after that, but we continued to play Mother and Child on Grandma's front porch.

The Easter Shoes

Mama took me shopping to buy an Easter outfit. She told me she wanted me to have new clothes and shoes, not just for Easter, but to wear to Sunday school for a long time.

We found a pretty cotton pique, a pale yellow dress, and a lightweight woolen spring coat. I loved the color of the coat. It was a new shade called fuchsia. I tried on some hats, and the one I liked best was a natural-colored straw, trimmed with a black grosgrain ribbon that wrapped around the crown and was tied in a small bow in the back with two ribbons streaming over the brim.

I picked out a small black patent leather pocketbook that had a shoulder strap. It was exciting to have my own pocketbook, especially one with a long strap I could wear over my shoulder.

A few days before Easter, I had everything I needed but my shoes. Because I had a narrow foot, Mama hadn't been able to buy shoes for me when she bought everything else. My only shoes were dark red leather. I'd been wearing them to church, but the color would clash drastically with a fuchsia-colored coat.

Mama had ordered shoes for me from the store where she usually bought my shoes, but there was no guarantee they would come in before Easter.

About three days before Easter, in desperation, Mama took me to a different shoe store to see if they could fit me in a pair of black patent leather shoes. They had only medium widths, but they said their dress shoes usually ran narrower than others. I tried on the shoes that looked very much like the ones she'd ordered, except the strap across the instep buckled in the middle instead of on the side.

I hoped they'd fit, and they almost did, but they were a little loose.

The shoe salesman was aware of our dilemma and was trying to come up with a way to make the shoes fit so I'd have new shoes for Easter. "I can put more holes in the strap." He did, and I tried on the shoes again. They did fit better, but the strap was now off-center, and there was too much of it hanging on one side of my foot. "You can wear thicker socks," he suggested.

"Do you have thicker socks?" Mama inquired.

He did, but they weren't dress socks and didn't look right with the shoes. "You can try wearing the shoes a half size smaller." He tried the smaller size, and the shoes didn't slip up and down on my heels, but my toes were touching the end of the shoes, which Mama said didn't allow enough room for growth.

"I'd get those, Shirley, but I can't afford to buy a pair of shoes that you'll get hardly any wear out of and that don't fit properly. The other shoes will come in; you just might not have them in time for Easter."

The situation seemed hopeless, so we left with no shoes. As we were walking to the bus, Mama sighed. "I just hope and pray that the other store gets in the shoes before Easter, or I don't know what we'll do."

On the Friday morning before Easter, Mama let me know, "You're just going to have to wear your dark red shoes. There's nothing else we can do."

Everyone in the Sunday school class would have new shoes except me, but that was all right. My dark red shoes could be polished to look like new. If I had to wear dark red shoes with a fuchsia coat, I'd just have to do it, even if the colors did clash. That's the way I was thinking on Friday morning, but I was really hoping my new shoes would come in. Every time the telephone rang, I hoped it was a call from the shoe store.

It was almost time for Daddy to get off work and come to pick up Mama when the telephone rang again.

"What time is it? Can they be calling from the shoe store this late?" Mama wondered.

"It's a quarter of six, and I think they close at six. You answer the phone in case they're calling about the shoes, Florencie."

Please, please, let it be the shoe store, I thought.

Grandma and I stood beside Mama as she answered the telephone. "Thank you very much. I'll pick them up tomorrow."

We were happy that my shoes had come in. Mama didn't usually come to Grandma's on Saturday, but she came to take me to try on the shoes.

"Don't forget to take the book of ration coupons," reminded Grandma.

Daddy drove Mama and me downtown to the shoe store and waited outside in the parking lot for us. When we went inside, the shoe saleslady buckled the shoes on my feet, felt the toes of the shoes to see how close my toes were to the end, and had me walk across the carpet to see if they were slipping on my heels. Then, she asked me to stand on the shoe x-ray machine to see for sure if the shoes were a good fit.

I peered into the top of the machine to see the bony skeleton of my feet through a bright green light at the bottom. Then, the saleslady looked and said the shoes seemed to be a perfect fit.

When Mama paid for the shoes, she gave the saleslady cash and the ration coupon book. The lady tore out the coupon for shoes, rang up the sale, and handed Mama her change and the ration book. She gave me a pink, helium-filled balloon.

There were enough ration coupons for shoes for my family because Grandma and BeeWee never bought any new shoes. When their shoes became worn, they took them to a shoe repair shop, where they could get new heels, new soles, or both. Even if BeeWee had holes in the soles of his shoes, he took them to a shoe repair shop for new soles rather than buying new shoes.

Scuffed shoes could be shined at a shoeshine stand to look almost new, but BeeWee could shine his own shoes to make them look new. He called it a spit shine because he actually spit on his shoes and mixed the spit with the polish. That wasn't something he made up—some other men liked spit shines, too. There were shoeshine stands in a lot of places downtown. Some barber shops had a shoeshine stand, and a lot of boys would set up their own shoeshine stands on the streets.

The idea of spitting on your shoes, then mixing it with the shoe polish as you shined your shoes made me feel queasy, but the finished product did make your shoes look nearly new.

Easter Sunday

On Easter morning, Grandma got me up earlier than usual because she and BeeWee were planning to help me to dye Easter eggs.

After breakfast, Grandma cleared the dishes, rolled back the white oilcloth, and spread newspapers on the table. She set out the green glass punch cups that were always kept on the top shelf of the cabinet. There was a package of Easter egg dye. There was a small cellophane package of colored tablets inside that BeeWee unwrapped and let me drop one-by-one into the punch cups. Grandma handed BeeWee the apple cider vinegar bottle and a spoon, which he used to measure the vinegar, and he let me pour it into each cup. The tablets fizzed until they dissolved.

Grandma poured warm water from an aluminum kettle into each cup, and BeeWee stirred the mixtures. Then, Grandma set a bowl of hard-boiled white eggs on the table. BeeWee showed me how to put an egg in the wire egg holder that came in the box and to lower it into each cup of dye. Next, we went back to the first cup and raised the egg to see if the color was dark enough. We did that with each egg until we dyed all of them and set them on paper towels.

BeeWee showed me how to put transfer pictures of bunny rabbits, ducks, lambs, crosses, and flowers on the colored eggs. Grandma had been washing dishes while we dyed the eggs. When we were finished, Grandma said we had to get dressed for Sunday school.

After we were all dressed and ready to go, Grandma and BeeWee surprised me with an Easter basket and a stuffed bunny.

When Sunday school was over, we came straight home. Grandma and BeeWee put the cool, colored eggs in my Easter basket, and BeeWee took pictures of me outside.

Crissy came over, dressed in her Easter outfit, carrying her Easter basket and a stuffed bunny. BeeWee took pictures of Crissy and me together, standing up, holding our baskets and bunnies, and sitting on the front steps with the baskets and bunnies beside us.

I was amazed that Crissy had shown up when she did because we'd never played together that early on a Sunday. The most amazing thing of all was that we were dressed almost exactly alike. Our coats were not made the same, but they were the same fuchsia color, we each had black patent leather shoulder strap pocketbooks with matching shoes and natural-colored straw hats, but hers had a wider brim than mine.

It was definitely not planned by our mothers or my grandmother because they didn't even know Crissy's mother. I guess Crissy and our mothers, and I just had the same taste in selecting clothes and shoes. We said we liked each other's outfits, but we didn't talk about the similarities. Our attention was drawn to the contents of our Easter baskets as we poked through the green cellophane grass to see what we had.

Grandma said I could have one piece of candy and one hard-boiled egg while she was preparing our Sunday dinner, and I could have more later.

We had our usual delicious Sunday meal with fried chicken, creamed potatoes, and butterbeans. Then I went back outside.

Crissy came back, and we sat on the steps in the sunshine, still wearing our Easter outfits. We talked and ate candy from our baskets for the rest of the afternoon.

I went into the house at five o'clock to eat supper and to watch *The Shadow* at five-thirty. Grandma listened to the news, and then she, BeeWee, and I sat in the living room to listen to the Sunday evening radio programs.

From the time I woke up until I went to bed that night, it was one of the happiest days of my life.

Easter Monday

The next day was Easter Monday. After BeeWee went to work, Grandma took me to City Park. She and I walked to the park, which was ten blocks away, at the end of 35th Street. I wore my play clothes because I was going to play on the playground at the park.

When we first got there, we sat on a bench in the gazebo at the front of the park. After about five minutes, Grandma and I walked along a path to the playground for children twelve and under. I had fun playing while Grandma sat on a bench and watched me. Then we went into the snack shop that looked like a log cabin, and Grandma bought a small Coca-Cola and a small bag of roasted peanuts in the shell for herself and a cola snowball and a small bag of popcorn for me. We enjoyed sitting on the bench, eating our snacks.

Afterward, we went to the duck pond to see the ducks. The large, fenced-in pond was at the bottom of a grass-covered hill.

We sat on one of the benches at the top of the hill and watched the ducks and some children who seemed to be having fun rolling down the hill.

"Grandma, can I do what those children are doing?"

"I guess it'll be all right."

I rolled down, and it was so much fun. I did it over and over until Grandma said it was time for us to go home. We walked the long walk home in the late afternoon. It was cooler, not as sunny, and we were both tired but happy because we'd had a wonderful afternoon.

Memorial Day

By the first of May, BeeWee was putting the screens back in the windows to prepare for the warmer days ahead.

On Memorial Day, he always drove Grandma to the flower stand near the Granby Street bridge, where she bought bunches of freshly cut flowers to put on her father's, her mother's, and her brother's graves at Elmwood Cemetery.

BeeWee drove through the entranceway to the cemetery, which was surrounded by an old red brick wall. Grandma said the tall, black, wrought iron gates were kept open during the day and closed at dusk. BeeWee drove slowly down the narrow, winding dirt lane until he reached the Reid family plot, where Grandma's father was buried. She showed me the American flags that an organization had put on the graves of veterans. Then, she filled a clean mayonnaise jar with water from the faucet by the road, put in one bunch of flowers, and set it in the center of the ivy-covered grave. After that, she did the same for her brother.

Next, BeeWee drove down the dirt lane, turned right, and stopped at an ivy-covered grave on the corner, which was where Grandma's mother had been buried. Grandma said it still made her sad to think that her mother wasn't buried beside her father; because the Reid family plot was filled to capacity by the time she died. That was because the grave beside Grandma's father had been reserved for her mother, but unfortunately, her brother had died of consumption at an early age. Mary Loveley Reid didn't want her son to be buried in a grave by himself, so she gave up her grave for him to be buried beside his father instead of her.

I didn't understand such things; I just knew it made me feel sad to know that Grandma was sad. Grandma had tears in her eyes, and so did I.

Making Mud Pies

June began with wonderful weather, and I enjoyed being outside every morning. I especially liked to sit on the bottom step of the back steps and make mud pies.

Grandma gave me two old tin pie pans, an old, dented tin measuring cup, and an old tablespoon. BeeWee pumped a bucket of water for me to mix with the soil that I dug up in front of the gas and electric meters that were covered by a little white house BeeWee had made. There was a hinged door on it for the meter man to open and read the meters. The back of the roof had hinges so it could be lifted up from the front.

One day, I lifted the little roof to look down at the meters and saw something I would never have expected—it was a mother cat with her kittens! I was so thrilled to see those fluffy little fur babies! I wanted to shout to BeeWee, who was in the woodshed, to come to see them, but I didn't want to scare them away. I just looked at them a little bit longer and then lowered the roof as quietly and as gently as I could.

BeeWee and Grandma didn't mind if I dug a hole in the back yard as long as it wasn't in front of the steps and if I filled in the hole and smoothed it over before I went in the house. I put soil in each pan and mixed it with just enough water to make it as thick as dough. Then, I smoothed the tops and set them in the sun to 'bake.' The wisteria vine covered the back half of the yard. The area near the steps got sun on sunny days.

I had fun until some large, fast-flying green bugs started buzzing and whizzing around me. BeeWee said although they were big and noisy, they were just insects called June bugs, and they wouldn't hurt me.

Before BeeWee walked up the steps to go in the house for lunch, I told him about the kittens. He lifted the roof and was surprised to see them, too.

"BeeWee, would you like to buy a pie?"

"Do you have an apple pie?" BeeWee played along.

"I have one right here," I showed him.

"How much is it?"

"It costs five cents."

"Then I'll take it." BeeWee pretended to hand me a nickel.

I picked up the other mud pie I'd made and offered it to him. "Would you like to buy a peach pie, too?"

"You've got a peach pie? I like peach pie. Is it five cents?"

"Yes, it is."

"Well, I'll take that one, too." He pretended to hand me another nickel.

I enjoyed the playful conversation between BeeWee and me. I loved him, and I thought he was a good grandfather.

New Neighbors

The next day, I was sitting on the back steps, making more mud pies, when I heard someone say, "You'd better watch that spider on the fence. If it writes your name, you'll die."

I looked around to see who had spoken, but I didn't see anyone.

"I'm up here," yelled someone with a girl's voice.

I looked up and saw a little girl at a window in the second-floor apartment; I shouted back, "I didn't know you lived there."

"I don't live here yet. My family is moving in today. If you look out front, you'll see the moving van."

I stood up and looked around the side of the back porch. There was a big, long-moving van in front of the apartment building.

"I've got to go now to put away some of my things, but don't forget to keep an eye on that spider to see if it's writing your name," she warned.

There was a large web with the biggest spider I'd ever seen in the middle of the fence. It was black with long legs. I kept looking over at the spider, but I didn't see my name on its web yet. I wondered if it would wait to write my name after dark, and I wouldn't even see it.

When BeeWee came along and said it was about time for us to go in for lunch, I was still worrying about the spider. "BeeWee, do you see that big spider on the fence? If it writes my name, I'll die, and I'm afraid it'll write my name after dark, and I won't see it." I was almost crying.

"Where did you get such an idea?"

"There's a new girl who lives in the apartment, and she told me."

"I don't know why she'd say such a thing. That spider won't write your name, and it won't hurt you. It's a garden spider that is helpful because it eats insects like mosquitoes. The kind of spider you need to be afraid of and never touch is a small black spider that has a little red dot on it. It's called a black widow. If you ever see one like that, Sugie, don't touch it because it's poisonous."

I was glad BeeWee told me the truth about the spider. Now I wouldn't waste a lot of time worrying about the spider writing my name.

"Are there any black widow spiders around here, BeeWee?"

"It's always possible, but I haven't seen one in years."

The next morning, I was playing Tarzan in the back yard with Darrell when the little girl came to the window again. "Hi. My name's Martha. What's your name?"

"My name's Shirley."

"How old are you?"

"I'm five years old."

"Is that all? I'm six, and I have a sister who's thirteen and a brother who's eighteen. My brother just graduated from high school and joined the army," Martha bragged.

I'd never heard anyone say there was anything wrong with my age before. I didn't think there was anything wrong with being five, but I could tell that Martha thought I was too young, so she might not want to be my friend.

While I was thinking about her remark, Darrell spoke up and said his name was Darrell, and he was five years old, too.

"I didn't ask you," she shot back at him.

Last night, Mama and Grandma had said I should ask the new little girl next door to come over to play because her family seemed to be nice, and since she didn't have a yard, she might enjoy playing with me in Grandma's back yard.

Remembering Mama and Grandma's suggestion, I offered, "Would you like to come over and play Tarzan with us?"

"No. I don't play Tarzan. I don't climb trees, swing on vines, or yell."

"We don't always play Tarzan. Sometimes we play Cops and Robbers or Cowboys and Outlaws."

"I don't play those games either. I'm not a tomboy like you."

"What's a tomboy?" I had never heard of it before.

"It's a girl who plays with boys and plays boys' games."

Darrell and I had played together before there were any girls on the street for me to play with. I was the one who had shown him how to play Tarzan. Martha made it seem like something girls shouldn't do.

When she walked away from the window, I said, "Darrell, I didn't know you were five years old."

"I'll soon be five," he clarified.

"When is your birthday?"

"It's in October."

Since I had asked her to play and she didn't want to, Darrell and I went back to playing Tarzan by ourselves. When I went into the house to eat lunch, Mama wanted to know if I had asked the new girl to play, and I said that I did. "Why didn't she come over?" Mama wanted to know.

"She said she didn't play with boys and didn't play Tarzan."

"At least you asked her, be sure to ask her again," Mama pushed.

"I'll ask her, but I think she thinks I'm too young because she's six and I'm five."

"Be sure to keep asking her to play because she seems like such a nice girl."

I didn't know if I agreed with Mama about Martha being nice because she didn't say very nice things to me.

Three's a Crowd

That afternoon, Crissy came over, and we played Mother and Child on the front porch.

Martha came out on her front porch and asked if she could play.

"Sure. Just bring a doll baby, a carriage, and your mother's old clothes, shoes, and pocketbook," I told her.

She came over and said she had everything except a carriage because they didn't have enough room in their apartment for her to bring her carriage from the place where she used to live.

Martha said we weren't playing Mother and Child the right way. She said we should have a family with a mother, a father, and a young child, instead of being three mothers with three babies.

As we continued playing, I was disappointed to learn that Martha expected me to be the father. "Why should I be the father? Fathers are older and taller than mothers, so you should be the father because you're older and taller."

"Not always. My mother is older and taller than my father," argued Martha.

"I don't believe it. Do you believe it, Crissy?"

Crissy shook her head from side to side.

"How old is your mother, Shirley?"

I had no idea why Martha wanted to know, but I told her anyway. "She's twenty-four."

Martha jumped in. "My mother's twenty-four, too, and my father's younger and shorter."

Martha's father might have been a little shorter than her mother, and he might have even been a little younger, but my mother was about as young as a mother could be. Martha's parents had to be older because they had gray hair, and Martha had said her brother was eighteen.

Wanting to prove my point, I asked, "How old is your mother, Crissy?"

Crissy shrugged her shoulders.

"But isn't she younger than your father?" I hoped.

Crissy nodded her head up and down.

"Don't you talk?" Martha cut with her words.

Crissy nodded her head up and down again.

"You be the child since you're smaller and you don't really talk. We'll pretend you're two years old," Martha decided.

Crissy shook her head from side to side.

"Let's just try it. You'll see that my way is much better. Let's get our babies ready to go for a walk, but not you, Crissy. Remember, you're only two years old, so you don't get the babies ready, and you just wear your own clothes because you're a child."

Crissy shook her head from side to side and wouldn't take off her mother's clothes and shoes. She got her doll baby dressed the way she always did.

"Shirley, you need to take off your mother's clothes since you're the father."

"I don't want to, Martha. I still want to be a mother."

Crissy put her doll in her carriage, and when she turned to get her mother's pocketbook to put under her arm, Martha started pushing the carriage down the sidewalk. Crissy caught up with her and grabbed the handle of the carriage to stop it.

"You're just selfish," Martha accused.

Crissy shook her head from side to side.

We all stood on the sidewalk, looking at each other.

Playing Mother and Child had been so much fun for Crissy and me because we liked pretending to be mothers, so it was no fun when Martha wanted to be the only mother.

We stopped playing and sat on the steps for a while. No one said anything, and we were getting hot, sitting there in our mothers' dresses in the hot summer sun. Crissy never went home before I had to go in for lunch, but she took off her mother's dress and shoes, put everything in her carriage, and pushed it toward her house. Then Martha and I took off our mother's dresses and shoes, and Martha went home.

The next morning, I played by myself, making mud pies in the back yard.

Martha came to the window and said, "Are you watching that spider? I think it's starting to write your name."

"It's not going to write my name. My grandfather said spiders don't write people's names," I was happy to tell Martha.

The word 'grandfather' slipped out before I had time to think about it. BeeWee was in the woodshed making fishing lures, and I hoped he hadn't heard me since he wanted to be called BeeWee.

I wouldn't want to say or do anything to cause BeeWee to stop talking with me. I was impressed with how much he knew about the outdoors. His telling me about the writing spider gave me the confidence to stand up to Martha. I really loved him for how much he taught me.

Martha Invites Me Over

Martha wanted to know if I could come to her apartment that afternoon to play with her paper dolls. I went inside to ask Mama, and she said that would be fine.

When Martha invited me over, I was surprised. I didn't think she wanted to play with me anymore. I was excited to play paper dolls with her. I thought this might be what we needed to bring us together as friends because we finally had something in common to enjoy.

Martha brought out a medium-sized, old cardboard suitcase, set it on the rug in the middle of her living room floor, and opened it. It was filled with a large collection of paper dolls.

"Where did you get so many paper dolls?"

"Most of them belonged to my sister. She gave them to me."

I especially liked the movie star paper dolls and their beautiful clothes. Martha played with the Judy Garland paper doll and pretended to be her. I played with the Lana Turner paper doll and pretended to be her.

We dressed our dolls in tennis clothes and pretended they were going to the tennis court to play tennis. Then, we pretended they changed clothes and went to a restaurant to eat lunch. Next, we dressed them in evening gowns and furs and pretended they were going out for the evening for dinner and dancing.

The only reason we knew what movie stars did was because of going to see them in movies.

"Isn't this a lot more fun than playing Mother and Child?"

"Oh, yes," I blurted out, thinking only about the last time we'd played. Then I felt bad because I said 'yes' without thinking. I really liked playing Mother and Child with Crissy as much as I liked playing paper dolls.

I wondered if Martha, Crissy, and I would ever be able to play Mother and Child together, with all of us pretending to be mothers. Crissy would probably like playing paper dolls, too, but I doubted that Martha would ever ask her.

Then, Martha went on to say, "Isn't this better than playing with that little girl who doesn't talk?"

If I had said 'no,' Martha might not invite me to play with her paper dolls anymore, which I really liked to do.

The following Sunday afternoon, I realized I didn't have to worry about whether Crissy and I would still be able to play Mother and Child. She said she was going to have to start staying with her parents in their store every day except Sunday because her parents didn't think her thirteen-year-old brother was watching her well enough.

Although I missed Crissy, I was very happy that she and I could still be together on Sunday afternoons.

Martha and I played paper dolls together when she invited me to come to her apartment some afternoons during the rest of the summer.

I still played with Darrell most mornings. He'd ask if he could come over when he saw me in the yard. We still played Tarzan, but we also particularly liked to play Cowboys and Outlaws. We pretended to have guns by making a fist and extending our index fingers. We used brooms for horses. It was fun galloping around Grandma's yard on my broom horse. I could easily pretend Grandma's yard was an old western town since there was no grass, and the weathered woodshed and garage reminded me of old western buildings.

My favorite cowboy was the Durango Kid, played by Charles Starrett. I'd seen him in movies at the Visulite theater. I told Darrell I'd be the Durango Kid every time it was my turn to be a cowboy.

At first, Darrell and I argued a lot. Each of us wanted to be cowboys because they were the good guys. Darrell wanted to be the cowboy, capture me, and take me to jail, but I wanted to be the cowboy and have a shootout with him until he pretended to be the wounded outlaw who fell to the ground. He decided he preferred being the outlaw because he liked falling on the ground.

Crissy and I played together on Sunday afternoons, which worked out fine because I never saw Martha on Sundays.

All the children on the block played hide-and-go-seek almost every night during the summer. We met at the oak tree in front of the apartment building and didn't hide anywhere past Grandma's driveway or the other side of the apartment building. It was creepy on the other side of the apartment building because it was pitch dark over there. We played until the nine o'clock gun went off, then we all went home.

I liked the experience of making one friend at a time, so I could really get to know each one. I learned not to expect all of them to want to play together all the time, except for a game like Hide and Seek, which was more fun with a group.

BeeWee Finds a New Fishing Spot

The whole family missed going to Lynnhaven, especially BeeWee, who liked going there to fish two or three times while he was on his two-week vacation every July.

We couldn't go to Lynnhaven because of the gas shortage and rationing. The sticker on the car was good for barely enough gas for BeeWee to drive to and from work and to run errands on payday every two weeks. There wasn't nearly enough gas to drive to and from Lynnhaven, which was a long distance away. We could only dream about it that summer.

There was a place nearby where BeeWee could fish, but the fish didn't bite until after dark when the streetlights were shining on the water. BeeWee said the lights attracted the fish. It was on the other side of the creek where he always went to catch minnows in his bucket to use for bait to fish at Lynnhaven. The new place didn't have a beach, and it was after dark when we got there. We went after supper, so we didn't take food. Mama and Aunt Nita didn't go.

Grandma and I sat on a bench beside a streetlight and watched BeeWee fish. There was nothing to do but sit there and wait. I got tired of looking at the dark water and waiting for BeeWee to catch a fish, so I turned around, with my feet and legs on the side of the bench, and looked at the houses across the street.

The houses were large and stately, with two stories. Some were dark, and some had lights on, but the window shades were pulled down at all but one house. That house stood out from the rest because the shades were raised to a few inches from the top of the two windows in the dining room, and bright lights were on inside. I'd never seen such a bright room.

I sat across the street and stared at everything in the room. There was a large, brightly lit crystal chandelier above a long, shiny mahogany table with eight matching chairs that had red, cushioned seats and backs. A rectangular-shaped mirror with a wide, ornate, gold leaf frame was hanging on the wall above a shiny mahogany buffet. There was a large silver teapot and some other silver on a silver tray on the buffet. A tall, wide, matching china cabinet with gleaming glass doors was centered on the opposite wall. I could see a set of fancy white dishes decorated with red flowers. Wide gold rims were around the edges of the cups and the dishes.

My eyes must have been as big around as the saucers in the china cabinet because I'd never seen anything like that room. At first, I felt as though I shouldn't be looking into someone's window, but then I thought they would have pulled down the shades or turned out the lights if they didn't want anyone to look.

Now I understood why Grandma thought the furniture that had belonged to her mother was old, plain, and faded. She never said she didn't like the furniture, though.

Grandma's Tiffany design chandelier with colored glass red apples, green pears, purple grapes, and green leaves over the round oak dining room table had three small round, seven-and-a-half watt white light bulbs. Grandma kept two of the three bulbs unscrewed enough so that only one bulb came on when the light switch on the wall was turned on, except for Thanksgiving and Christmas dinners.

I was shocked to see that fancy room because I didn't know anyone lived that way.

Grandma's house was the place for me. She didn't mind if I climbed on the big, wide oak buffet and sat on the top shelf. The wood was heavy, sturdy, and wasn't easily scratched. I'd enjoyed swinging on my swing that hung from the big hooks at the top of the dining room doorway for as long as I could remember. I rode my big tricycle in all the downstairs rooms and kept it parked in the corner of the dining room.

I told Grandma I was glad my great-grandmother bought the house and the furniture. I was glad she planted the wisteria beside the woodshed, the pink crepe myrtle tree, the blue hydrangea bushes beside the driveway, the orange day lilies beside the white clapboard house, the white snowball bush in the back yard, and the pale-yellow daffodils that were our first sign of spring every year.

Then, she told me more about my great-grandparents. According to Grandma, my great-grandmother, Mary Elizabeth Loveley, met my great-grandfather, Charles Campbell Reid, when she worked in a store near The Reid Steam Bakery. He was a bachelor who frequently went into her store to buy boxes of candy for the young women he was seeing. They'd talk with each other while she wrapped the candy as prettily as she could. He soon realized she was the young woman he loved and wanted to marry. She'd always secretly loved him, too. After a short courtship, they married when she was twenty-seven and he was forty.

His parents had come from Glasgow, Scotland, and started the bakery, which was very successful, so she and my great-grandmother could afford to have a fine home, with fine furnishings, in a fashionable section of the city. Grandma remembered the beautiful crystal chandelier that hung in their house.

They had a son and four daughters. Then, my great-grandfather found out that one of his partners in the business had been spending more money than they were taking in. He lost the business and his home.

"Papa was so disappointed that he moved the family from Norfolk to Portsmouth and took any job he could get," Grandma told me.

"I remember when you said he was a good man. Your mother and the children loved him very much. You took his lunch to him and sat with him while he ate. He must have really liked that, Grandma."

"Honey, you have a good memory. Your great-grandmother loved you when you were a baby, and she'd love you now."

I admired my great-grandmother for working as a young woman and overcoming adversity in her life. Her husband lost his business and their house. She adjusted to a lower standard of living in Portsmouth and, in time, watched her twenty-one-year-old son die slowly of consumption, which was eventually called tuberculosis. Grandma told me James Reid was his parents' only son and that he had been a bank teller who had to leave his job because of his illness. My great-grandfather, Charles Campbell Reid, died about two years after their son, leaving her with four young daughters.

Mary Elizabeth Loveley and her daughters pulled themselves up by their own bootstraps, so to speak. She bought the house in Norfolk, and the girls went to work to help her. She started the Thanksgiving and Christmas dinners for her family, and Grandma continued the tradition for her own family.

Almost everything I knew about her, I heard from Grandma. She said that after selling her house and furnishings to Grandma and BeeWee, she moved to Tampa, Florida, to live with her oldest daughter, Mary, and her family. She enjoyed traveling on the train from Tampa to Norfolk every year to spend the late spring and summer with Grandma and her family. She wrote letters to Grandma in beautiful handwriting.

If there were any pictures of my great-grandmother, I never saw them. Grandma said she had dark hair, was tall, trim, and energetic, sometimes dancing to music she heard on the radio. Grandma said she seemed to be healthy until a few months before she passed away in the summer of 1937, at about the age of seventy-nine.

It meant everything to me to know that the women in my life were who they were. I am so proud of them for hanging in there, so to speak, and being such strong women. It made me feel good to know there were strong women in my background.

I'm so glad Grandma told me about her wonderful mother. Of all the people who had passed away before I was old enough to know them, my great-grandmother is the one that I would love to have known the most.

After fishing for a while, BeeWee said the fish weren't biting, so he was ready to go. Grandma asked if we could go to Karp's Pharmacy so she could run in to get peach ice cream cones. He took a shortcut through Colonial Place, and a man walked out into one of the dimly lit intersections and waved his hands for us to stop.

BeeWee was in the precarious position of not being able to drive through the intersection without hitting the man, so he raised his window and slowed down as though he was going to stop. When the man walked over to the car, BeeWee stepped on the gas and drove away as quickly as he could.

"I thought you were going to stop and talk to that man, Clarence, and I was scared to death."

"I couldn't keep driving and hit the man. I didn't want to drive backward and risk hitting one of the cars parked on both sides of the street. I slowed down so he'd think I was going to stop. I figured he'd get out of the middle of the street and walk over to the car. Then, I could drive through the intersection," BeeWee explained.

"What do you think he wanted, BeeWee?"

"I think he was up to no good," Grandma remarked.

"You never can tell, and I didn't want to take any chances."

"I'm glad you didn't take any chances, BeeWee because I was scared."

BeeWee stopped at Karp's, and Grandma went inside to get the cones. It was the only drugstore near us that sometimes had peach ice cream in the summer.

"What kind of ice cream do you want tonight, honey?"

"I want peach, but if they don't have it, I want chocolate."

BeeWee handed Grandma a quarter to buy the cones and told her to be sure to get each of us two scoops of ice cream on our cones.

The drugstores that sold ice cream always had only strawberry, chocolate, and vanilla, so peach would be a special treat. When I saw Grandma come out of the drugstore, I opened the car door. She was carrying two towering cones of peach ice cream. She handed me the two cones to hold while she got in the car and closed the door.

Then, she handed BeeWee his change of nickel and took her cone. The ice cream was firm, the way I liked it, because it lasted longer. I liked to take my time enjoying bites of my ice cream rather than having to hurry and lick a melting cone before it dripped.

BeeWee never ate ice cream. We stopped by Robbins' Confectionary and ate our ice cream while we waited in the car for him to go in and buy two bottles of beer to drink when we got home.

He pulled into the driveway and let Grandma out so she could open the front door, go through the house, turn on the back porch light, and open the back door for us.

Every night BeeWee turned out the car lights, stopped the car, got out and unlocked the garage doors, opened both of the doors as wide as they'd go, got back in the car, parked it in the garage, locked it, closed and locked the garage doors, and went in the back door.

As soon as we reached the back yard, he noticed something unusual. "Well, I'll be! Someone's standing beside the woodshed."

"How can you see someone in the dark, BeeWee?"

"I can't see the person, but I can see the light of the cigarette the person is smoking. See that little red light beside the woodshed?"

I saw it and started getting scared.

"It's nothing to be scared of. It's probably just a neighborhood boy who's sneaking a smoke because he doesn't want his parents to know he smokes," explained BeeWee.

I was worried about him when he got out of the car to unlock the garage. After he parked the car in the garage, I slipped across the front seat and got out on his side of the car. Then he closed and locked the car doors, closed and locked the garage doors, and we walked to the house.

Grandma had turned on the light at the back of the house, but it was so dim that there was only light over the steps. The person beside the woodshed was probably watching us, but we could only see the light on the tip of the cigarette.

I felt relieved when we were inside the house, and the doors were locked.

We all sat at the kitchen table. Grandma had finished her ice cream cone and was at the sink running faucet water into small glasses for us. We didn't like ice water. I ate the last bite of my ice cream cone, the crunchy little triangle of melted ice cream at the bottom.

BeeWee positioned the bottle opener over the cap of the beer bottle and lifted it up. It came off in his hand. He poured the beer into a glass and started drinking it. I liked to see the white foam at the top of the glass.

"Grandma, do you think the person beside the woodshed could be the man who was in the middle of the street?"

"I don't think so." She gathered the usual things she took upstairs every night.

They didn't seem concerned, so I wasn't scared, but I thought there were two mysteries.

We went upstairs; I put on my pajamas and went to bed. Then, Grandma went downstairs to wait for Aunt Nita so she could open the front door as soon as she saw her come up the front steps.

I fell asleep, still wondering why the man was in the middle of the intersection, waving his arms for BeeWee to stopand why someone was standing beside the woodshed. They were both still mysteries to me.

Adventures with My New Friend, Jerry

I couldn't wait to tell my new friend, Jerry, about the two mysteries. He was shorter than I was, and I thought he was about a year younger. It always seemed as though I would never meet someone exactly my age. They were always either younger or older, but I was just glad to have other children to talk with and to play with. Jerry lived in Martha's apartment building, and I met him when I was leaving her apartment one day. We started talking, and, at the time, I liked the way we could carry on a real conversation. After I left Martha's apartment, we sat on the ground, with our backs to the other side of the apartment building, and talked.

When I told him about the person standing beside the woodshed, Jerry said he thought it was a German spy who had escaped from a prison camp in the area. I hadn't heard about any prison camps or spies being captured and held as prisoners in our area. Jerry thought we should wait until our families were asleep one night, about midnight, slip out of the house, and try to find out who it was.

When we talked about slipping out of the house at midnight, it sounded like something that would be exciting, but on the night when we planned to do it, I was afraid to even walk downstairs into Grandma's dark house.

The next day Jerry told me he was sorry that he fell asleep before the time we agreed to meet. I told Jerry I didn't think I could ever carry out our plan because I was too scared of the dark.

"You're scared of the dark? You're not scared of the dark when we're playing Hide-and-Go-Seek."

"That's because it's before nine o'clock at night, most of the children on the block are playing with us, and Grandma's sitting on the front porch," I explained.

He let me know he wasn't afraid of the dark, but he was afraid of what his mother would do if she found out he'd sneaked out of the house at midnight or any other time since she didn't even allow him to leave the apartment house premises during the day. "I still want to do it because I like adventures."

"What kind of adventures do you like, Jerry?"

"If you mean traveling somewhere on an adventure, I haven't been anywhere except when my family moved here so my daddy could get a job at the navy yard. My daddy doesn't have a car, so we rode on a bus for a long time. There are other ways to have adventures without traveling. Walk up the steps to the second floor, watch me, and I'll show you what I can do." Jerry climbed the fence beside the apartment house woodsheds and grabbed the wooden clothesline post that held the pulley clotheslines for one side of the apartment building.

Ladies who lived on the second and third floors of the apartment building washed their family's clothes, stood on their back porches, hung them on the lines, and pulled one of the double ropes to move them out over the woodsheds to dry in the air and sunshine. I'd sat on the woodshed roof in Grandma's yard and watched Martha's mother hang out clothes, but there were no clothes hanging on the lines now.

The next thing I knew, Jerry let go of the clothesline post, ran across the long, silver-colored, slanted metal roof above the six woodsheds, and grabbed the clothesline post on the other side. "I dare you to do it," he challenged me.

No one had ever dared me to do anything. I figured he dared me because he didn't think I could do it, so I wanted to show him that I could.

I climbed up the fence to the woodshed, grabbed the clothesline post, and looked down. The roof looked very slick.

If I slipped off, the worst thing that would happen was that I'd fall into the Harris's back yard. They lived directly behind the apartment building and had a pretty yard covered with the thickest green grass in the neighborhood. I thought the grass would cushion my fall.

What could be worse than a fall, though, would be Grandma or Mama looking out the back kitchen window toward the apartment building and seeing me running across the roof over the woodsheds. I'd surely get a switching from Mama if she saw me. They didn't even know about Jerry. They thought I was still playing with Martha.

"Jerry, I don't think I should do it because Mama will switch my legs if she sees me."

"Aw, you're just chicken," he taunted.

"No, I'm not. I climb up on the roof of my grandfather's woodshed all the time, and it's higher than this one."

"This roof is slanted and slippery, though. You're afraid of falling because you're a girl. I thought you were different, but you're just as scared of everything as other girls are."

I let go of the post and ran across the roof as fast as I could, somehow thinking that if I ran fast, I wouldn't fall. When I got to the other side and grabbed the clothesline post, I stepped past Jerry, who was still holding on, and I climbed down the fence. I ran to Grandma's and knocked on the front door, hoping that she and Mama hadn't been looking out of the back window.

"Why are you so out of breath?" asked Mama when she opened the front door for me.

"I was running." I walked straight into the living room and plopped down on the nearest chair, feeling relieved that they didn't see me.

The Sunday Afternoon Drive

Despite the gas shortage and rationing, BeeWee told me he thought he had enough gasoline to take Grandma and me for a Sunday afternoon drive once in a while up Hampton Boulevard and back. Now, when we went for our ride, we saw olive-drab military vehicles driving to and from the base, sometimes in long caravans. Sometimes there were white signs on them with bright red letters.

"What do those signs say, BeeWee?"

"Those signs say 'Danger' to warn people not to get too close because the trucks are carrying explosives. Explosives are dangerous because they can blow up. They try to move them over the weekend when traffic isn't as heavy as it is during the week," BeeWee explained.

"I didn't know that, Clarence. Maybe it isn't safe for us to be riding on Hampton Boulevard on Sunday afternoons anymore."

"I don't think we need to worry because I don't think it'll be long before President Roosevelt tells us we can't do any pleasure driving at all."

Grandma was more at ease. "Well, if that's what you think, maybe we'd better go for rides as long as we can."

BeeWee was usually quiet during the Sunday drives, so I knew he felt strongly about what he was saying. I wondered how much longer it would be until we had to give up our occasional Sunday rides. I always liked to look at everything along the way. I was learning about some more of the ways that war affects a country.

Seeing Jerry Again

The next day, I really wanted to tell Jerry about seeing the explosives signs on the military vehicles, but I decided it would be better if I didn't say anything about the war.

When I talked with Jerry, he said he wasn't surprised that I ran across the woodshed roof because he had thought all along that I could do it. I was glad to hear that, but I was hoping he wouldn't dare me to do it again. He didn't dare me to run across the woodshed roof again, but he soon thought of another dare.

The porches on the back of the apartment building were concrete and had black iron steps that led from the first floor to the third floor. There was a concrete sidewalk in front of the woodsheds. The six families who lived in the apartments used the back steps when they took the trash to their big, round, galvanized trash cans beside the woodsheds. They also used those steps to take their coal scuttles filled with coal or ashes to and from their woodsheds and their furnace rooms.

The six apartments each had a furnace room with a coal stove, and each family was responsible for heating their own apartment. The apartments were all alike, so I knew there were radiators because they were in Martha's apartment.

I found out about the furnace rooms when I asked Grandma about the coal trucks that backed into the apartment driveway beside Grandma's house to deliver coal all winter. The coal truck driver used a long chute to put coal in a woodshed.

Each resident, including those who lived on the third floor, came down the back steps with a coal scuttle of ashes, emptied them in their big trash can, walked to their woodshed, filled the empty scuttle with coal and kindling wood, and took it to the coal stove in their furnace room. Some coal was inevitably dropped on the concrete walkway.

Jerry's new dare was for me to walk up the back steps to the second floor and slide down the black iron pole that supported the iron stairway.

"You can't dare me to do something that you won't do yourself."

"Oh, I've done it lots of times," Jerry bragged.

"Then do it again so I can watch you. I'm not doing it unless I see you do it first," I insisted.

"Come on upstairs, and I'll show you how to do it."

When I looked down, it was a long distance to the concrete walkway covered with small pieces of coal.

Once I fell on coal on the sidewalk leading to Grandma's driveway, where the coal truck driver backed in to deliver coal. I was running from a neighbor's dog that was chasing me. I headed for Grandma's driveway to try to get to the back yard. The driveway wasn't paved, but the dirt was hard and coarse with little pieces of coal, and I scraped the palms of my hands and my knees when I went down. Tiny bits of coal imbedded themselves into my hands and knees, and I got up and ran to the front door. Mama carefully cleaned them out with warm water on cotton. Then she picked up the small bottle of orange-colored mercurochrome and dabbed it on the wounds with the little glass applicator attached to the bottle top. Each wound stung for a long time afterward.

Thinking about that incident made me decide I wouldn't take the dare, even if Jerry did slide down the pole.

He slid down the pole with no apparent effort or fear, but I still had no desire to follow him. After all, Mama and Grandma didn't even know Jerry or his family. They thought I was still playing with Martha.

Since Jerry's mother didn't allow him to leave the apartment house property, he wouldn't be able to go for Mama and Grandma if I fell and hurt myself. I'd just lie there and suffer.

"Go ahead. I dare you to do it," he persisted.

"No. I don't want to because I might fall and hurt myself, and Mama and Grandma wouldn't have any way of knowing because they don't know I'm playing with you. I've got to go now."

"Aw, you're just saying that because you can't do it."

"I don't care what you think. We used to sit and talk. I liked that. Now you just keep daring me to do things that might make me hurt myself. I've got to go, and I don't think I'll be back anymore." I ran off to Grandma's house.

I was proud of myself for refusing the dare but not proud of the fact that I was playing with Jerry when my family thought I was still playing with Martha. It wasn't that I didn't want to tell them about him; I'd just forget it after I got back to Grandma's.

Each apartment had a window in the kitchen, but everyone had their shades and curtains closed, I guess, so they wouldn't be startled when they saw someone on the stairs outside their window. That's why Martha's mother didn't see me and Jerry's mother didn't see him. Otherwise, I'm sure that Martha's mother would have called Grandma on the telephone.

If Martha's mother had called Grandma, she would have told Mama. Mama would have been mad and gotten a switch to thrash my legs until she drew blood. I would think I deserved it for not being where I was supposed to be and for doing what Jerry dared me to do.

It Started with Shoes

By the middle of August, Martha was talking about looking forward to starting school. One day, she was wearing a cute pair of brown leather shoes that laced on the sides. "They're my new school shoes," Martha showed me. "I'll be starting school soon."

"When do you start?"

"I start in September, after Labor Day, so I might not be able to play with you anymore after that."

"Why not?" I tried not to sound as though I felt like crying.

"When I go to school, I'll make new friends who'll be my age. I'll learn how to read, but you won't be able to read," she bragged.

"I have some books that Mama and Grandma bought me, and I can read some words in those books. I can even read some words in the newspapers," I said proudly.

"I don't mean that, silly. I mean, I'll learn how to read schoolbooks. You won't have schoolbooks because you won't be going to school."

When I went home, I told Mama and Grandma what Martha had said, and I asked if I could start school, too.

"You can't start school until next September because you're not old enough, but you will be needing new shoes anyway, so I might be able to get you a pair of shoes like school shoes," Mama offered.

I was happy to hear that, and I kept asking Mama when we were going downtown to shop for shoes. "Mama, are you sure we have a ration coupon for shoes? Didn't we use it for my Easter shoes?"

"We have another ration coupon. The government knows children's feet grow and their shoes wear out."

When Mama and I got to the shoe store, I looked in the show window, where they had children's shoes on display, to see if I could find a pair of shoes like Martha's, and there they were. The same shoes were on display on a shelf in the back of the store, where the children's shoes were.

We sat down next to a stool where the shoe saleslady sat to measure my feet. When Mama told her which shoes I wanted, she said they came only in medium width.

"Can we order a pair in a narrow width?" Mama inquired.

"That shoe doesn't come in a narrow width."

"Do they make any school shoes in narrow widths?"

"Oh, yes. The shoe company makes a very good-looking brown leather, oxford-style school shoe. I'll check to see if we have it in your size."

Although I was disappointed, I was glad to hear they might have some kind of school shoe in my size.

When I first saw the shoes, I didn't like them because I thought they were too plain. Mama said she liked them better than the other style, and after the saleslady checked them to be sure they fitted me properly, Mama said she'd take them.

"I don't like them, though, Mama," I pleaded.

"What is it you don't like about them other than the fact that they're not like Martha's?"

"I don't like the way they don't tie on the sides. That's what I liked so much about Martha's shoes. I don't like the way they look so big, and I don't like that they have shoelaces because I don't know how to tie them."

The saleslady explained, "Your shoes look big to you because your foot has grown, and you wear half a size larger than you did before. When you are learning to tie your shoes, it'll be easier for you to have the laces in the center of the shoes than on the sides. I think you'll like the shoes once you get used to them, and they come in narrow widths in sizes that should take you all the way through elementary school."

"It sure is good to hear that." Mama breathed a sigh of relief, and then she turned to me. "You can't help having a narrow foot. I have narrow feet, too, but this is the only school shoe in your width, so you'll just have to get used to it. You would've had to learn to tie the shoes like Martha's. You'll have to learn to tie any school shoes."

"All right." I agreed with Mama that I had no choice, but I was secretly very unhappy to think I'd have to wear big, brown shoes that I thought were ugly for the rest of this year and all seven years of elementary school.

Mama bought me a new short-sleeved maroon and white printed cotton dress and a pair of maroon socks to match the dress. That more than made up for being disappointed about my shoes. I liked the dress and socks a lot.

We went into Woolworth's dime store because Grandma had given Mama some change to buy her a quarter of a pound of Spanish peanuts. They were small, round peanuts with red skins. The lady behind the counter scooped up a few peanuts, weighed them, and put them in a small white bag.

Then, Mama said she'd buy me a quarter of a pound of whatever kind of candy or peanuts I wanted, so I looked at all the candy and nuts behind the glass counter and decided on the orange slices because I couldn't get them anywhere else. Only the downtown dime stores had them.

As we were walking through Woolworth's, I saw a thick book that caught my eye, and I stopped. When I opened the book, I saw more words than I had ever seen in one place in my life. "What is the name of this book, Mama?"

"It's *Webster's Dictionary*."

"I love it. Mama, will you buy it?"

"But it's not a storybook that we can read to you, and it doesn't have any pictures, so I don't know what you see in it."

"I'd like to have it because it has so many words. I can learn to read the words."

"All right. It won't hurt to have a dictionary in the house."

The dictionary was a hardcover book that was much more expensive than a little Whitman book would have cost. I could never understand why stores that were called dime stores, or five and ten cent stores, sold mostly things that cost a lot more than that, such as dictionaries, pots and pans, dishes, aprons, towels, and a variety of other things.

When we got back to Grandma's, Mama had me try on the dress, socks, and shoes to show her. I looked in the wardrobe mirror, and I liked the dress, the maroon socks, and even the shoes. Mama was right. They did look better than Martha's shoes.

"I like everything. You look just like a little schoolgirl," Grandma said with a big smile.

"I even got a book with a lot of words," I showed Grandma.

The next day, Mama had me wear my new dress, shoes, and socks for BeeWee to see. She even braided my hair.

BeeWee smiled. "I can't believe it. My little Sugie looks like a schoolgirl."

After breakfast, I went outside and started climbing in the snowball bush that was more like a small snowball tree because Grandma's mother had planted it, and it had grown a big, strong trunk. The flowers had white petals that grew in a round shape on the snowball bush. BeeWee came outside with his camera and took a picture of me climbing in the tree. Then, I had to go inside and change from my new clothes and shoes to my play clothes.

The next time I went to Martha's apartment, I wore my new shoes.

I waited a long time for her to say something about them, but she didn't say anything. Finally, I said, "Did you notice that I'm wearing new school shoes?"

"They're not school shoes."

"They are school shoes," I insisted. "The shoe saleslady said they are. She said they even come in sizes for older school children."

"They're only school shoes if you wear them to school," she shot back.

"You said your new shoes are school shoes, and you haven't worn them to school," I reminded her.

"I will be wearing my shoes to school."

"Oh," I said, sadly accepting that Martha was right. "Do you like my shoes?"

"They're all right, but I like mine better. Mine tie on the sides."

"I like yours, too. I wanted to get shoes like yours, but I have narrow feet, and they don't make those shoes in narrow widths," I informed her.

Martha looked at my shoes. "Yes, you do have long, narrow feet."

I looked down at my feet, and they suddenly looked longer. "What size are your shoes?"

She told me her size, and it was larger than mine.

"Your feet are longer than mine."

"But I wear a medium width, so my feet don't look as long as yours."

For the next few days, I was very conscious of my feet and kept looking down at them.

"Why have you started looking down at your feet when you walk?" Mama wanted to know.

"I don't know."

"You need to look where you're going so you won't bump into something," Mama cautioned.

Martha started school and said she was learning to read and do arithmetic.

During the day, I tried to read the words in my picture books, comic books, and newspapers. I turned the pages of my dictionary and looked at the words until I came to some that I could read. I just wished I could read more of them.

I sat on Grandma's porch and watched for Martha to come home from school each afternoon, but when she saw me, she ignored me and walked straight into the apartment building.

One afternoon when I saw her coming down the street, she was walking with another girl, who was her height, but a little slimmer, with short brown hair that was softly curled on the ends. She had a small, pretty face and bluish eyes.

Martha looked my way as she walked into the apartment building with her friend, and I sat there, wishing she would at least speak to me.

The next time I talked with Martha, I asked her about the girl.

"Her name is Alice. She's my new friend from school. She's a 'nice' girl." She emphasized the word 'nice,' as though she thought I wasn't a nice girl.

Martha hardly ever played with me anymore, so I started playing with Darrell again.

We played Cowboys and Outlaws again in Grandma's back yard. Our horses were still brooms. We liked galloping around the yard on the brooms, pretending to be either a cowboy or an outlaw. Darrell still liked to be the outlaw, so he could pretend that I shot him off of his horse, and he fell to the ground.

Sometimes I liked pretending I was a lawman, and when Darrell stepped out from behind the woodshed, I shouted, "Drop your gun and stick up your hands. I've got you covered." I did it because I knew he was expecting to pretend he was shot.

"Aren't you going to shoot me?"

"I'm a lawman who doesn't believe in shooting outlaws," I told him to walk in front of me to the jail, which was on the side of Grandma's house, between the back porch and the fence.

Darrell didn't like being caught and taken prisoner because he didn't get to pretend to be shot and fall on the ground.

When I was the outlaw, I preferred being taken prisoner because I didn't like falling on the ground.

It was amazing that Darrell turned out to be a much better friend to me than Martha was. He started out as a bully, but he did a complete about-face. I always, in the back of my mind, wondered if he would ever bully me again, but he never did. Martha was never a true friend because she didn't know how to be a friend—friends don't talk to each other the way that Martha talked to me.

The Hurricane

One morning BeeWee told us that we might get a hurricane.

"What is a hurricane, BeeWee?"

"It's a storm."

"You mean like a thunder and lightning storm?" I wondered.

"There might be some thunder and lightning in it, Sugie, but a hurricane usually has strong winds, rain, and flooding."

"I'm scared of storms." I moved toward Grandma.

"Clarence, you're scaring the child."

"Sugie asked me what a hurricane was, and I was telling her. I wasn't trying to scare her."

"BeeWee didn't scare me, Grandma. I was already scared of storms."

Mama had been listening from the back of the table and added, "Speaking of being scared, I remember being scared to death when the hurricane of 1933 hit Norfolk."

"I know you were scared. We were all scared. It was the worst hurricane we ever had," remembered Grandma.

Bee Wee recalled, "That's because it hit on high tide and caused a lot of flooding."

"I hope we never have another one like that." Mama sounded a bit worried.

"Why do we have to have storms, BeeWee?"

"It's just a part of nature."

"I like the plants and animals part of nature, but I don't like storms," I decided. I got more and more scared as I heard the storm was moving closer to Virginia.

"Don't worry. We might not get the storm. Sometimes it hits Florida or North Carolina before it gets to us," Grandma informed us.

The hurricane hit some other places and was weaker before it reached Virginia, but we had a lot more wind and rain than I had experienced before. It poured down rain, and the strong wind blew and sounded eerie. It kept blowing the tree limbs of the big gum tree, causing them to thrash against the side of the house. We heard something that sounded like metal blowing around, and Grandma thought it sounded like a trash can lids.

She and I sat quietly side-by-side on the sofa. The wind eventually died down, and the rain stopped. Grandma told me the hurricane was over, and we went upstairs to bed.

The next day, everything was quiet and still again.

After breakfast, BeeWee and Grandma went outside to clear the yard of twigs and small branches that were blown off the trees by the wind. They checked the side of the house where the tree branches had blown against it, and it wasn't damaged. BeeWee thought we were lucky that no large tree limbs had fallen in the yard and no slates had been blown off the roof.

My Halloween Costume

By October, the weather was cool enough to wear a sweater outside.

Mama bought me my first Halloween costume, but I didn't like it because it was a Dutch boy costume. She told me they didn't have anything else in my size and it would look cute once I tried it on.

I tried it on and hoped I'd like it when I looked at myself in the mirror, but I didn't like it at all. There was nothing cute about the short, baggy blue pants and the plain short-sleeved white shirt. "Mama, did they have something for a girl in the next size?"

"This is two sizes larger, and it was the only costume they had," she explained. "I was lucky to get this costume because they said it was left from last year. I guess they're not making new costumes because of the war."

No wonder the costume was left from last year, and no one had already bought it this year. I wanted a costume, but I almost wished that Mama hadn't found that one.

About a week before Halloween, Grandma got a telephone call from Martha's mother, who said Martha's dancing school was having a Halloween party, and she had no costume to wear. Grandma told Martha's mother that my mother had bought me a new costume, and we would be happy to let Martha use it to wear to her dancing school party.

I'd hardly played with Martha since she started school, so her mother invited me to come over to play with her shortly before Halloween, probably to be nice to me for letting Martha wear my costume.

Even though I didn't like the costume, I didn't like the idea of Martha wearing it before I did. I wouldn't have minded if Crissy wore the costume before I did, but I cried into my pillow that night after Grandma told me that Martha would wear it first.

Mama and Grandma thought Martha's mother was nice, which she was. They assumed Martha was nice because her mother was nice. They just didn't know Martha the way I did.

As we played with her paper dolls, Martha didn't hesitate to tell me that she was learning to read and that her friend Alice was a nice girl, emphasizing the word 'nice.' She also made sure to tell me that she took dancing lessons, which was why she was invited to a Halloween party, and that my grandmother was letting her wear my new costume even before I wore it.

She was so busy bragging that she didn't think to ask me anything about the costume.

Martha's mother returned the costume to Grandma before Halloween and thanked us.

It was cold on Halloween night, so I had to wear my clothes and leggings under the costume and my coat over it.

Mama told me, "Leave your coat open, so people can see your costume."

I was happy that it turned cold so I could wear the costume over my clothes, and I was even happier that I could wear my coat over it.

Mama noticed that I cheered up. "Are you satisfied with your costume now?"

"Oh, yes, I am." I was satisfied because I could wear my coat.

Grandma smiled. "You're lucky to have a costume."

"I know," I agreed, still thinking I was lucky that I could wear my coat over it.

When people asked me what I was, I didn't mind saying I was a Dutch boy. I never really minded being a Dutch boy. I just didn't like the way I looked in the baggy costume. The costume might have looked better if it had not been two sizes too large.

Martha and her mother came to the door when I went trick-or-treating at their apartment.

"Who is this?" Her mother asked me, pretending not to know who I was.

"I'm a Dutch boy."

Martha seemed pleased to say, "I should have known you'd be a boy."

The next time I played with her, I confronted her. "Why did you say you knew I'd be a boy on Halloween? You were a boy, too, because you wore my costume first."

"I never wore it because I didn't go to the party."

"Why didn't you go?" I thought I might very well know the reason.

"I decided I didn't want to go."

I wish I could have seen Martha's face when she saw the Dutch boy costume, especially if her mother had made her try it on.

If the weather hadn't turned cold on Halloween night so I could cover the costume with my coat and wear my leggings under the baggy blue pants, I might have decided I didn't want to go trick-or-treating. Mama had gotten me a costume, though. That was nice of her. She couldn't help that it was the only costume left.

I did have a good time that night, my first time going trick-or-treating.

We Have Each Other

The day before Thanksgiving, Grandma's house smelled like roasted turkey, just as it had the year before. Grandma had managed to buy all the ingredients and was staying up late again to cook a wonderful Thanksgiving dinner.

By the time we sat down to eat on Thanksgiving afternoon, Grandma had the big, round oak dining room table set with the ivory lace tablecloth and the white dishes and silver-plated utensils we used every day. She had rounded up the three oak dining room chairs and three of the four white wooden kitchen chairs and put them around the table.

Besides the delicious roasted turkey and dressing, there were seasoned collard greens, soft hot baked sweet potatoes with butter, Ocean Spray jellied cranberry sauce, hot bakery rolls with butter, and coffee with pure cream. Even though we enjoyed our fill of these delicious foods, I think we all managed to save enough room for a small slice of Nolde's pound cake.

After dinner, BeeWee and Daddy sat in chairs in the living room, smoked cigarettes, and talked shop, which was what they called their usual conversation about their jobs.

Mama, Aunt Nita, and I helped Grandma to clear the table by taking everything from the dining room table to the kitchen table. Then, Grandma told all of us to go sit in the living room because she would take care of washing and drying the dishes and putting everything away.

Mama and Aunt Nita were hardly ever in the house at the same time, but now they were sitting on the sofa and talking about clothes, people they both knew and movies they'd recently seen.

I got on my tricycle, and BeeWee noticed that my knees were hitting the handlebars. "Sugie, you don't need those wooden blocks on the pedals anymore. I'll take those off in the morning."

I must have grown a lot since last spring when I needed the blocks so my feet would reach the pedals.

I spent some time riding my tricycle around in the house, but I spent most of my time in the kitchen, talking with Grandma. While everyone else talked in the living room, Grandma scraped the plates, pots, and pans and washed the mountain of dirty dishes. She never came into the living room after Thanksgiving dinner because she was still working in the kitchen, even when Mama and Daddy came to say they had to leave because Daddy had to go to work in the morning.

After they left, BeeWee told us he was going to "hit the hay," and Aunt Nita said she was going to bed because she had to get up early to go to work.

I went back into the kitchen and sat at the table to be with Grandma as she finished up. "Grandma, I know you're tired because you worked so hard cooking a big, delicious dinner and washing so many dishes."

"My mother used to cook the same Thanksgiving dinner for all of us and wash all the dishes afterward."

"I wish I'd known her because she must have been like you, Grandma."

"Well, that's mighty nice of you to say. I did have a good mother. She went through a lot, but she didn't let it get her down. You were too young to know her, but she knew you. She held you in her arms and said you were a pretty baby. The poor thing was sick by then, and she died the summer after you were born."

"I'm sorry, Grandma."

She leaned over and gave me a hug. "Thank you, honey."

Grandma finally finished in the kitchen, and we went upstairs to go to bed.

Getting Ready for Christmas Again

By the next morning, Mama was back, and she was talking about Christmas.

"It seems early to me to be thinking about Christmas shopping," Grandma commented.

"I think we should get our shopping done early this year because the buses and the stores are going to be packed with servicemen," Mama insisted.

She took me shopping a couple of times, and each time we waited at the bus stop as several buses passed us because they were crowded. Sailors were standing in the aisle and even standing on the steps at the front and back doors. The downtown sidewalks and the stores were as crowded as Mama said they would be. Sometimes a young serviceman asked Mama her opinion about a gift he was trying to buy for his girlfriend or asked her size because his girlfriend was about Mama's size.

By the beginning of the second week in December, Mama saw in the newspaper that fresh, live Christmas trees were advertised, and BeeWee took us to buy one on December 16th, the day after his payday.

The day we went for the tree was almost as cold, damp, and windy as it was the year before when Mama and I sat in the car.

When we stayed in the house, I never noticed the odor of the coal stove, but after being outside in the cold air for a while and going back in, the smell of coal burning in the Arcola stove was the first thing I noticed.

Grandma always worried about going out when there was a fire in the stove, but there was nothing else to do. If she didn't start a fire because we were going out, the house would be unbearably cold when we came home. She let the fire go down as much as she could before we left home, but she couldn't put it out because the fire remained in the red-hot coals for a long time.

It felt good to return home to a warm house after being outside in such cold weather. When I was cold, I always sat on the radiator in the living room or the dining room or pulled up a chair beside the Arcola stove in the kitchen and sat with my back to the side of it. That felt so good.

As soon as we got home, Grandma put on a pot of coffee and heated the pot of kidney bean soup she had cooked that morning. BeeWee had just enough time to nail the iron tree stand to the floor, put the tree in it, test the strings of lights, and arrange them on the tree before he washed his hands and sat at the table to eat. We all liked Grandma's kidney bean soup. Even though BeeWee would never say he liked it, he obviously did because he didn't leave a drop in his bowl.

Aunt Nita came home from work instead of going out with her friends because she liked to decorate the tree and had promised to let me help her again this year.

Grandma brought two drawers of ornaments downstairs and set them on the living room floor. Aunt Nita and I took each ornament from the old white tissue paper wrapping.

Aunt Nita took off her shoes and stood on a chair to put the star on the treetop. Then she hung the smaller ornaments on the top branches as I handed them to her. I asked her if I could stand on the chair this year to help her.

We got along fine until it came time to put icicles on the tree. Aunt Nita said she tried to buy new tinsel, but the stores didn't have it this year. "It's a good thing we save the tinsel every year, or we wouldn't have any for this year."

"Why do people put tinsel on Christmas trees?"

"Don't you remember what I told you last year? The tinsel is supposed to look like icicles." She carefully placed each strand on the branches.

Then, for some reason, I started tossing tinsel on the tree.

"What in the world are you doing?"

"I'm pretending that it's snowing on the tree."

"Stop it because tinsel isn't supposed to be thrown on the tree. If you don't want to put on one icicle at a time, just let me do it."

"I don't know why I did it, Aunt Nita unless I thought it would be fun and would look good, but it wasn't fun, and it doesn't look good. I'll put on one icicle at a time from now on," I promised.

"Okay. I'll try to fix it while you're doing that."

We finished the decorating, Aunt Nita turned out the lights, and we stood back to admire the tree.

"I'm going to get Grandma so she can see how the tree looks." I ran to the kitchen.

"You certainly did a good job of decorating the tree," said Grandma as she walked into the room.

A few days later, Mama took me to the department store downtown where we'd seen Santa Claus before. When Mama told me we'd get off at the next stop, I was thrilled to think we were about to see Santa. We stepped off the bus and headed for the store, where there was a crowd of people standing on the corner. Mama explained that they were looking at Santa and we'd see him soon.

I could hardly hold back my excitement as we approached him. There he was, sitting on a huge chair, wearing his red suit and hat, both trimmed with white fur and shiny black boots. He had a full, snowy white beard and mustache and bushy white eyebrows.

Although he was behind the glass of the three-sided corner store window, we could hear him say, "Ho, ho, ho. Merry Christmas!" After watching him for a few minutes, I asked Mama what time it was because I didn't want to miss Santa's radio program from the North Pole.

"There's plenty of time before Santa comes on the radio, but we need to cross the street and start waiting for the bus. People who work downtown will get off work soon and crowd into the buses. I want us to get home before dark, too."

"Then let's go," I said, anxious to hurry home.

We got to Grandma's house before dark and long before Santa came on the radio. He reminded everyone children could send letters to him at the North Pole. I'd be glad when I learned how to write so I could send him a letter.

I liked hearing Christmas music on the radio. My favorite children's Christmas songs were still *Up on a Housetop* and *Jingle Bells*. All the radio programs began to be about the characters getting ready for the holidays. The soap opera characters on the afternoon programs and the characters on the evening programs were all getting ready for Christmas, just as we were.

One day, Grandma and BeeWee took me Christmas shopping. The store had creaky wooden floors and was as dim inside as it was in Grandma's house. The cloudy day made it seem like nighttime. It was cold in the store, too, so my heavy winter coat, leggings, and hat felt good.

Mama said I was outgrowing my leggings, but she made them last one more winter so I'd have something to keep my legs warm. She cut off the straps that went under my feet, and she cut off the shoulder straps.

There were counters in the store with a variety of items that would make good, useful Christmas gifts for people like BeeWee and Daddy, such as men's white work socks and white handkerchiefs. Grandma explained men could always use those as she helped me to pick out a gift for each member of the family.

Grandma pointed out that BeeWee would like a new pair of white work socks, and it was all right if he knew I was giving them to him because he liked getting new work socks. Then, she said Daddy might like to have a new handkerchief because any man could use a nice, new white handkerchief.

There were gifts for ladies, such as boxes of candy and delicately embroidered handkerchiefs. Grandma suggested that I get long narrow boxes of peppermint patties for Mama and Aunt Nita. I wanted to get one for her, too, but she said she didn't eat candy. "I don't expect you to buy me a gift, honey. I'll be happy if you give me a hug."

Giving Grandma a hug was something I would do anyway, so it didn't seem like enough for someone who did so much for me. Of everyone in the family, I'd rather give a gift to Grandma than anyone else. I felt sad to think that I wouldn't have a gift for her, so I asked BeeWee if I could buy her something. He said he thought she'd like the box with a nice white handkerchief that had pretty blue flowers embroidered in one corner. I thought it would make a nice gift for her, too, so he bought it.

Mama put the Christmas lights in the windows, but we didn't know yet if we'd be able to turn them on. Grandma said too many lights burning in windows might light up the country more and make us a better target for enemy planes.

Aunt Nita wrote Christmas cards to almost everyone she knew, and Grandma wrote them to her sisters, some of the neighbors, and her Sunday school teacher. The mailman brought Christmas cards every day. Cards and postage stamps weren't expensive. I thought it would be nice to be a grownup and have a job so I'd have my own money to pay for gifts for my family and to buy Christmas cards to send to people I knew.

The Christmas Holidays

Christmas morning was just as it had been the year before, except that Santa Claus brought me different things.

Santa left me a child's mahogany-colored roll-top desk and chair. He must have known how anxious I was to start school. Now I could play school. I got a new doll, a game, a big thick book of bedtime stories, and a round tin box divided into sections with different kinds of hard, filled candy. I'd seen one like it at Robbins' and asked Santa to bring it to me. There was raspberry candy that was shaped like raspberries, filled peppermint straws, and shiny white flat squares that had a chewy, black walnut filling. I'd never had so much hard candy. It would be especially good for eating on Sunday afternoons while I was listening to *The Shadow.*

BeeWee was happy in the morning but became depressed again this year because Mama didn't come over to watch me open my presents.

Grandma had been in the kitchen most of the night before, preparing Christmas dinner for the family, and the aroma of roasted turkey filled the house as it did every Thanksgiving and Christmas.

Mama and Daddy came over in the afternoon, Aunt Nita came home from work, and we all sat in the dining room and stuffed ourselves with Grandma's magnificent meal.

When we exchanged gifts, I hugged Grandma and told her I loved her. Then I gave her the handkerchief. She seemed very surprised and said how pretty it was.

During the holidays, I tried to think of something I could make for Grandma, and I finally came up with what I thought was a good idea. I'd make her a rug to stand on at the sink because she stood there for so many hours washing dishes and clothes.

I wondered how I'd make it, so I thought of what we had on hand. Grandma had a stack of old newspapers on the porch, and I'd seen Aunt Nita use a needle and a large spool of white thread when she made the little coat for my doll. I could tear some newspapers into strips, stuff them between two pieces of material, and sew around the edges to keep the newspaper strips from coming out.

I asked Grandma if there were two pieces of material I could use because I had a good idea for something she needed that I could make for her. She found two pieces of cotton material and let me use her needle, thread, and my small, blunt-edged scissors that would hardly cut the thread.

Grandma helped me to thread the needle. She said she had always had a hard time threading a needle because it was hard for her to get the thread through the eye. I thought it was funny for the tiny hole in the top of the needle to be called an eye. We laughed a lot when she was having trouble doing it, but she finally got the needle threaded. I made the mat and put it on the kitchen floor in front of the sink.

"Thank you, honey. It's just what I need," she told me with a big smile.

I liked sewing. I thought I would like to do it again sometime.

I enjoyed listening to *The Shadow* on Sunday afternoons even more now that I had my big round tin of candy. It would be a good box to save after I finished all the candy. There was no telling how long that would take.

It was cold outside, but I rode my tricycle up and down the sidewalk during the week. I didn't stay outside as long as I would have in warmer weather. I would knock on the door, and Mama would come and take the tricycle into the house.

When I got inside, I asked if I could make myself a catsup sandwich, which consisted of a slice of fresh white bread that Mama or Grandma sliced for me and some catsup that I shook out on it. Mama and Grandma said I was hungry between meals because I was growing.

When I woke up in the middle of the night, sometimes with a leg ache, Grandma would say that was because I was growing, too. Grandma had a remedy for everything, including my leg aches. "I have two kinds of liniments. One liniment is strong, and the other is medium, but they're both too strong for your tender skin," she explained. She sat on the side of the bed and rubbed my leg with camphorated oil until the aching went away, and I started drifting off to sleep. Camphorated oil was clear and had almost no scent.

The house was as cold during the night as it was last winter. The sheets and pillowcases were freezing when I first got in bed, but I began to warm up when I pulled the woolen blankets under my chin, and Grandma added heavy woolen winter coats to the bed. I wore my same long, rose-colored chenille bathrobe to bed, too. I always wore my socks. They helped to keep my feet warm, so I didn't take them off when I went to bed. In fact, sometimes I kept on my rose-colored bedroom slippers over my socks to keep my feet warm and quickly threw them on the floor by the bed before I fell asleep.

"Are you getting too warm, honey?"

"I'm getting hot, and I can't turn over on my side."

Grandma laughed and started putting the coats back on hangers and hanging them on the hook on the little room door. She was so busy trying to help me get warm; Grandma hadn't gotten in bed herself.

I was usually asleep before Aunt Nita and BeeWee came home. If I was awake, Aunt Nita and I would scratch each other's backs.

Grandma probably turned on the oven and opened the oven door to heat the kitchen just before BeeWee came home. Or, maybe he wouldn't have felt as cold as I did because he always wore his Union suit under his blue denim coveralls.

Grandma kept the side bedroom windows up about a foot, with a metal ventilator screen in them, in Aunt Nita's room and hers and BeeWee's room in case there were any dangerous fumes in the house from the coal stove.

She also thought it was healthy for us to have some fresh air in the rooms while we were sleeping, so she always raised another window in each bedroom about two inches.

Mama said Aunt Nita had asthma when they were growing up. They shared a bed in the same bedroom that Aunt Nita has now. During the night, Aunt Nita sometimes had trouble breathing. Mama said she was afraid Aunt Nita would lose her breath, so she ran to get Grandma. Grandma would rush into the room, raise the front bedroom window as high as it would go, and help Aunt Nita to the window so she could inhale fresh air. Mama said the fresh air would help Aunt Nita to breathe.

"Mama, I've never seen Aunt Nita have trouble breathing."

"I think she outgrew asthma."

I was glad she didn't have asthma anymore because it must have been scary for Aunt Nita to think she might lose her breath.

New Year's Eve

On New Year's Eve, Grandma let me stay up to listen to Guy Lombardo's orchestra play for a dance at a hotel in New York City. I liked listening to the big band music. I pictured the ladies wearing beautiful, long, satin evening gowns and the men wearing black tuxedos like movie stars wore when they danced together in the movies.

Just before midnight, the orchestra played *Auld Lang Syne,* and they started a countdown when it was about five minutes until the New Year. I felt sad because it was almost the end of 1942, a year that I thought had been pretty good for us even though our country was at war.

Another year of our lives was almost over, a year we could never get back.

When the countdown ended, everyone shouted, "Happy New Year!" Grandma and I wished each other a Happy New Year, too.

The year 1942 was gone forever, but I wanted to remember it.

"Grandma, I liked 1942, and now it's gone."

"It's gone, but it will always live on in our memories," Grandma remarked thoughtfully.

I moved closer to Grandma. "Does that mean we'll always be able to think back to 1942?"

"Yes. We'll always be able to think back to 1942." Grandma looked down at me, smiling.

"Can we remember every year?"

"We can remember every year."

"Good, because I want to remember everything in my life." I hugged Grandma.

Part III – 1943

New Year's Day

It was cold on New Year's Day, so cold that as I sat on the sofa in front of the living room windows, I felt the cold air coming through the cracks, where the windows didn't fit tightly enough in the frames. It was dim in the room, too dim to look at books without turning on a light. Grandma wouldn't want a light on anyway.

I stood up and turned around so I could get on my knees and rest my elbows on the back of the sofa. Then I parted the lace curtains in the middle so I had a clear view of the outdoors. The sky was gray, and the big oak tree next to the sidewalk was bare, having lost its leaves in the fall.

There wasn't a person in sight except for those who drove the few cars that passed by. They were probably people who had to be out today since gasoline was still rationed.

Grandma walked into the room. "It surely is a cold, dreary day. Your arms must be getting chilly, honey. If you feel cold, you can sit in the chair by the radiator."

I was getting colder, so I moved to the high-back chair in the corner, my favorite spot in the living room. It was BeeWee's favorite spot, too. When he occasionally sat in the living room; that's where he always sat. It was warmer by the radiator, but I don't think that's why BeeWee sat there. I think he preferred sitting in the high-back chair because he was tall. He wasn't extremely tall, though. I once heard him say he was five feet eleven and a half inches, but he looked taller because he was slim.

New Year's Day was different from other holidays because we didn't celebrate in any way. Some people had the day off, and others had to work. Daddy had the day off, so Mama stayed with him instead of coming to Grandma's house. BeeWee had to leave for work at two o'clock, so he was taking his afternoon nap, and Aunt Nita was working until four o'clock.

Aunt Nita promised she would write down our New Year's resolutions when she came home. I looked forward to that because I enjoyed spending time with her.

While I was waiting for Aunt Nita to come home, I took off my shoes, pushed the chair closer to the radiator, and sat on top of the radiator with my feet in the chair. When Grandma came back downstairs, she said, "Honey, if you're that cold, why don't you come and sit in the kitchen? I've got the oven on, and it's warm back there."

"Oh, I'm not that cold, Grandma. I just like to sit on the radiator."

Grandma smiled and kept walking toward the kitchen.

Sitting on the warm radiator was a good spot where I could relax and think. I had hoped rationing would be over by now, but the war was still going on. I wished it would end soon so we could go back to Lynnhaven. In March, I'd be six years old. I was especially excited about this birthday because I would start school in September. I could hardly wait to learn how to read. Oh, I could read a lot of words, but I wanted to be able to read sentences so I could read whole books. I wanted to read the way Grandma, Mama, and Aunt Nita read to me.

After thinking for a while, I put on my shoes and went to the kitchen to talk with Grandma, who was washing clothes in the kitchen sink. I thought she was washing underwear or stockings because I saw the box of Ivory flakes on the drain board. She always said it was milder than soap powder for washing underwear and stockings.

"What are you washing, Grandma?"

"I'm washing my bloomers."

I thought the word 'bloomers' sounded funny, but I didn't laugh. "What are bloomers?"

"They're underpants." She finished washing them and walked to the back porch to hang them on the line to dry.

I almost laughed out loud when I saw that they were much, much larger than Grandma. I wondered why they were so big, but I wouldn't think of asking my grandmother about the size of her underpants. I hoped it would be all right to ask, "Grandma, why do you call your underpants bloomers?"

"I've never thought about it, but I guess it's because ever since I was a little girl like you, that's what we called girls' or women's underpants."

"Oh."

It was icy cold on the porch, but we were only out there for a couple of minutes before we came back into the kitchen. I stood with my back to the Arcola stove to warm up for a minute before I sat down at the table. I liked to hear Grandma talk about her life, so I asked, "Grandma, where did you live when you were a little girl my age?"

"I lived here in Norfolk," she answered as she put away the box of Ivory flakes.

"Did you live in this house?"

"No. The house hadn't even been built then. I've told you the story about Mama and Papa and how Papa's business partner had caused them to lose the business that their parents had started and even to lose their fine home. Papa was so disappointed that he didn't want to live in Norfolk anymore. They moved to Portsmouth, and Papa had to take any job he could get." Grandma got teary-eyed. "Mama made his lunch every day, and we walked to where he was working and sat with him while he ate. He was such a good man. We were all crazy about him. Mama bought this house after Papa died. Poor Mama lost Papa and my brother within two years of each other."

"Which one died first?"

"My brother died first. He had tuberculosis. They called it consumption, then. There wasn't a thing the doctor could do for him. If you got consumption in those days, you just stayed at home and wasted away." Grandma paused for a moment. "Mama and Papa had four girls and one boy. We girls loved our brother so much. He was such a fine young man. It upset us so much to see him suffer, and we felt so hurt when he died."

"How old was he, Grandma?"

"He was just twenty-one years old."

"What was his name?"

"He was named James, after Papa's father. After Papa died, Mama didn't want to live in Portsmouth any longer. She wanted to move back to Norfolk, and she heard about a man building houses for a price she could afford, so she bought this house."

"How old were you then, Grandma?"

"My three sisters and I were all young girls in our teens, but we had to quit school and work to help Mama."

"What kind of job did you have?"

"At first, I took care of people's children, and then, when I was old enough, I got a job as a cashier in one of the grocery stores owned by David Pender. They're called DP stores now," she explained.

"I didn't know you ever had a job like that, Grandma."

"Oh, I never minded working. I would have gladly kept working after I was married, but your BeeWee didn't want me to work."

"Why didn't he want you to work, Grandma?"

"He thought if a married woman worked, it looked as though her husband couldn't support her. He thought the man should be the breadwinner in the family."

"What is a breadwinner?"

"The breadwinner is the one who earns the money for the family."

I followed Grandma as she walked back to the porch to hang up her stockings. She began to prepare our main meal of the day. "Are you getting hungry, honey? It's almost time for lunch. As soon as I set the table and take up the food, we'll eat."

In a few minutes, Grandma, BeeWee, and I were sitting down to a delicious meal of pork chops boiled with white turnips. We had black-eyed peas and stewed tomatoes with them.

"Now, Sugie, be sure to eat all your black-eyed peas, so you'll have good luck this year."

"Will black-eyed peas bring me good luck, BeeWee?"

"They will if you eat them on New Year's Day."

"Then, I'm going to eat every black-eyed pea on my plate." I began eagerly scooping up as many on my spoon as I could and shovel them into my mouth.

Grandma and BeeWee chuckled, and Grandma told me, "It's an old custom that people have believed in for as long as I can remember."

"I love all of this food, Grandma. I can cut my pork chop myself with the side of my fork, and I love these white turnips and stewed tomatoes."

"Mama used to make this meal every New Year's Day," Grandma reminisced.

BeeWee gave Grandma a kiss on the side of her face, "Well, I'm off to work." She handed him his lunch on his way to the door.

I finished eating while Grandma cleared the table and started washing dishes.

Grandma worked so hard. The skin on her hands and wrists was dry and rough during the winter because she almost always had her hands in water and went outside in the cold air.

Besides hanging out clothes, she brought in all the coal and kindling wood from the woodshed. She always kept a scuttle of coal and a scuttle of kindling wood on the back porch. She used the kindling wood to start the fire in the coal stove. Then, she used a small shovel with a long handle to shovel the coal from the scuttle into the stove.

She took the trash from the kitchen to the small, galvanized trashcan by the woodshed every day and set the can at the curb to be emptied on trash collection days. She came inside and washed her hands. Then, she opened a large white glass jar of rose water and glycerin hand cream that she rubbed on her hands. It was pink and smelled good, but it didn't stay on long enough to soften her skin.

As Grandma was cleaning up, I rode my tricycle around the house, pretending that each doorway was a corner with a stop sign so I'd stop and look both ways. All the while, I was listening as the big black clock on the black marble dining room mantle struck every hour. I knew that at four o'clock, Aunt Nita would get off from work and catch the bus to come home.

Aunt Nita finally came home, and I was so glad to see her. She smiled. "Are you looking forward to making New Year's Resolutions?"

"I sure am." I could barely contain my excitement.

"Okay then, give me about five minutes to take my things upstairs and get some paper and a pencil, and I'll be right back." She soon walked downstairs, looking pretty and smelling of sweet cologne and chewing gum, as she usually did. "Would you like some gum, Shirley?"

I liked it when she offered me gum. This time she had spearmint.

"Let me turn on a light so we can see what we're doing." Aunt Nita turned on the switch of the new lamp she'd bought. The light bulb in that lamp was bright, and I liked the way it lit up the room. All the rest of the light bulbs in the house were dim in comparison. The lamp was on the same table that the young servicemen set their hats on. Then, Aunt Nita asked, "Would you like to hear some music?"

"I sure would."

Aunt Nita walked across the room to the record player and put on a record. It was one of her favorites, *Don't Sit Under the Apple Tree*, by the Andrew Sisters. It was about a serviceman telling his girlfriend not to sit under the apple tree with anyone else but him until he came home from the war. The music played in the background as I thought of my resolutions, and Aunt Nita wrote them down.

When Aunt Nita asked for my first resolution, I said I was going to mind my own business and tell the truth all year.

"Wait a minute. That's two resolutions. Give me time to write them down." She laughed. She didn't ask me why I decided on those resolutions, but she seemed to be very happy that I did. After she had written down those two, she asked, "Do you have another resolution?"

While I thought about my answer, she walked to the record player because the record had stopped playing. "Is there a record you'd like for me to play?"

"Will you play *You Are My Sunshine*? That's my favorite."

"I sure will. Just give me a minute or two, and I'll find it." She thumbed through the records, and in a little while, we were listening to Bing Crosby sing my favorite song.

After thinking more about it, I told her, "My other resolution is that I'm starting to school this year."

"Shirley, that's not a resolution because you have to start school. You can make it a resolution by saying that you resolve to try to do your best when you start school."

"All right," I agreed. I didn't ask Aunt Nita about her resolutions because I knew from last year that she wouldn't tell me. She had said she never told anyone her resolutions.

"When you start school and learn how to write, you can write your own resolutions, and no one will know what they are."

"Why wouldn't I want anyone to know?"

"In case you can't live up to your resolutions, you'll be the only one who knows," she confided.

Grandma came into the room. "Nobody can sing better than Bing Crosby!" she exclaimed. "Juanita, I know you're planning to eat out with your friends, but I think you'd better let me warm some black-eyed peas for you to eat before you leave."

"Don't worry, Mama; I'll eat some while I'm out."

"Well, don't forget you've got to eat black-eyed peas on New Year's Day, so you'll have good luck all year," Grandma reminded her.

"I won't forget. I'll be sure to eat some." Aunt Nita turned off the record, put it away, and closed the lid of the record player. "I've got to get ready to go now, or I'll be late." She hurried toward the stairs.

I called out after her, "Bye, Aunt Nita!" Aunt Nita was at home for such a short time; I always felt sad when she had to leave.

"Come on in the kitchen, and we'll eat our supper, honey. We'll finish all the leftovers from lunch."

"Good. I loved what we had for lunch, Grandma."

"Well, I know you did, honey. I'm glad you enjoyed it."

I loved having leftovers from lunch since everything Grandma cooked was delicious, and she and I usually just split a can of soup for supper and had bread and butter with it. I had a small glass of milk, and she had a cup of hot water with a little evaporated milk in it. She never drank coffee after lunch.

Grandma and I finished eating, and she washed and dried dishes while we listened to the news on the radio.

When BeeWee was at work, I always sat in his place at the table, which was at the end, directly across from Grandma's place. Grandma liked to sit near the stove because she was always getting up from the table to check on the food she was cooking.

It was warm in the kitchen, and the overhead light was brighter than the lights in the other rooms. It was about forty watts.

After a certain time in the early evening, Grandma started letting the fire in the Arcola stove go out for the night. She didn't put in any more coal, but she opened the stove door and used the poker to spread the coals around in the stove to cool until the fire in them began to go out.

We spent the rest of the evening listening to funny radio programs. Then, at nine o'clock, we got ready to go to bed. It was a lot easier to prepare to go upstairs in the winter because Grandma didn't have to raise awnings and bring glider cushions into the house.

When we got upstairs, it was very cold. All the radiators in the house were cold after the fire went out. Then our winter bedtime routine began. I hurried and slipped into my pajamas. The material was cold, and I was shivering, so Grandma said I could also sleep in my chenille robe. When I got in bed between the sheets, they were freezing, and the pillowcase under my face was freezing, so I drew myself into a ball by pulling my knees up under my chin and wrapping my arms around my legs to keep myself in that position.

In the meantime, Grandma piled winter coats on top of the woolen blankets and chenille spread until I was weighted down, but I was getting warmer. Grandma put on her chenille robe and slipped under the covers beside me. As I warmed up, I took my arms from around my legs and eased my legs down toward the foot of the bed.

When I eventually got warm, I began to notice the weight of the coats. Grandma expected it and asked me if the coats were getting too heavy. When I said yes, she chuckled and got out of bed, picked up one coat at a time, put it on a hanger, and hung it back on the hook on the little room door until all the coats had been removed from the bed.

I was warm and comfortable as I fell asleep. By the time I woke up the next morning, the bedroom was warm because Grandma had gotten up early and started a fire in the coal stove. The mornings were nice. I liked seeing the light of day through the lace window curtains. Even more, I liked seeing Grandma beside the bed and hearing her voice.

Each day of winter was as cold as it was on New Year's Day. Grandma continued the evening rituals with the woolen coats and the morning coffee all winter. I knew I was a very lucky little girl to have a grandmother who was so loving and thoughtful.

Riding Tricycles on Cold, Sunny Days

Even though the weather was cold, I bundled up and went outside to ride my tricycle on sunny days. I liked the way the sun felt on my face, and it warmed everything enough to take some of the chill out of the air.

At first, Crissy came and walked beside me while I was riding my tricycle. I offered to let her ride it or stand on the back of it. When she stood on the back, I found out that I couldn't pedal that way.

A few days later, I looked up the street and saw a little girl riding a tricycle toward me. As she came closer, I was happy to see that it was Crissy. She and I were such good friends that we didn't have to say anything about her turning up with a tricycle. I was just glad she had gotten one so we could ride together.

We rode as far as I was allowed to go in both directions. After riding for a while, we parked our trikes in front of Grandma's house and sat on the steps in the sunshine and talked. Mama eventually came outside to take my trike inside and tell Crissy it was time for me to eat lunch and take my bath and a nap.

It felt comfortable in the house, and there was an aroma of some good food Grandma was cooking. I took off my coat, hat, and mittens. Then, I sat on a living room chair and took off my shoes so Mama could pull off my leggings. The leggings were getting harder and harder to get off because I was growing, and I'd had them since I was three years old.

The first year, the leggings were so big that they came down over the tops of my shoes, and the shoulder straps had to be crossed in the back and buttoned in the last buttonhole in the front. The second year, they fit just right with the shoulder straps not crossed in the back and buttoned in the first buttonhole.

This year, Mama cut off the straps because they were too short now that I had grown taller. "If you can just get through the winter with this coat, hat, and legging set, I'll buy you a new coat next winter when you're in school," Mama promised.

I was always uncomfortable in the third year; I had to wear a coat. Getting through the winter in a three-year-old woolen coat would not be easy. I would need help getting it on and off. I could hardly wait to get a new coat the next year.

Grandma's Chicken and Dumplings

When I went into the kitchen, I could see what smelled so good. Grandma was boiling chicken because she was making chicken and dumplings for lunch. I liked to watch her put the flour, shortening, salt, and water into a large mixing bowl to make dough. She kneaded it and shaped it into a big ball. She got her wooden cutting board from the bottom of the white Hoosier cabinet and set it on the table. She set the ball of dough on the board, flattened it with the palms of her hands, and rolled it with her rolling pin. Then she cut the dough into strips. She used a large spoon and lifted the chicken from the big black cast iron Dutch oven to a large bowl. Then she dropped the strips of dough slowly into the pot of boiling chicken stock, a few at a time.

I can honestly say that it was at this time that I decided I wanted to cook just like Grandma someday. I especially wanted a rolling pin and all the other kitchen utensils that she used. Until then, I had just thought about eating the food.

In a few minutes, Grandma set her largest white bowl in the center of the table, with a big spoon for all of us to take turns digging in. Mama put a heaping spoonful on my plate, spread it out to cool a little, and cautioned me to watch out for bones, even the small ones.

Mama and I each took one bite and told Grandma how much we liked the meal and how perfect it was for a cold day.

Grandma smiled and said, "It makes me happy to try to warm everybody's bones on a cold day."

Grandma did a lot more than warm my bones with her good cooking; she warmed my heart with her love and kindness every day.

Roller Skates

Sometimes when Crissy and I were riding our tricycles in the afternoon, we saw older children roller skating.

I asked Mama how old I had to be to skate.

"You can skate when you're six if I think you're ready then," she remarked as she combed my hair.

"What do I have to do to get ready?"

"You have to prove to me that you can be a good girl and follow directions." She parted my hair on the side and put a barrette in it to keep the hair out of my face.

"I'll be a good girl and follow directions."

"I'm glad to hear you say that, but you'll have to show me that you mean it. I don't think I need to remind you of some of the things you've done in the past." She put the comb on top of the chest of drawers.

"I'm older now than when I did those things, and I want to be good. I've always wanted to be good," I promised.

"You know right from wrong, so we'll just have to see what happens between now and your sixth birthday."

Mama said I knew right from wrong, but sometimes I wasn't sure. What could I do when I wasn't sure, like the time when I got the idea to try to read Aunt Nita's letters? I'd thought I was doing something good and got myself into a big mess. What might have kept me from doing that? I knew not to go into other peoples' things anymore, but I was going to have to be very careful not to do some bad thing I didn't know was bad until I'd already done it.

By the first of March, I was almost certain Mama would think I'd been good because no one said I had done anything wrong, and I hadn't been punished for anything. I started thinking a lot about getting skates for my birthday and began picturing myself skating up and down the sidewalk.

When it was closer to my birthday, I asked Mama if I could have a party and invite Crissy, Martha, Darrell, and Jerry. She bought a package of invitations and wrote one for each of them. About two weeks before my birthday, I gave them out to everyone except Jerry. They were all excited about the party and said they would come if their mothers would let them, and they were sure that their mothers would.

I would have to give Jerry his invitation the next time I saw him, which was every time I played with Martha.

The next day was Saturday, so Martha didn't have to go to school, and she invited me to her apartment to play paper dolls. It was fun sitting on the rug in the middle of her living room, where she would spread out her movie star paper dolls and their clothes. As usual, we pretended to be movie stars; I was Lana Turner, and she was Judy Garland.

We pretended not only to be movie stars, but we pretended to be anywhere we wanted to be, like Hollywood, California, where the weather was warm, and we could wear bathing suits and go to a swimming pool.

When I left Martha's apartment, Jerry opened his hallway door and whispered, "Hi."

I waved to him and handed him the invitation without saying anything because, if I did, his mother would hear me, and he'd be in trouble for opening the front door. I didn't think Jerry had played outside with anyone all winter.

The Fight

In the winter, I didn't go behind the apartment building because the coal trucks backed into the driveway to deliver coal to the six families in the building, who each had a furnace room and ordered their coal on different days, so the trucks came frequently.

Crissy didn't come to play with me the next morning, so I went out in the back yard for the first time that winter. There were a few days in March when it wasn't quite as cold, and this was one of them.

Since the first of March, Grandma, BeeWee, and Mama had been saying that spring was right around the corner, and daffodils seemed to burst into bloom overnight. Sunny days were brighter, and the sunshine was warmer.

Darrell saw me in the yard and wanted to know if he could come over to play.

We'd been playing Cops and Robbers for a few minutes when a woman came from the back of the apartment and looked toward the yard. She walked down the alley by the building, heading for the street. She had short, gray hair, wore glasses, and was wearing a short-sleeved cotton house dress, the way all of the ladies on the street dressed when they were not going to church or taking care of business.

I didn't know who she was, and Darrell didn't see her because he was facing me. Darrell and I continued to play until I heard him say, "Uh oh." Then, I saw the woman in the driveway walking toward the back yard.

Darrell started running toward the other side of Grandma's house, probably so he could climb the fence and run across Grandma's front yard to get to his house. I ran behind him, but I stopped at the backyard fence.

I thought the woman was coming behind us, but when I got to the back edge of Grandma's house, I saw that she had gone the other way, so I didn't go any farther. She had stopped on the sidewalk between the apartment building and Grandma's house. She looked so angry when she came face to face with Darrell that he started hollering for his mother.

Darrell's mother came running out of her house and stopped beside the woman and Darrell.

I wasn't sure whether the woman had been coming after both of us or just Darrell, but I wasn't taking any chances. I was frozen in the same spot. It entered my mind that I had somehow gotten into trouble, but I didn't know what I could have done. I worried that whatever it was might mean that I wouldn't get skates for my birthday.

The two women exchanged a few words, but I couldn't hear what they were saying. Then, the older woman shoved Darrell's mother. His mother shoved her back. When the woman grabbed a handful of Darrell's mother's hair, they started fighting.

I finally got scared enough to move and run toward the back of the house and knock on the back door to get in to tell Mama and Grandma about it. Grandma came to the door and asked me what was wrong, and I told her, but by the time she and Mama got to the front door to look out, the fight was over, and no one was there, so they could hardly believe that such a thing had happened.

Then, I worried that they would think I was just making it up. Grandma and Mama didn't even know about it. They didn't see it or hear it, maybe because I was knocking at the back door. I was always afraid I would not get the skates I wanted for my birthday.

When the fight broke out in front of Grandma's house, at first, I couldn't move because I was scared. When I finally knocked at the back door to tell Grandma and Mama to go to the front door to see what was happening, the fight was over, and the women had left. Mama and Grandma didn't believe there had been a fight because when I was younger, I had "cried wolf" a couple of times to get their attention.

The Next Day

The next day, when I was riding my trike in front of the apartment building, I was surprised to see Jerry open the front door of the building and walk toward me. "Is your mother letting you play out front now?" I asked.

"No. She just wants me to tell you that I can't go to your birthday party," he said.

I was too disappointed to know what to say. Then, I blurted out, "I'm sorry. I thought you were my friend, or I wouldn't have invited you."

"I am your friend. My mother won't let me come because she thinks Darrell will be there. You did invite him, didn't you?"

"I invited him, but what difference does that make?"

"My mother already didn't like Darrell because of something she saw him do one day when he was in the back of the apartment building. She tried to talk to him, but he ran away from her. She was in a fight with Darrell's mother. It happened near the front of your house. Didn't you see it?"

"I saw it, but I didn't know what it was about, and I didn't know the lady was your mother," I explained.

"I have to go back upstairs." Jerry began walking toward the door.

I understood why Jerry's mother wouldn't let him come to my party, but I felt sorry for him because I knew he really wanted to come. I'd miss him being there, too. Jerry was so much nicer than Darrell. I wished I hadn't invited Darrell in the first place because I'd rather have Jerry at my party. When I went in the house, I told Mama what Jerry had said and asked her if I could tell Darrell not to come.

"Don't say one word to Darrell about not coming," Mama said sternly. "You've already invited him, and you can't invite someone and then take back the invitation. That would be a cruel thing to do, and I'm sure his feelings would be hurt."

Grandma added, "Remember the Golden Rule. Always treat other people the way you'd like to be treated."

"I will, Grandma."

My Sixth Birthday

On March 17th, Mama began setting the table for my party. First, she arranged a big paper tablecloth on the round dining room table. Next, she started opening packages of paper birthday plates, cups, and napkins. After setting each place, she opened a bag of cute little baskets and put two of them beside each person's plate. Then, she put salted peanuts in one and little white mints in the other. They looked like miniature Easter baskets.

I was filled with joy and excitement about my party from the time I saw Mama setting the table, but by lunchtime, I was so excited I could hardly eat.

"I knew the closer it got to the time for your party that you would be excited, so we're having lunch an hour earlier than usual. I just fixed hamburgers, beans, and fried potatoes so you can eat quickly," Grandma explained.

Mama added, "Grandma and I want to clean up the kitchen and put everything away before the children come, so you go ahead and eat."

BeeWee and Mama finished eating and said they had to go somewhere.

"Where did they go, Grandma?"

"I think they went to the store."

It occurred to me that it might have something to do with my birthday, and Grandma wasn't supposed to tell, so I didn't ask any more questions.

In a few minutes, I found out that BeeWee had taken Mama to the bakery to pick up my birthday cake because they came back with a square white box, and Mama asked if I would like to see my cake. She pointed out, "It's devil's food with white icing, your favorite kind of cake."

It was a round-layer cake with "Happy Birthday, Shirley" written with green frosting letters in the center. White frosting flowers circled the top and the bottom of the cake, and green frosting shamrocks filled some of the space around my name.

"The green shamrocks are for Saint Patrick's Day," Mama explained.

"Well, what do you think of your birthday cake?" BeeWee was anxious to know.

I suddenly realized I had been standing there with my mouth open in a big circle. When I found my voice, I exclaimed, "It's beautiful!"

BeeWee pulled out his pocket watch to take a look at the time. "I wish I could be here for your party, but you know your BeeWee has to go to work."

"Mama, I want to save a piece of cake for BeeWee."

"Oh, don't worry, we'll definitely save some cake for BeeWee."

A few minutes before the children were to arrive, Mama set the cake in the center of the dining room table and put six small pink candles on it. The pink candles looked good with the pink trim on everything else on the table.

BeeWee said he wished he could take a picture of me standing beside the table, but there was no way to take an indoor picture because there wasn't enough light.

I thought about my birthday party when I invited Aunt Nita and her friends because I didn't have any friends of my own. I really thought her friends were my friends, too. I didn't think of inviting them this year because I knew they were just being nice to me because I was Aunt Nita's niece. Although it was fun, I felt embarrassed when I thought about it on this birthday.

I began to worry that my friends wouldn't come. I knew Mama would be sad if they didn't come after she prepared for them. Soon, all three of them came to the party, so I was happy.

Mama struck a match, lit each candle, and said the children could sit down at the table, but I had to stand to make a wish and blow out the candle. "Make a wish, but don't tell anybody what you've wished, or the wish won't come true. Then, take a deep breath and blow out the candles. If you blow out all the candles, your wish will come true."

I took a deep breath and blew on the flames as hard as I could, but as I started running out of breath, I began to realize that having a sixth candle on the cake made a big difference. I was nearly breathless when I blew out the last flame.

Then, they sang *Happy Birthday* to me. After that, Mama sliced the cake and put a big slice on each of our plates. Grandma came from the kitchen with a pint block of vanilla ice cream that she had opened and cut into four equal slices.

Grandma handed Mama a quart bottle of ginger ale that she had opened in the kitchen; Mama poured some into each cup and said we could start eating.

The devil's food cake was soft and fresh, with yummy white frosting, and the vanilla ice cream tasted perfect with the cake. I was saving my peanuts and mints to eat last, but when I looked up at my friends, I noticed that Darrell had put his peanuts on his ice cream and was eating them together. Crissy was looking down, eating from her plate.

Martha was eating, but each time she raised her spoon to her mouth, she looked up and watched Darrell. When she saw that I was looking up and she had caught my eye, she pointed toward Darrell. "Darrell's playing with his food. He dumped his peanuts on his ice cream, and he's eating them together."

"I like peanuts with ice cream. What's wrong with that?"

"My mother says its bad manners to mix your foods," Martha shot back.

"My mother doesn't mind." He scooped up another spoonful of ice cream mixed with peanuts, shoveled it into his mouth, and happily chomped away.

Crissy looked up, but she didn't say anything, and neither did I.

When we finished eating, Mama quietly announced that we could sit in the living room while I opened my presents.

Martha handed me a card and a gift that was flat, with something small and hard on the top, under the ribbon. It was a paper doll book and a small, silver-colored pair of blunt-edged scissors. I thanked Martha and told her I could hardly wait to cut out the paper dolls and clothes.

Crissy gave me a card, a coloring book, a small box of Crayola crayons, and a box of two small white handkerchiefs with pretty colored embroidery in one corner of each of them. I thanked her and told her I would like to color the pictures and use the handkerchiefs.

Before the party, Grandma and Mama told me to be sure to thank each person for their gift and to tell them I liked it, no matter what it was. They also told me not to expect a gift from everyone because they didn't have to give me a gift just because they came to my party.

Grandma gave me a card and a small, white tissue-paper-wrapped box from her and BeeWee. I thought it was from the jewelry store because that's how the store wrapped its gifts. I was sort of hoping they'd gotten me a new signet ring since BeeWee had no way of fixing the one they gave me last year. I just kept it in the ring box it came in and looked at it from time to time.

I knew it couldn't be a ring, though, because the box was too long for a ring. I lifted the lid and the long piece of cotton that covered the gift. It was a small, pretty gold cross on a thin gold chain.

"It's beautiful, Grandma. Thank you. I love you and BeeWee."

"We love you, too, honey. I'm glad you like it," Grandma said with a smile.

Mama told me she was going to set it on the top shelf of the living room mantle so it wouldn't be thrown out accidentally with all the wrapping paper. She said I was only to wear it to Sunday school and to take it off and put it away when I got home.

Aunt Nita gave me a card with some money and a note that said Grandma could hold the money and use it for us to go to some movies or to spend at Robbins' store. She had left it for me before she went to work.

I thought that was a good idea because I knew Grandma didn't have much money. She never spent more than a nickel on herself at Robbins'.

Thinking back to my birthday presents, I didn't see any other gift, which disappointed me because even though I wasn't sure Mama and Daddy would give me skates, they had always given me something.

Darrell didn't give me a gift, but that was okay because I knew he was happy to come to my party; and that he was having a good time. I knew he liked me because he played with me all the time. He and I just liked each other as playmates, not even as friends.

"I'll just get the blindfold for Pin the Tail on the Donkey, and we'll be ready to start the game." Mama got up and walked out of the room. When she came back, she had a wrapped box. "I found this in the hall. I wonder what it is."

Darrell leaned toward me and whispered, "I think she's playing a trick on you. I think it's from her."

Grandma was standing between the living room and the dining room with her arms folded and a smile on her face, so I was beginning to think that Darrell was right.

Mama handed the box to me. I was trying not to get my hopes up because it could contain something like a pair of rubber boots, which I could use, but I could have more fun with a pair of skates. When I finally got the paper off the box and opened it, there was a shiny new pair of skates and a card from Mama and Daddy.

I knew my mouth was gaping open, but I was speechless.

Darrell leaned over again. "I was right. I figured it out because your mother was the only one who hadn't given you a present."

I wondered why Darrell said that since I hadn't gotten a present from him.

Crissy and Martha sat like young ladies, saying nothing.

I was happy to get the skates, and I thanked Mama. I would have liked to put them on and skate at that very moment, but I was having my party, and Mama said we could walk to the back hall to play Pin the Tail on the Donkey. She handed each of us a paper donkey tail and a straight pin. She offered to help us to pin it on the tail when we decided where we wanted to put it. Then, holding a large, clean white handkerchief to use for a blindfold, she asked which of us would like to have the first chance to pin on the tail.

Crissy, Martha, and I stepped back, and Darrell stepped forward. "I'd like to go first," he volunteered.

Mama put the handkerchief over his eyes, tied it behind his head, and turned him around twice. We were bent over with laughter as Darrell put the tail all over the donkey and eventually settled on a spot on the donkey's side. Mama helped him with the pinning, and he laughed louder than any of us when Mama took off his blindfold, and he saw where he'd pinned the tail.

When we had all taken a turn, Darrell ended up being the winner because he had gotten closer to the tail than any of us. Mama gave him a small prize and then gave each of us a small cardboard horn and one of those rolled-up things that go straight out like a long tongue when you blow it.

We had fun blowing the horns and blowing the roll-ups at each other for about five minutes, and then Mama said it was four o'clock and time to put on coats to get ready to go home. She said she would put more salted peanuts and mints in our little baskets if we wanted to save them, which we all did.

Everyone remembered their manners as they said they had a good time, and we thanked them for coming.

After they all left, I asked, "Mama, can I put on my skates now?"

"You can't put them on this afternoon because I'm too tired to help you with them. I'll help you with your skates tomorrow after I've had a chance to rest," she promised.

My birthday party was wonderful; I liked everything about it! Everyone was so nice to me, and I could tell that my family and friends were having fun. It was as nice as a party could be, and it meant a lot to me that Mama had taken care to make it such a special day. I had a great time, and I couldn't wait to learn to skate.

Learning to Skate

The next morning, Mama and I sat on the sofa as she showed me how to use my skate key to adjust the shiny steel skates over my shoes.

BeeWee sat in the high back chair across from us and put my skate key on a strong piece of string so I could wear it around my neck.

Grandma stood between the living room and the dining room, watching us as she dried her hands on a kitchen towel and reminisced, "Florencie, this takes me back to when you and Juanita used to skate."

"I know. I always liked to skate, and I think Nita did, too."

"Juanita liked to skate, but she couldn't skate every time she wanted to because of her asthma," Grandma recalled.

"I know. Now, Shirley, hold on to me and try to stand up on your skates," Mama instructed.

I didn't know how hard it would be to stand on skates until I stood up, the wheels started rolling, and my feet almost went out from under me. Mama let me hold on to her as I slowly walked on the skates in the living room, dining room, and hallway several times.

Grandma and BeeWee watched for a while, and then Grandma said she had to go back to the kitchen to prepare lunch. BeeWee said I was doing a good job of walking on the skates, but I needed to push off on one skate and then the other so the wheels would roll. I tried it, but when the wheels started rolling, I still felt as though they were going to roll out from under me. I got scared. "I can't do it. If that's what I have to do, I can't skate."

"You'll learn. This is just your first day, and it takes time," BeeWee explained.

Mama said it was easier for her to learn how to skate on one skate first, and then if she started to fall, she could catch herself on her other foot. I tried it and soon learned to skate so easily with one skate that I tried skating on both of them. After a few days of holding on to Mama, door frames, stairway railings, and the heavy draperies in the hallway, I could skate without holding on, so I thought I was ready to skate on the sidewalk.

"There's nothing to hold onto on the sidewalk, so take your time and just skate in the front of the house. Don't skate toward the street, or you'll roll downhill and won't be able to stop yourself," Mama cautioned.

It was a sunny day, but it was still cold outside, so I was bundled up from head to toe and probably wouldn't hurt myself if I fell. I did all right, holding Mama's hand at first, then letting go and skating as slowly as I could.

Darrell came outside and sat on his steps to watch me. "I wish I had a pair of skates, but my mother said I have to wait until Christmas."

I thought if Darrell ever got a pair of skates, he would just put them on and skate on the sidewalk without any help from anyone.

I skated every day.

On cold, sunny days, I skated on the sidewalk, and on rainy days, I skated in Grandma's house. Crissy began coming to watch me almost every time I skated outside. She followed me around on her tricycle.

"Crissy, why don't you ask your mother to buy you a pair of skates so we can skate together?"

She shook her head from side to side.

When the weather became less cold, I was getting hot and sweaty in my winter clothes. Mama told me I could begin skating without having to wear my woolen leggings and my hat.

It was much more comfortable not wearing tight leggings and a hat. I was able to skate faster and turn around on the sidewalk instead of having to step onto the grass to stop and then step back on the sidewalk. I was skating smoothly and thinking how easy it was when I came to Mrs. Marshall's driveway, where coal trucks had delivered coal all winter. Evidently, a small piece of coal was on the sidewalk, and one of the wheels on my skates hit it.

Kerplop! I fell on the sidewalk and skinned my knees, which felt as though someone had scraped the skin off with sandpaper.

When I eased myself into a sitting position on Mrs. Marshall's lawn, I looked at my knees and saw the skin was badly scraped off, and there were tiny bits of coal in the bloody scrapes. This was worse than any time when I fell on the sidewalk because the scrapes were deeper and bloodier. They were more painful, too.

I didn't feel like skating back to Grandma's because my knees hurt too much. They felt stiff. I took off my skates and walked gingerly and stiff-legged to Grandma's house with the skates in my hands.

When Mama and Grandma saw me, they didn't seem very surprised, but they quickly helped me to take off my coat, and then they gathered the supplies Mama needed to treat my scrapes. She used cotton dipped in a small enamel basin of lukewarm water to clean the coal from the wounds. I knew she was being as gentle as she could, but it was still about to kill me to wait for the wounds to dry. Then, she opened the little glass bottle of Mercurochrome and took out the glass applicator.

"Mama, please don't put Mercurochrome on my knees. It stings even when you put it on scratch. It's going to burn me up if you put it in these deep scrapes."

"I have to do it to kill whatever germs may be on your knees and to help them to heal," she explained.

"Grandma, please don't let her do it."

"Honey, your mother has to do it. I'm sorry it's going to burn, but it'll keep your knees from getting infected, and they'll heal faster. Just turn your head so you won't see her putting it on, and it'll be over before you know it."

When my ordeal was over, Mama told me I could sit in the living room, prop up my feet on the stool, and color. "I don't want you to skate on the sidewalk until your knees heal."

"Don't worry. I'm never going to skate on the sidewalk again."

I didn't have to wait for my knees to heal to go outside, so I went out the next morning and sat on the edge of the porch. Instead of bending my knees, I extended my legs over the steps. I thought the warm sunshine made my knees feel better.

Something whizzed by, and I saw that it was Darrell skating up the sidewalk. When he passed by again, going in the opposite direction, I noticed the wheels weren't rolling at all. He was going fast, but he wasn't really skating. It was the way I walked on my skates when I first got them. Worst of all, the way he was leaning forward, he looked as though he was going to fall on his head.

I couldn't help smiling each time he went by because I knew he thought I was impressed with his fast "skating." He "skated" to the steps, sat down on the bottom step, and took off his skates.

"Didn't your mother say you'd have to wait until Christmas to get skates?"

"She did say that, but my uncle gave me his old skates so I can practice before I get new ones." He examined his skates as he talked. "I might not even need new skates now that I have these. They're fine except for being a little rusty, but I don't care about the rust. How'd you skin your knees?"

"I fell when I was skating," I admitted.

"Oh." I could tell by the look on his face that he was concerned about it. Darrell picked up his skates and walked home.

On the first day of skating, I fell and skinned my knees. At that time, I wanted to give up skating, but I changed my mind the next day. Skating was too much fun to quit. I had heard that if, at first, you don't succeed, try, try again, and I agreed. Skating on the sidewalk was one of the most enjoyable things I ever did.

Ocean View Amusement Park

In April, BeeWee went fishing after his work shift at the piers and caught some fish that Grandma cleaned and cooked for breakfast. It was good to wake up to the aroma of fresh fish being fried in the kitchen again.

While we sat at the table eating our fish, BeeWee talked about wanting to go back to Lynnhaven in July to fish for flounder and any other fish he could catch. We all said we wished the gasoline shortage would be over before BeeWee's vacation in July, but Grandma didn't think it would be over by then, so we shouldn't get our hopes up.

Needless to say, when July came, we were still having air raids, using ration coupons, and having a gasoline shortage. Since we were still at war, there was no chance of our going to Lynnhaven for the second consecutive year.

BeeWee took us to City Park so I could play on the playground several times while he was on vacation. Grandma, Mama, and BeeWee sat on a park bench and watched me. I wanted to seesaw, but there was no other child nearby. Mama agreed to seesaw with me, but it didn't work very well because I couldn't get her side of the seesaw to go up.

Then, we went to the park store that looked like a small log cabin; and I got my favorite cola snowball and a small bag of popcorn. Grandma got her usual nickel bag of roasted peanuts in the shell and a small Coca-Cola. BeeWee and Mama didn't want anything.

Another day, we went to the Ocean View Amusement Park, and Mama took me to the Fun House. It was sort of spooky because we got in a blue wooden rowboat without oars, and the boat moved slowly in a narrow lane of water. There were some sections of darkness where we heard loud laughter. Other sections were dimly lit and had ghoulish-looking faces staring at us and making eerie sounds. I liked it a lot.

Next, Mama took me on the merry-go-round, which she said had always been her favorite ride. She showed me which horses went up and down, and I climbed up on one of them. She got on a horse beside mine. I liked the way the horses moved up and down as they went around and around. I liked the mirrors in the center so I could see myself; I liked the bright lights, and I especially liked the music. I could see Grandma and BeeWee watching us, and I waved to them each time we passed. They smiled and waved back.

Then, for the first time, I got pink cotton candy and enjoyed pulling off big pieces that melted in my mouth as soon as I shoved them in. My hands got sticky, but it was worth it.

Last, we all went to a booth that had little plastic ducks floating by in the water. For a nickel, I was given a small net to fish out a duck. There were prizes on shelves at the back of the booth, like big stuffed chimpanzees and other animals in sizes that ranged from small to huge. I'd seen a few people walking around in the amusement park, carrying those chimpanzees. There were also many other prizes. The prize that caught my eye was a small, colorful glass bird that automatically dipped its beak into a small glass of water. I didn't expect to win a big chimpanzee, but I thought since the bird was small, I might win it.

I held the scoop and looked at the ducks for two or three minutes before I scooped up one of them and waited for the lady behind the counter to match the number with the prize. She didn't even go to the shelves at the back of the booth. Instead, she pulled a shoebox from under the counter, poked through it, and handed me a tiny prize. Naturally, I was disappointed that I didn't get the glass bird or any one of the prizes on the shelf, so I asked what I had to do to win one of those prizes.

"I told you. The number on your duck has to match one of the numbers on those prizes." She sounded irritated to have to repeat herself.

Mama said one turn was enough, but I wanted to try again. She reluctantly paid for me to scoop another duck, and I was given another tiny prize from the shoe box. Although I wanted to keep trying until I won the glass bird or a stuffed animal, Mama insisted that I had to stop, and she'd tell me later why I couldn't try again.

After we walked away, Mama explained, "I don't want to come out and say that dishonesty was involved, but it stands to reason that they are in business to make money, and they can't afford to be handing out expensive prizes to every other person who spends a nickel or a dime. If someone stands there for a long time and spends a lot of money, they'll probably eventually be handed a prize that's equal to the amount of money they've spent. Then, other people see the person with a good prize and think they can win one."

Grandma, having carefully watched the whole encounter, added, "I think you get more for your money buying an ice cream cone than taking a chance on a duck, but I can see that it's something a child would enjoy."

Deep down inside, I knew they were right, but on the surface, I was thinking that if we went to the amusement park again and I netted another duck, I might be luckier and win the glass bird or one of the stuffed animals on the shelf.

Summertime Traditions

After his breakfast every morning, BeeWee painted the dark green trim on the house before it got too hot. I watched BeeWee paint until my neck began to hurt from looking up at him, then I skated on the sidewalk.

I began skating again because it was so much fun. I just had to be careful about looking out for pieces of coal on the sidewalk that stopped my skate wheels and made me fall. I skated until I got hot and sweaty.

Mama wanted me to ride my tricycle every day because she thought this would be the last year I'd be able to ride it. It was the largest tricycle they had made, and BeeWee had been adjusting the seat and the handlebars as I grew. Now the seat and handlebars were as high as they could go, so my feet fit comfortably on the pedals, and my knees just barely touched the handlebars.

Crissy and I rode from one end of the block to the other, usually pretending we were driving cars. She was short, so she'd be able to ride her tricycle after I outgrew mine.

BeeWee fished at night where he fished last summer, and he caught enough fish for us to have fried fish for almost every meal. Although, Grandma still fried chicken every Sunday afternoon with creamed potatoes, which were mashed with milk and butter until they were creamy, and butterbeans.

I liked fried spots so much I could have eaten them for every meal forever. Grandma prepared different vegetables to go with them, like fresh snap beans and boiled potatoes, succotash (which was fresh corn and butterbeans), lettuce and tomato salad, or pork and beans. She had the knack of knowing how to prepare everything in the most delicious way without ever measuring anything or following a recipe.

At BeeWee's new fishing spot, Grandma and I sat on the bench and watched him fish. One day, on the way home, he stopped by Arp's Pharmacy for Grandma to hurry in to get peach ice cream cones for us. Then, BeeWee stopped by Robbins' Confectionary for his beer and drank it before he went to bed.

I was disappointed if there was a thunderstorm in the evening and we had to stay at home on BeeWee's vacation nights. Since the sofa was still in the front of the windows, Grandma and I still sat together in the high back chair during storms. It was a close fit now that I was bigger. We had to sit sideways, but we liked being together.

BeeWee sat on the front porch in the high-back green rocking chair at the beginning of the storm, but it made Grandma nervous. I knew she was nervous because she sniffed a lot. "Storms have always made me nervous. I don't understand why your BeeWee likes to sit on the porch and watch them. I just wish he'd come inside before he gets struck by lightning," she told me with a worried voice, and then she sniffed some more.

She didn't like keeping the awnings down during a storm because they'd get wet and she couldn't raise them, but BeeWee told her to leave them alone, that they'd be all right. I think he said that so the awnings would keep the rain off of him. BeeWee enjoyed sitting on the porch, listening to the loud crashes of thunder, and watching the long, bright streaks of lightning zigzag from the sky to the ground. He came inside if the wind started blowing rain on him. Then, he went to the kitchen, drank his two bottles of beer, and said, "Well, I think I'll turn in." We all said goodnight, and BeeWee went upstairs to go to bed.

For years to come, thunder and lightning storms scared me. I was just as scared as I had been when I was a little girl until I had my own children. By that time, I tried my best to just be in a secure place until the storm was over.

As a mother and grandmother, I carried on the tradition of eating fried spots at least once every summer. We would buy fresh spots from a local seafood shop in Norfolk, and I wanted to share the wonderful experience of eating fried spots with my family.

Getting Ready to Start School

Around the first of August, Mama took me downtown to buy shoes and clothes to wear on the first day of school. I got the same kind of brown leather, laced Stride Rite shoes that I got last year.

I liked having the shoes all year, even though Martha had let me know they didn't make me a schoolgirl. It was good to have the shoes a year before I started school because everyone in the family taught me how to tie the laces. They had their own methods, but I learned something from each of them to put together what I thought was the easiest way for me. They didn't care whose method I used as long as they didn't always have to tie my shoes for me. I was happy with myself when I learned to tie my shoes.

I was getting bigger, so I expected my new shoes to look longer each year, but I still dreaded seeing the new shoes on my feet when the saleslady tied them and told me to walk across the room. It always took me a few days to get used to them.

Mama handed the saleslady the ration coupon book and the cash, and the lady rang up the sale. Then, she went to the back room and came back with a helium-filled balloon and tied it to my wrist.

We left the shoe store, and Mama took me to the Cinderella Shop to look at clothes. She bought me a red skirt with straps over the shoulders to hold it up, a white blouse, a navy-blue cardigan sweater, white underwear, and white socks.

"This is enough to get you started with a new outfit for the first day and a sweater for when it turns cool. You can wear your last year's cotton dresses that still fit," she told me.

I was happy with the new shoes and clothes, especially my first skirt.

When we got back to Grandma's, Mama informed me, "I want you to start wearing your new shoes when you're in the house so you can break them in before school starts."

I put on the shoes again and still couldn't believe how long they looked. It never occurred to me that my whole body was growing just as fast as my feet were.

As September and the opening of school drew closer, I thought I'd burst with excitement. I couldn't believe I was finally going to learn to read. That had always been what I looked forward to when I thought of starting school. I hadn't given any thought to the other subjects, my teacher, or my classmates.

My First Day of School

On my first day of school, I was ready early, so I walked into the back bedroom and stood before the long mirror on the left side of the tall wardrobe with the mirrored double doors to see how I looked. I studied the reflection of the little round-faced girl with long, dark blonde hair and blue eyes. The soft, red jersey skirt had red straps over the shoulders with red, white, and blue embroidered flowers on them. The white blouse had short, puffy sleeves and a round collar that was embroidered with the same flowers. I liked my new outfit.

Then, it struck me for the first time that I'd changed a lot. I'd grown a lot taller since I began staying with Grandma, and I knew I'd continue to grow. I wouldn't be a little girl much longer. It wouldn't be long before I'd be too big to sit on BeeWee's knee on his paydays when he put his arm around me, gave me a shiny half-dollar, and nuzzled his chin against my cheek. I'd miss sitting on BeeWee's knee, and I was already too big to sit on Grandma's lap when she read a story to me. I'd still find ways to be close to her, though.

My eyes became moist with tears, but I didn't want to cry and have to go to school on the first day with red eyes and a stuffy nose. I wondered why I was noticing my reflection in the mirror and thinking about these things on my first day of school. My eyes misted with tears again, so I turned away from the mirror and went downstairs.

A few minutes before I left for school, Mama told me she had gone to the same school, and some of the teachers she had were still there. She said I might get one of those teachers and that I should be good and pay attention to the teacher's directions.

Grandma offered her advice, too, "You shouldn't ask too many questions, or the teacher will think you're dumb."

BeeWee agreed with her.

When it was time to go, I kissed Grandma and told her I loved her. She gave me a hug and said, "I love you, too, honey."

Then, BeeWee drove me to school and waited outside while Mama took me to my classroom.

My first-grade teacher was standing at the door smiling sweetly at the children who were entering her classroom. She was young, no older than Mama, so I knew she couldn't have been one of Mama's teachers. The teacher introduced herself as Miss Trueheart, and I immediately thought it was a pretty name that suited her perfectly because she was pretty and seemed to be nice. She was tall and trim, with medium brown, softly curled hair, and she wore a long-sleeved white cotton blouse with a full red skirt. Her red lipstick was the same shade as her skirt.

She showed me where to sit, which was in a middle seat at a low, rectangular-shaped wooden table for six. I pulled out the small wooden chair and sat down. Mama told me she was leaving and would pick me up at the front door after school. I watched as other children came in and quietly took their seats.

When it seemed that all of the seats in the room were filled, Miss Trueheart closed the door and walked to her desk, where she stood to welcome us to first grade. She began by explaining that she was going to call the roll and each of us should answer "present" or "here" when she called our name.

I thought I'd have more time to decide how I'd answer, but she quickly got to the "Ds" and called my name, so I just said, "Here." Then, I noticed that all of the girls were very properly answering "present", and the boys were saying "here." I wished I had said, "Present."

Halfway through the morning, we had Little Recess, a time for us to go outside and walk around or play for fifteen minutes. I walked onto the playground by myself and stood to watch the children who were sliding down the big slide. A couple of boys walked by and smiled at me.

Miss Trueheart soon had us line up in a girls' line and a boys' line to go to the restrooms, which she referred to as the girls' basement and the boys' basement because they were located in the basement. Then we went back to the classroom.

In a few minutes, Miss Trueheart took us outside to play games on the grass. We played one game each of The Farmer in the Dell, A Tisket, A Tasket, and Ring Around the Rosy. I liked the games, mostly because I got to play and laugh with the other children.

When we went inside, Miss Trueheart explained this was just a half day of school, and all first graders attended for half days during September. She gave us a school supply list and said we needed to give it to our parents so they could buy the supplies for us to bring to school the next day.

After school, BeeWee and Mama were waiting for me. BeeWee drove us to Robbins' Confectionary to buy the supplies. We picked out a jar of paste, a flat square box of eight Milton Bradley fat crayons, two fat pencils with erasers, a thick writing tablet, a pair of metal children's blunt-edged scissors, a wooden foot long ruler, and a brown canvas book bag with a leather handle. It was thrilling to finally have school supplies and be a real schoolgirl.

The next morning after breakfast, BeeWee sharpened my pencils for me with his pocketknife, the way he always sharpened pencils.

It made me happy to pack all my supplies in my book bag and bring them with me to school.

When I got to my classroom, I put everything on my desk and hung up my book bag in the cloakroom. I wondered why it wasn't called the coat room because that's where the teacher said we would hang our coats when the weather was cold enough for us to wear them.

Since most of us had our supplies, we began doing some work, such as learning some of the alphabet and numbers and even writing some of them. I could recite the letters of the alphabet and the numbers to at least the number ten, read a lot of words, write my first name, and tie my shoes. When I realized some of the children couldn't do those things, I felt smart.

I used my tablet, which was a larger wide-ruled pad of paper, and my fat pencil to practice writing the ABCs, which I could write, but they were lopsided and shaky looking. The teacher told us we could take our tablets and pencils home to practice our writing as long as we brought them back each day. I was excited to have my first homework.

We were given small sheets of unlined newsprint paper and instructed to fold them several times to make columns so we could write our numbers. I wrote the first column from zero to ten, but I had some trouble writing the numbers from eleven to twenty in the second column. I definitely didn't know my numbers as well as I knew my ABCs.

We were allowed to take our papers home, so I practiced writing the numbers at home as well as my ABC's and the teacher said I was doing very well. I didn't understand that we were learning to read by learning our ABCs and the sounds of the letters first, so I kept wondering when we would learn to read.

Sometimes I passed Martha in the hall or saw her on the playground at recess time, but she always ignored me. She and her friend Alice walked around together, Martha with her nose in the air.

The two boys who had smiled at me on the first day of school started chasing me every time they saw me. I couldn't figure out why they chased me, but I was running so much during recess that I was out of breath and hot when it was time to go inside. I told Grandma about being chased, and she said the boys probably just liked me.

I explained, "I just want them to stop because I don't like to spend my whole recess running. They even chase me from the playground to the other side of the building. I'm always out of breath, hot, and tired from running when I go inside."

"Well, it's dangerous for you to run to the other side of the building because that's just an alley for coal trucks to deliver coal and for the trucks that deliver food and other supplies to the school," Grandma insisted. "Tell me their names, and I'll call their mother."

"How can I find out their names?"

"Just ask them, honey."

"How will you know their telephone numbers?"

"I'll look them up in the telephone directory."

The next day, when they walked over to me instead of running, I quickly asked, "What are your names?"

They told me their first names, but they said they had the same last name, so I thought they were just making up a last name. Before I could ask them about it, they chased me again.

I told Grandma. That night, after we ate our soup, she looked up the last name under several different spellings until she found one that she thought she'd try to call. Grandma dialed the number and began talking to someone. I heard her saying, "Well, that's nice, I'm glad to know they like her, but they have her running around during her recess every day, and she doesn't have a chance to relax before she goes back in the building. They're chasing her to the other side of the building, and I'm afraid she'll be hit by a truck." Grandma stopped talking and listened to the man on the other end of the telephone. She assured him, "Oh, thank you for taking care of it but don't be hard on them. No harm has been done."

After she hung up the phone, she turned to me and said she talked with their grandfather. He told her the boys were brothers, and they lived with him. He assured her they wouldn't chase me again. They obviously didn't like me anymore because they ignored me after that.

After BeeWee drove us to school for a few days, Mama said we were going to start walking to school. She explained that she wanted me to practice the route I'd take because I'd soon be walking to and from school by myself. I was terrified of crossing the wide, busy boulevard by myself, but she said if we walked three blocks up the boulevard, there was not only a traffic light but there was a policeman to help the children cross.

I got used to the police officer, and Mama told him I would soon be walking by myself. He was a tall, middle-aged, stocky man who wasn't friendly, but he did a good job of blowing his whistle and stopping the cars for the children to cross the street. He was also at the corner when school let out in the afternoon. It wasn't long before I started walking by myself and going to school for a full day.

Mama tied my lunch money in the corner of one of the pretty handkerchiefs Crissy had given me for my birthday, and I kept it in my dress or skirt pocket until lunchtime.

The cafeteria was unlike any place I'd ever seen. There was an aroma of food cooking, but it didn't have the distinctive good smell of any one food like Grandma's cooking had. It smelled like a combination of all the food that had ever been cooked there.

The cafeteria manager said she would assist us because it was our first time. I took a tray and asked for the hot plate, which consisted of meatloaf, white rice with gravy, and green peas. A cafeteria worker placed a warm, buttered roll on the edge of the plate in the gravy. I didn't like for my roll to get soggy. The cashier put a small carton of milk and straw on my tray and asked if I wanted ice cream. I said I did, and she set a small cup of vanilla with a flat wooden spoon on the tray.

A lot of children were already sitting at long tables, eating their lunch. I followed my classmates to our long table, and we all sat together to eat. I'd never had meatloaf, rice with gravy, or green peas, but it was all very good. By the time I finished half of the food on my plate, some children were leaving the table, throwing away their trash, and going outside for Big Recess.

The screen door leading to the playground was opening and closing behind children every minute, a constant reminder of the fact that they were going outside and I wasn't. By the time I opened my ice cream, a girl who had been sitting at the table next to mine was getting up to throw away her trash. I didn't want to be the last one to leave, but I had been looking forward to eating my ice cream, which turned out to be so melted that it was more like a cup of milk than a cup of ice cream. I drank it and threw away my trash.

I finally went outside. I still didn't have a friend, but I liked walking around in the sunshine and watching some of the children line up and go down the big slide.

So far, I really enjoyed my new school and being in first grade.

One Sunday afternoon, when Grandma was sitting at her place at the kitchen table reading the newspaper, she saw a familiar name and came into the living room to show me a picture. "I saw this name and thought it might be your teacher. Isn't her name Miss Trueheart?"

I looked at the name and the picture. "It is Miss Trueheart. What does it say about her?"

Grandma read me the announcement of Miss Trueheart's engagement. She was planning to get married soon.

In school the next morning, one of the girls raised her hand, and when she was called on, she said, "I saw your picture in the paper yesterday, Miss Trueheart. My mother wants to know if you're going to move away after you get married."

Miss Trueheart smiled at first, hesitated a moment, then looked very serious. "Since you've brought it up and asked me about my future plans, I'll say this to the entire class. I'm engaged to be married to a wonderful man, and when we're married, I'll have to move from Norfolk to be with him." She went on to tell us that even though we'd have a new teacher, we'd stay in the same room.

I didn't want her to leave, but she was happy about getting married, so I was happy for her.

My Second First-Grade Teacher

Although I was sorry my teacher left, I didn't have any reason to believe the new teacher, Mrs. Bowles, wouldn't be just as nice as Miss Trueheart.

The new teacher was standing behind her desk one morning as we entered the room. She was as tall as Miss Trueheart and about the same size, but she was middle-aged with long, frizzy black hair. She was fairly nice-looking, with a ruddy complexion, and she wore thick face makeup and red lipstick. She wore a rayon dress that fitted her nicely, but when she started looking mean and yelling at someone who walked in late, I forgot the color of the dress. I began to worry that she'd yell at me, too.

Although I got through the day without being yelled at, I was still worried enough to mention it to Mama when I got home from school.

Mama advised me, "As long as you listen and follow directions, I don't think you'll have a thing to worry about."

"Mama, the boy she yelled at this morning had just walked in the room!"

"You said the child was late; some teachers don't like students walking into their room late."

"But, Mama, she didn't even ask the boy why he was late. She just yelled at him. She yells at children about every little thing."

"She hasn't yelled at you, has she?"

"Not yet, but when I see her looking mean and yelling at other children, I'm afraid all day that she'll yell at me."

"Those children must be doing something to cause her to raise her voice to them." Mama tried to convince me that everything would be all right. "I still think you have nothing to worry about. Miss Trueheart never yelled at you, did she?"

"Miss Trueheart never yelled at anybody." I wasn't completely convinced that Mrs. Bowles wouldn't yell at me, but I knew that there was nothing more that could be done right now.

The next morning Mrs. Bowles said she was going to call the roll, and when she called our name, we were to stand if we lived in Benmoreell. I had never heard of Benmoreell. I always knew the name of Grandma's street, but I had never heard my family mention the name of the section.

I didn't know what to do. I thought Mrs. Bowles would get mad and yell at me if I lived there and I didn't stand. I didn't have time to think about what would happen if I didn't live there, and I stood because she had come to the D's and called my name.

When I stood, she gave me an angry look and said in a hateful voice, "Sit down, Shirley. You don't live in Benmoreell. I'm surprised at you for telling a falsehood."

Everyone turned and looked at me with expressionless faces that didn't reveal whether they had pity for me or if they thought I was the biggest liar in the world. I felt tears coming to my eyes, and I looked down at my desk so no one could see how I felt.

Mrs. Bowles finished calling the roll and was speaking to the class, but I was still looking down, trying to stop crying, so she spoke in an angry voice again, "Look at me when I'm speaking to you, young lady." She had a mean expression on her face that matched her voice.

I brushed away my tears with my hands and forced myself to look at her.

It was almost time for Little Recess, and I was so upset I knew I would burst into tears if anyone mentioned it on the playground or in the girls' basement.

What would I do if Mrs. Bowles yelled at me again? I would probably burst out crying. I was sure she would yell at me again because she already thought I was a liar and thought I didn't pay attention to her when she was speaking to me. We hadn't even had Little Recess yet, and she'd yelled at me twice.

If Miss Trueheart had been here, this would never have happened. I wished she hadn't moved because she was nice, and she'd never yelled at anyone. I wished I didn't have to go to school anymore if it was going to be like this. I wondered what Grandma, BeeWee, and Mama were doing, and I started missing them.

When we lined up and went outside for Little Recess, I walked away from everyone else to the edge of the playground. I didn't consider what Grandma, BeeWee, and Mama would think when they saw me or what the teacher and the other children would think when I didn't return to the classroom.

I left the playground, crossed the busy boulevard by myself, and walked the block to Grandma's.

When I got to her house, BeeWee's car wasn't in the driveway. As I climbed the steps and walked across the porch, I hoped Grandma and Mama would be there, but I really didn't think they would because whenever BeeWee went out in the morning, they always went with him.

Instead of knocking on the screen door, I tried it to see if it was locked. I hoped it would be locked since that would mean someone was there, but when I grabbed the door handle and pulled it, the screen door opened. I was disappointed, so I sat on the steps to wait for them to come home. Probably five minutes went by before I became calm enough to realize that it was probably BeeWee's payday, and they would be gone for the rest of the morning, cashing BeeWee's check at the bank, paying bills, buying groceries, and getting something to eat.

I wondered what I should do next. If I sat on the steps until they came home, I'd be there long enough for one of Grandma's neighbors to see me and wonder why I wasn't in school. Maybe Mama wasn't even with them. Maybe she was at her house.

As I walked back to the boulevard, I glanced across the street at the school. If I crossed the street there, I'd have to walk on the sidewalk beside the school, and someone would see me. The fourth-grade classroom had tall windows that went all the way down to the floor. If I walked past the tall chain link fence that surrounded the playground, a child might glance toward the windows, see me, and tell the teacher. The principal might come out, grab me by the arm, and take me back to Mrs. Bowles' classroom; then, I'd be more upset than ever.

I'd also been afraid to cross the street where there was no traffic light when I first left school, but I was so anxious to get away that I just looked both ways and ran across when I didn't see any cars coming from about a block away in both directions.

I decided to walk the three blocks to the street that had the traffic light, where I crossed in the morning before school and in the afternoon. Mama's house was on the same street, about three long blocks from the light.

Finally, I spotted the two-story white duplex where Mama and Daddy lived upstairs. I climbed the back steps to the small porch with the swing. Passing behind the swing, I walked to the door and looked through the glass. I could see into the kitchen, but I didn't see Mama, so I knocked on the door.

The big, bushy, brownish cat that hung out here because Mama fed it table scraps was nowhere in sight. I was glad because, on the few occasions when I'd been here, it hissed at me, so I hoped it wouldn't show up when it heard me knocking on the door.

Mama didn't come to the door, so I figured she was with Grandma and BeeWee. I thought about what I'd do next and decided to sit on the swing for a few minutes to wait for them to get back to Grandma's.

Then, I took the same route back to Grandma's and saw the car pull into the driveway just before I got to the house. Boy, were they surprised to see me.

They took in the groceries and started putting them away as I told them what had happened.

Luckily for them, they'd already eaten barbecues at one of the barbecue stands, where there was curb service, instead of bringing barbecues or Chinese food back to the house to eat, as they sometimes did on payday.

Grandma said Mama should go to the school and talk with the principal to see if there was anything he could do because I was afraid of the teacher. BeeWee was ready to do what he could to help. "Come on, Florencie. I'll drive you there and wait for you. I don't need to take a nap every day."

"What do you think will happen, Grandma?" I asked as she finished putting away the two weeks' supply of groceries.

"I don't know, honey. I don't know," she replied, sniffing nervously.

In a few minutes, Mama and BeeWee came home, and BeeWee went upstairs to change from his suit to his work clothes. Mama came into the kitchen and announced, "The principal was very nice. He said he was sorry about what happened, and he doesn't want you to be scared, so he's putting you in another teacher's room."

I was so relieved. "I'm glad he didn't say I had to go back into the same room because I never want to see that teacher again."

"The principal had someone get your book bag and supplies from your desk, so you won't have to go back in that room," Mama assured me.

I was happy to know that the principal was putting me in another teacher's classroom. I hoped I would like the other teacher and have a good experience with her.

My Third First-Grade Teacher

"The principal told me your new teacher is someone with many years of experience as a first-grade teacher." Mama explained, "She's nice, and she's very strict. She requires her students to take a nap every day, so I'll have to buy you a mat before you go back to school. She has a sink in her room with shelves above it for drinking cups. I'll have to buy you a glass, write your name on adhesive tape, and stick it to the glass."

BeeWee had to go to work, so Mama walked to the variety store a few blocks away and got the mat and the glass. The mat looked soft and comfortable. I thought I'd like to rest in the middle of the day, the way I used to do, and I'd like to have my own cup for water.

Mama informed me the principal wanted her to be sure to talk with me about the danger of my leaving school without permission and crossing busy streets by myself. She assured the principal that she would talk with me.

Miss Odum was an older teacher who had brown eyes and dark brown, slightly graying hair that she wore pulled back in a bun. She wore dark crepe dresses and black shoes with medium-height thick heels. She spoke in a soft voice and expected us to do the same. We walked into the hall on our tiptoes, with our fingers over our lips.

I looked forward to nap time because I wanted to use my new mat, but I became a little self-conscious about it when I saw it was different from all the other children's mats. Theirs were about an inch thick, and mine was about three inches thick, like a bed pillow. Theirs were all solid-colored, like red or blue, and mine was navy blue and white striped with red fringe around the edges. When no one said anything about it, I didn't worry about it anymore.

I tried to go to sleep, but I couldn't. I didn't know if the other children were asleep or if they were just being quiet. I understood what Grandma meant when she sometimes said it was so quiet you could hear a pin drop. I'm not sure about a straight pin being dropped, but you could have heard a large safety pin if it were dropped in the room during nap time.

One day, Miss Odum handed each child a tagboard card and a small sheet of lined newsprint paper. She gave us oral directions for doing the exercises. We were to use crayons to show our answers. Either I misunderstood the directions, or I wasn't listening in the first place, but I put my answers directly on Miss Odum's tag board card in crayon.

Miss Odum was walking around to check our progress when she saw what I'd done, and she quietly told me I should have shown my answers on the sheet of paper instead of on the card. I was so nervous; my hands started sweating.

The boy who sat on my left at the table said to Miss Odum, "Why don't you leave her alone? Can't you see you're making her nervous?"

Miss Odum showed the kind of teacher she was by saying, "I'm sorry if I sounded harsh, Shirley. I certainly didn't mean to. Your work is very nice; just remember to write on your paper next time instead of writing on the card."

I thought Ted was the nicest boy I'd ever met for standing up for me, even to the teacher. That was the first time I'd thought of a boy as being my boyfriend.

I'd been in Miss Odum's class for about two weeks, and everything was going well. She was even teaching us the sounds of the letters so we could learn to read the stacks of Dick and Jane readers on her shelves. She even read books to us, like *To Think That I Saw It on Mulberry Street* by Dr. Seuss.

I liked my third first-grade teacher even better after she clarified the directions for me. Although I had made a mistake, she was nice about it instead of yelling at me. I was glad to finally be back on track for my first-grade year.

I Did a Very Dumb Thing

I did a very dumb thing, the dumbest thing I could do. I left school again and went to Grandma's house. I am not sure why I did it except that one morning I just started missing Grandma, Mama, and BeeWee.

They were at home when I got there, and Mama asked me why I had left school, but she was mad when I told her the reason. "Shirley May Dawson, you're going right back to school." Mama grabbed my arm and started leading me toward the front door. Grandma and BeeWee didn't say anything.

BeeWee drove us there and waited outside. Mama knocked on the teacher's door to let her know where I'd been. Then, Miss Odum stood there and watched Mama pull up my dress in the back and spank me on my bottom until I cried. "Now you go back into that room, and don't you ever leave school again until you're dismissed by the teacher."

I slunk into the room, sniveling and using my fingertips to brush the tears from my eyes. I wiped my nose on the back of my hand and then took out the handkerchief in my pocket and wiped off my hand. My lunch money was still tied in the corner, but lunchtime was over. I knew it served me right not to eat lunch after what I'd done. I was too upset to eat anyway.

To my surprise, the other children seemed to feel sorry for me, and Miss Odum didn't say a word.

The next day, when we had Little Recess and Big Recess after lunch, the children were nice to me, and I had friends after that, like Patricia, Virginia, and Patsy. Ted was already my friend, and a boy named Teddy became my friend, too.

I had a good feeling about being in Miss Odom's class. I liked her and the students because they were all nice to me. I really needed and appreciated that. I felt comfortable in this class.

November 1943

During the month of November, our class went to the music teacher's room and sang *Over the River and Through the Woods*. I liked the song because it was about going to Grandma's house for Thanksgiving.

I was looking forward to Thanksgiving Day at Grandma's. Everyone at Grandma's house was busy getting ready. BeeWee had taken out the screens in the living room windows, and he and Grandma had cleaned the windowpanes until they were almost sparkling. Grandma had washed and starched the lace curtains, and Mama had put them on the curtain stretchers. BeeWee had stood on his tall ladder to hang them back at the windows.

By the afternoon before Thanksgiving, the house was ready for the big day, and the aroma of roasted turkey filled the air. Grandma sat at her place at the table, peeling the potatoes and cutting the potatoes, celery, and onions into small pieces. When everyone else was sleeping, Grandma was in the kitchen cooking. As usual, I didn't know what time she finally went to bed.

On Thanksgiving Day, our family sat down to another delicious meal lovingly prepared by Grandma. BeeWee, Mama, Daddy, Aunt Nita, and I were there, and we all enjoyed eating, talking, and just being together at the table.

Decorating for Christmas in the Classroom

From the day after Thanksgiving, everyone started talking about Christmas. The newspaper had a daily countdown of the number of shopping days until Christmas, and the radio stations started playing Christmas music.

When I returned to school on the Monday after Thanksgiving weekend, we began making Christmas decorations for our classroom. Miss Odum passed around tag board patterns for us to trace with our pencils on colored construction paper. As we cut out our trees and decorations, she walked around the room, watching to see if we were using our scissors properly.

I wanted to learn to cut smoothly instead of choppy, the way I had cut out some paper doll clothes from the book Martha gave me for my birthday. I had cut out only two outfits because I couldn't cut the edges smoothly, the way Martha's older sister had cut out her paper doll clothes.

Glancing around at the other children at my table, I saw that some cut smoothly, and some cut the way I did. After Miss Odum demonstrated the proper way to cut, I realized what I was doing wrong and corrected it.

She also taught us to use a small amount of paste and spread it out with the brush instead of putting down a big blob and sticking a decoration on it.

When we completed the paper Christmas trees, she set them out for the paste to dry thoroughly overnight and hung them around in the room the next day. They made our room look pretty.

Wartime Weariness and Silent Night

One morning when I went into the kitchen to eat breakfast, I was surprised to hear the conversation between Aunt Nita, Mama, and Grandma. Aunt Nita had usually already gone to work by the time I woke up, but she would occasionally switch hours with someone and go to work at a different time.

Aunt Nita lamented, "How can we have a merry Christmas this year? Nothing's been the same since Pearl Harbor was bombed two years ago."

Grandma tried to reassure her, "Life has to go on, Juanita."

"Life is going on, but what kind of life is it? We live in fear of being bombed every time a plane flies over the house or when we have an air raid. Everything is still rationed, too."

Mama added, "Nita, I'm surprised at you. I thought you liked meeting all the young servicemen."

"I do. It's just that I'm tired of the war. This will be the third Christmas it's been going on."

Grandma reminded her, "Be thankful for what you have: your health, a roof over your head, a good job."

"I am thankful for those things. It's just that I want more."

"That's the trouble with this world. People are never satisfied with what they have. They always want more. That's why we're having this war now. Some people weren't satisfied with what they had," Grandma concluded.

Aunt Nita explained, "I was satisfied living in peace. I graduated from high school in January 1940, took a business course, got a job at the telephone company, and saved money for a down payment on a car."

"We know all that, Nita. You've done very well. You should be proud of yourself and happy."

"How can I be happy, Florencie? I'm twenty-one years old, and I can hardly ever drive a car because of the gasoline rationing. I have to wait at the bus stop for buses that are so crowded; people are standing all the way to the door. There isn't room for even one more person to get on, so they don't stop."

Grandma remembered, "There was something in the morning paper about improving the crowding on buses in the afternoons."

"Is there really? I'd like to see it," Aunt Nita said hopefully.

Grandma walked over to the chair by the back door, where she kept a stack of newspapers that she hadn't finished reading, and picked up the one on the top. "Here it is." She handed it to Aunt Nita.

Aunt Nita read it and relaxed a little. "You see what I mean. I hope it helps."

Mama, who had been reading the notice with Aunt Nita, became frustrated. "I don't know when they think school children will shop and see Santa Claus if they're not allowed to ride the bus downtown in the afternoon. They're in school all day. I have to take Shirley downtown to try on clothes, and I want her to see Santa Claus."

"Well, Clarence and I do most of our shopping close to home. Clarence never rides the bus, and I don't have to ride it."

Aunt Nita interjected, "Mama, I've been meaning to tell you when you shop this year, I don't want you and Daddy to buy me a present."

"Juanita, you know perfectly well your Daddy and I always give you a Christmas present."

"Why don't you want Mama and Daddy to give you a present?"

"I just don't. They can't afford to keep giving me a Christmas present."

"Juanita, that's nonsense. We want to give you a present."

Aunt Nita turned toward Grandma. "I'm serious about this, Mama. I'll never forgive you if you buy me a present."

BeeWee, who had been quietly eating his breakfast, got up from the table and calmly stated, "If Juanita doesn't want a present, we won't give her one. She's old enough to know what she wants or doesn't want."

Aunt Nita smiled. "I'm going to work now. See you when I get home tonight."

Grandma walked to the front door with Aunt Nita and locked it behind her. When she returned to the kitchen, she observed, "Clarence, you were awfully quick to go along with Juanita about not giving her a present."

BeeWee chuckled. "I just told her that. You know what I was thinking? We'll surprise her. Nobody tell her, but we'll make her think we didn't get her anything. Then, we'll give her a gift last, after everyone has opened theirs, and surprise her."

"Well, I'm glad to hear you say that. I know Juanita well enough to know she'd be mighty unhappy on Christmas Day if we handed everyone a gift and didn't have anything for her."

I finally interrupted, "Mama, did you say you're taking me downtown to see Santa Claus?"

"I'll take you if they allow us to ride the bus downtown in the afternoon."

I looked in the paper at the notice they were talking about, but before I could try to read some of the words, I saw an ad about Christmas trees and asked Mama what it said.

Mama pointed out, "It says that fresh Christmas trees will be on sale at Orr's beginning on December 10th."

"Are you going to buy a Christmas tree this year, BeeWee?"

"I sure am, Sugie. I always buy a Christmas tree."

"How many days will it be before December 10th?"

"We'll get a tree, but not on the first day; they go on sale. We'll have to wait until my payday on December 15th," BeeWee explained.

One day the music teacher played a recording of a beautiful Christmas song so we could listen and learn the words. After school, I told Mama I'd heard a beautiful Christmas song, but I couldn't remember the title.

"Try to remember some of the words to tell me, and I might be able to figure out the title," she offered.

"It was something about night and a mother and a child," I recalled.

"I'll bet you heard *Silent Night*."

"I think that was it."

"That's always been one of my favorite Christmas songs," Mama shared with me.

As we practiced the song in the music room every week, I learned the first verse and sang it often during the days before Christmas.

Christmas Shopping and Crowded Buses

Somehow Mama and I were able to ride the bus downtown to look at clothes one afternoon. They must have decided to allow parents to take children downtown on the buses in the afternoons after all.

I wore size six, but Mama wanted to see if my next size in a dress should be size 6X or if I could start wearing clothes in the 7 to 14 sizes. Since the sizes at the Cinderella Shop only went up to size 6X, we went to a different store. I tried on a size seven brown corduroy jumper and a long-sleeved, yellow cotton blouse. I didn't like them at all because the jumper was way too big and hung down straight from my shoulders to the hem. The shade of brown was too dark, it had no pocket for my lunch money, and the material was stiff. I didn't like the shade of the yellow cotton blouse, which was also made with stiff cotton material. I didn't say that I didn't like them because Mama wasn't buying them anyway.

When we looked at coats, we discovered that the coats with matching leggings and hats only went through size 6X. From now on, my legs would be cold every winter. Mama said she had to buy the coat a size larger so I could get at least two years' wear out of it, but we didn't like their selection of coats.

Then we went to the children's department of Smith and Welton, a big department store. Mama had bought a nice black coat there at the after-Christmas sale last year, and she noticed they had a children's department. We rode the elevator to the fourth floor, where they had all children's clothes from sizes for newborn babies through size 14.

We found the perfect coat we both liked. It was navy blue wool, with a hood, and it had a red, heavy cotton lining. It was reversible, so I could turn it inside out to wear as a raincoat. It was a size 8, but I didn't mind because I could turn up the sleeves and have a red cuff that matched the lining of the hood. I liked it well enough to want to wear it for a long time, just as I had liked my coat, hat, and legging set that I'd worn for three years.

The shoe store was our next stop. Mama wanted me to have white rubber boots to wear on rainy days, but I wanted red rubber boots.

"Shirley, you don't understand that when you reverse the coat, it will be all red, and if you have red boots, you'll be wearing so much red that it won't look good."

I was not picturing myself the way she was. I was picturing the red boots looking wonderful with the navy-blue coat, with a little of the red lining showing around the hood and collar and the cuffs. "Mama, I might as well tell you now. I don't want to ever wear the coat on the red side."

"What? You let me buy you a coat that reverses, and you never plan to reverse it? I thought you liked the coat. If you don't like it, we should take it back right now."

"Mama, I do like the coat. It's just what I want to wear for a long time, but I never want to wear it on the red side because the wool side is itchy, and I would much rather have red rubber boots than white ones."

"All right, I guess I should be glad we like the coat, and you'll get a lot of wear out of it. You don't have to wear it on the red side, and you can get red rubber boots if the shoe store has your size. They'll be better anyway because they won't show dirt the way white boots would."

I was lucky the shoe store had my size.

We walked to Woolworth's five and ten cent store, and Mama bought me a quarter of a pound of orange slices from the candy counter. Then we waited for a bus for a long time until one came along that wasn't crowded to the front and back doors. There was standing room only, but two men got up and gave us their seats. I was glad because Mama was carrying packages and didn't have a free hand to hold my hand or to hold onto anything else.

Daylight was fading fast as we got off the bus and began walking to Grandma's house. The chilly air penetrated my sweater like a signal that it was time to start wearing my new winter coat.

When we got back to Grandma's, Mama told me to try on my new coat for her, and Grandma said she liked it. The hood was a little big, but I turned the front part of it back. I thought the red showing on the outside of the hood looked good with the red cuffs.

When Daddy got off from work and came to pick up Mama, we showed him the coat, and he liked the fact that it was big enough to last me for a long time. It was one of the few times when Daddy came to pick up Mama that he came farther into the house than the front hallway by the door.

Mama said he was always tired after work and wanted to go home to take a shower, go out to get something to eat and go back home. She said when he got home, he put on his pajamas, sat in a living room chair, and fell asleep.

The next time Mama took me downtown, we went to see Santa Claus in the department store window. I tried not to think about going to see Santa when I was in school that day, but I couldn't help it.

On the way downtown on the bus, I tried to look out the windows at various landmarks on the route because I wanted to see how close we were to downtown. I was sitting by the window, so I could see the landmarks on my right, but I couldn't even see the windows on my left because of all the people standing in the aisle.

The buses were crowded last year, but even more, people were packed in the aisles this year. There was a step at the front door to step up onto the bus and a step at the back door to step down off the bus. A couple of people were often standing on each step. When someone rang the bell to get off at their stop, the people standing on the steps had to get off the bus to make way for the person getting off.

They usually stepped back on the bus, but with so many people standing in the aisle, the bus driver sometimes couldn't see the back door. People who stepped out were sometimes left standing on the sidewalk, as the back door was shut before they could get on again. Mama and I were lucky to get seats again because two sailors stood up to give us theirs.

When we got off the bus, we heard *Jingle Bells* playing. There was a crowd of mostly women and children standing in front of the huge window, watching Santa Claus, who kept saying, "ho, ho, ho."

For a few minutes, we were in a wonderland, not thinking of the things that were always there to remind us that a war was going on. Then, we crossed the street and stood with all the other people at the bus stop and watched as crowded buses passed us by, bringing us back to reality.

As the sun set behind the silhouette of the downtown skyline, I began to worry that I wouldn't get to Grandma's in time to hear Santa Claus on the radio. That worried me every year.

"Shirley, you did the same thing last year. As soon as the sun started going down, you thought you were missing Santa Claus, but he doesn't come on until 7:30, so we have plenty of time to get home."

"But, Mama, if the buses keep passing us, we'll never get there in time."

"We will so stop worrying. You think it's later than it is because it gets dark earlier at this time of the year."

When we got to Grandma's, she was watching for us, and I told her how much I enjoyed seeing Santa.

I looked forward to going shopping and seeing Santa, and I was so happy that we were able to keep our tradition despite the bus restrictions that year. It was always magical to hear the Christmas music in the air when we got off the bus. This was just about the only time of year when I got to have this much quality time with my mother; I liked that we had a tradition together.

Radio Programs

Daddy picked up Mama, Grandma, and I ate our soup, and we listened to the news. Aunt Nita got off from work and came home to change clothes to get ready to go back out.

I kept asking Grandma about the time until she said I could use the telephone to dial 29311, the time number. She told me to listen to be sure that Mrs. Rayburn, the party line, wasn't talking before I started to dial. Mrs. Rayburn wasn't talking, but the operator had barely finished announcing the time before I heard her pick up the receiver of her phone.

Aunt Nita came downstairs, looking pretty and smelling sweet. "Would you like to have a stick of gum?"

"What kind do you have?" I asked, knowing that I would take any kind she offered.

"Dentyne." She held out the open pack so I could take the next piece. Unlike most gum, Dentyne was in a flat, red package, and each stick was short and thick. Instead of having a mint flavor, it had a cinnamon flavor. After taking the wrapper off the stick of gum, I plopped it in my mouth and began chewing.

"Thank you," she reminded me.

"Oh, that's right. I forgot to say thank you." I corrected myself, "Thank you."

"You're welcome. Be sure to chew with your mouth closed, too." I closed my mouth and continued to chew away. Aunt Nita always tried to teach me to speak properly and to have good manners.

She glanced at her watch. "I have to go. See you later, Shirley."

"What time is it, Aunt Nita?"

"It's seven o'clock," she said as she was putting on her coat. I couldn't believe how slowly the time was passing.

Seven-thirty p.m. finally came, and Santa Claus came on with the sound of sleigh bells. He said he was broadcasting from the North Pole to all the boys and girls out there. I was happy to know that I was one of the girls. He asked if we had all been good because he was coming to visit the good boys and girls. He went on to mention Mrs. Claus, his reindeer, and his elves, but I'm not certain what he said about them because I started worrying about whether he thought I had been a good girl.

The program only lasted for ten minutes, but when it was over, I sat with my elbows on the table and my face propped on my fists, pondering my fate. Why, oh why, did I always manage to do something bad during the year that could keep Santa from coming to see me? I wanted to be good, and regardless of what anyone thought, I really tried to be good.

"What's the matter, honey?" Grandma was surprised to see me so down after my nice day with Mama and Aunt Nita.

"Oh, nothing." I didn't want Grandma to know I was worried.

"I can tell something's wrong."

"Grandma, does Santa really not come to see boys and girls if they've been bad?"

"I don't know about that, honey."

"I remember when you told me about the switches and ashes, but do you know anyone who ever got switches and ashes?"

"No, I can't say that I do."

"But you did say he brought you broken toys and shoes that hurt your feet, didn't you?"

"Yes, but I always thought he must have fallen down the chimney, and that's what caused the toys to break."

"But why did he bring you shoes that hurt your feet?"

"You sure do have a good memory, honey. You need to stop worrying. Our favorite programs are coming on now, so let's listen to them and try to take our minds off of things that worry us."

"I'll try, Grandma."

Gifts for my School Friends

At school, we looked forward to our recess times each day of December so we could talk about Christmas. Some of the children said they were going to give me a present and asked me if I was going to give them a present, so I said yes.

I told Mama I was going to give a present to everyone who said they were giving one to me.

"It's going to cost a lot to buy so many presents. My mama and daddy always bought a gift for Nita and my teachers, but they couldn't afford to buy gifts for the children, too. Are you sure you want to do this?"

"I have to do it, Mama, because they said they're giving me a present."

"Some children just say that, so you'll get them a present."

The next day, I asked each of those children if they were really going to buy me a present and they all said yes. I was eager to tell Mama, "I asked the children again, and they said they're really giving me a present."

"Your Daddy's planning to sell your tricycle because you know you've outgrown it. This is a good time of the year to sell a tricycle. Since the tricycle is yours, we were going to save the money we get for it to buy something for you. If you want to buy gifts for the children, you'll have to use some of that money. Do you want to do that?"

"Yes." I was relieved that I would have a gift for each of them.

In a few days, Mama said Daddy got $15.00 for the tricycle.

Before we went shopping for the gifts, Mama explained, "I'm only doing this because you've already told some of the children that you're giving them a gift. It wouldn't be right to go back on your word. I just want you to promise me that you won't be disappointed when they don't give you a gift."

"But I even asked them to be sure and they said they're giving me a gift, Mama." Although Mama had tried to convince me they wouldn't give me gifts, I still thought they would.

We went to Rose's dime store, and I had fun looking around at everything in the toy and book section that I could possibly give a child. Then I said, "I think I'll get Patricia a—"

Mama interrupted, "Wait a minute. You're not getting something different for each child. That will take up too much time, and it might cause trouble. You said you promised gifts to seven children, so you can find something that you want to give, and we'll buy seven of them."

"I know what I'll get, coloring books!"

"If you get coloring books, you'll have to get crayons because they might not have any crayons at home."

"They're all girls, so I'll get paper doll books."

"Then you'll have to buy children's scissors because they might not have those at home."

"Mama, this is too hard to decide; I want you to decide for me."

"How about giving each girl a nice box of handkerchiefs?"

"I'd rather get them something that will be fun to play with, so I'll just get the coloring books and a small box of skinny crayons."

"I think you should give them a box of crayons like you use in school. They're nicer."

"No one really likes those, Mama. They're too fat."

"I'm getting tired, and we still have to pick out wrapping paper and gift stickers. Just get seven of everything; we'll get some white tissue paper and gift stickers and go."

Everything cost a total of $7.50, which Mama said was exactly half of the $15.00.

The next day Mama let me wrap the presents, write the girls' names and my name on the stickers, lick them, and stick them on the gifts. It was the first time I'd wrapped gifts, and it was fun.

It was the first time I'd bought a gift for another child. None of my friends in the neighborhood or at school had birthday parties. They never even mentioned their birthdays. I never thought I'd enjoy picking out gifts for other children, but I did. It gave me a special feeling like I was doing something good.

Decorating the Tree

Since I was in school all day on BeeWee's payday, I didn't get to go with Grandma, BeeWee, and Mama to pick out the Christmas tree, but I thought about it, and I wished I could be with them.

I hurried home after school, Mama opened the door, and I raced past her to take a look at the tree. It was just what I expected to see, a tree that was almost as high as the ten-foot ceiling.

BeeWee had bought a ten-foot tree and snipped off just enough of the top to make room for the star. He had strung the colored lights evenly over the branches before he went to work.

When Aunt Nita came home from work, we'd decorate the tree together. I could hardly wait.

Since Aunt Nita almost always ate at the telephone company cafeteria or in restaurants with her friends, Grandma prepared a meal she knew Aunt Nita would like.

There was the yummy smell of the steak, potato, and onion meal that Grandma was slowly baking in the oven. We hardly ever had to go to the kitchen to see what Grandma was cooking; the wonderful aroma of the food filled the house. Grandma set the hot, oval Pyrex dish on a pad in the middle of the kitchen table. The slices of steak, potatoes, and onions sizzled in the hot brown gravy. As always, she warned us not to touch the hot dish. We had butterbeans, which we usually only had on Sundays, and hot rolls from the bakery, which we usually only had on Thanksgiving and Christmas.

I enjoyed sitting at the kitchen table, eating with Grandma and Aunt Nita.

When we finished eating, Aunt Nita said, "The food was scrumptious, Mama."

Grandma chuckled. "Well, I'm glad you liked it. I wanted to fix something that would give you and Shirley plenty of energy to decorate the tree."

"It was delicious, Grandma."

"Thank you, honey. I'm glad you liked it. Now I'm going upstairs to get the ornaments so you and Juanita can get started on the tree." Grandma went upstairs and came back with a drawer of ornaments, which we unwrapped and hung on the tree with little wire hangers.

Aunt Nita reminded me that we should hang the smaller ornaments on the top branches, which I couldn't reach. Even Aunt Nita had to take off her shoes and stand on one of the kitchen chairs.

"I think you're old enough this year to take the paper off of the ornaments, one at a time, and hand them to me." She kept the box of little wire hangers in her pocket, slipped one on each ornament, and hung it on a branch.

Grandma went back upstairs to get the other drawer of tree decorations and soon brought it to the living room, placing it beside the first drawer. "You're all set now. I'm going back to the kitchen."

It seemed like forever before I got a chance to hang some ornaments. Aunt Nita finally stepped down, told me to take off my shoes, and helped me to stand up on the chair. "I'll put a hanger on each ornament, pass it to you, and you can hang it on the tree," she explained. I felt as though I was really growing up now that she was allowing me to stand on the chair the way she did. We both hung the largest ornaments on the bottom branches.

Aunt Nita took the silver-colored tinsel icicles out of a flat box and said, "I sure wish they'd start making tinsel again. We've used this so much there's no shine left. Go to the kitchen and ask your grandma to come here a minute."

Grandma had been washing dishes and came into the room drying her hands on a dish towel. A few tiny soap bubbles blew from her hands as she walked.

"Mama, do you think this tinsel is too dull to use again?"

"It's dull, but it's all we've got, Juanita. I don't think the tree will look the same without tinsel. We've always put tinsel on it."

"You're right. The tree wouldn't seem like our tree without it."

"Then that's that. I'll go back in the kitchen and put away the dishes." Grandma smiled and turned around to leave the room.

"Aunt Nita, will they ever make tinsel again?"

"They'll make it when the war is over."

"When will the war be over?"

"I don't know."

I thought Aunt Nita knew everything. That was the first time I had heard her say, "I don't know." "Why don't you know?"

"No one knows." Aunt Nita sighed. "I'm going to put the star on the top of the tree, then turn on the lights—No, wait! We'll have to turn on the lights during the day tomorrow."

"Can we turn on the lights for just a minute?"

"No, we can't. The government won't allow people to burn Christmas tree lights or window lights at night."

"Pretty please," I begged.

"No, and that's final. Someday you'll understand. Go get your grandma. Tell her we've finished decorating the tree, and we want her to see it."

"The tree looks grand," said Grandma as she walked into the room. "I'm glad you put on the tinsel." The tree did look pretty, but it would look beautiful with the lights on. I missed lying back on the sofa, with my head propped against the arm, gazing at the lights.

Aunt Nita looked over some of her records and asked, "Mama, would you like to hear *White Christmas*?"

Grandma chuckled. "You know me. I like to hear anything by Bing Crosby, especially *White Christmas*."

We listened to the record, and then Aunt Nita said she had to get ready to go to a movie with her friends.

Even though all Christmas lights had to be out at night, we could have the usual house lights burning unless there was an air raid warning.

Grandma let me keep the seven-and-a-half-watt bulb burning in the living room floor lamp so I was able to see the decorated tree. Lying on the sofa, I pictured how it had seemed like a wonderland when we turned on the window lights and the tree lights two Christmases ago.

Grandma came in and said, "I just wanted to see how you're doing."

"I'm doing fine, Grandma."

"I've always liked the smell of a fresh Christmas tree!"

I slowly inhaled the wonderful scent of the tree and wondered why I hadn't noticed it before. "It does smell good."

"Seeing the ornaments always reminds me of Mama." Grandma softly smiled.

"The ornaments are beautiful." Then, I thought about how BeeWee and Grandma looked forward to selecting just the right ten-foot tree each year, how BeeWee liked to string the lights, and how Grandma liked to bring out the drawers of carefully wrapped ornaments that had belonged to her mother, and Mama liked to take care of the window lights. Aunt Nita seemed to enjoy decorating the tree, and I had fun helping her. I wondered why it took me so long to realize that burning lights were only a small part of the Christmas decorations.

Long ago, a tradition was begun in this family, maybe it started with Grandma's mother, and maybe it started even longer ago than that. The joy, pride, and love that each person contributed to carry on the tradition meant the most. I was thrilled to become a part of it, and somehow, I knew I'd want to continue the tradition when I grew up and had a family of my own.

"Honey, do you want to look at the tree longer, or do you want to come back in the kitchen to listen to the radio?"

"I guess I'm ready to listen to the radio."

Giving Gifts

After she called the roll each day, Miss Odum asked the class to stand to say the Pledge of Allegiance. Next, she turned on a recording of *Onward Christian Soldiers*; we sang along with it and marched in place. Sometimes she allowed us to march around the room in a large circle, playing sticks in time to the music. Then we put the sticks in a box, went back to our seats, stood, and bowed our heads to say a short prayer to thank God for the day.

Finally, the teacher sold stamps to about six of us, who lined up at her desk. Each time I bought a ten-cent stamp, I knew I was a little closer to filling my booklet. When it was complete, someday, I'd be able to exchange it for a $25.00 U.S. Savings Bond.

Mama, Grandma, BeeWee, and the teacher said this was a good way for school children to contribute to the war effort, which was something everyone in the country wanted to do.

Some movie stars traveled across the country to sell bonds. Dorothy Lamour was one of the stars who sold millions of dollars' worth of bonds. Bing Crosby sang a song about bonds that began with "Buy, buy a bond...." Even my favorite cartoon character, Bugs Bunny, sang a song called *Any Bonds Today*?

Sometimes in school, the teacher asked us to stop what we were doing for a couple of minutes to crouch quietly under our desks. The teacher called it a drill, which I knew was not a game, yet I didn't know exactly why we did it.

I was learning to read more words, and I saw an announcement in the newspaper that had the word 'school' in it, so I asked Mama to help me read it. She said that the notice said Norfolk Public Schools would close for the Christmas holidays on December 17, 1943. Although I liked school, I looked forward to having a break before and during the holidays.

On December 17th BeeWee drove Mama and me to school. Mama went in with me to take a box of Whitman's Sampler candy to the teacher and to carry the gifts I had bought for the children.

I remembered what Mama had told me about not being disappointed if the other children didn't give me gifts. I tried not to show my disappointment when I gave out six gifts without receiving one in return, but I was disappointed.

A new feeling was building inside me. I felt embarrassed because I thought the children and the teacher were thinking I was a fool. Then, something good happened. When I gave the seventh gift to Patricia, she had one for me. I was happy enough to have hugged her, but I didn't. I just thanked her. She would never know how grateful I was to receive her gift. I immediately felt thankful for the gift I received from Patricia instead of feeling foolish and embarrassed about not receiving gifts from others.

After school, I couldn't wait to get home to tell Grandma and Mama about the gift. When I opened it, I was happy to see a box of two pretty handkerchiefs. I would have been happy no matter what the gift had been.

I'm glad Mama didn't say, "I told you so." Instead, she asked, "What do you think you'll do from now on when children at school say they're going to give you a Christmas present?"

"I won't believe them unless it's Patricia."

"What will you say when they ask you if you're going to give them a gift?"

I thought about it for a few seconds and replied, "I don't know. What do you think I should say?"

"I'm glad you asked me because I want to explain something to you. You were lucky this year because your Daddy was selling your tricycle; otherwise, we wouldn't have had the money for you to buy gifts for seven children. Next year, you'll need to tell them that you'd like to give them gifts, but you don't have the money to buy them. I honestly think some of those children who said they were going to give you a gift really wanted to do it, but they didn't have the money. They say it's better to give than to receive, and I'm glad you were able to do it this year. I'm just saying we can't afford for you to do it again."

"Okay, Mama."

I didn't have any bad feelings toward the girls who didn't give me a gift. I agreed with Mama; they probably did want to get me something. I was happy to have gotten them all coloring books, but I didn't want to plan to give gifts to friends in the future unless I could pay for them with my own money.

Countdown to Christmas

We could burn the lights on the tree during the day, so I stayed in the living room as often as I could.

From time to time, Grandma had bought me nice little Whitman books from Robbins' Confectionary. She read them to me, but now I was learning to read them by myself, not just to look at the pictures and read a word here and there. I read *The Three Bears*, *The Three Little Pigs*, and *Little Red Riding Hood* over and over again.

I was also beginning to really read my comic books. If I came to a word I didn't know, I'd ask Mama, Grandma, BeeWee, or Aunt Nita, whichever one was closest to me at the time. When I wasn't reading, I skated in the house.

Santa Claus was coming on the radio only one more time before Christmas. On the night of December 22nd, at seven-thirty p.m. I was glued to the radio, listening for my name because Santa had been calling out the first names of the boys and girls he was going to bring toys to. I still hoped he would mention my name.

He finally said my name! I was jumping up and down when I heard him say that parents should be sure that the fires were out in their fireplaces so Santa could come down the chimney without being burned.

Grandma and BeeWee didn't burn fires in the three rooms with fireplaces in the house: the living room, the dining room, or Aunt Nita's bedroom. I'd heard Grandma say the fireplaces had been covered for years because she was afraid they weren't safe for building fires.

The metal cover in the living room was decorated with a large-footed bowl of fruit, with clusters of grapes hanging over the edges. It was painted with a brass- colored paint, the same color as all the radiators in the house and the other two fireplace covers.

The metal covers in the dining room, and Aunt Nita's room were plain and were also painted with the same paint.

"Grandma, how can Santa get through a fireplace if there's a cover over it?"

"Santa's strong. He can push the cover away as if it's a piece of paper. In all the years we've been here, he's never had any trouble getting in the house, so you don't need to worry," she assured me.

"Okay. I just wanted to be sure."

As we continued listening to the radio, we heard some Christmas music, and I was hoping they'd play my favorite, *Up on a Housetop*, but they didn't play it that night.

Christmas Eve 1943

Grandma started her Christmas cooking on December 24th.

The heat from the turkey roasting in the oven fogged the kitchen windows, and I wrote Merry Christmas, with my index finger, on each window.

I looked at the stack of Christmas cards that Grandma, BeeWee, and Aunt Nita had received. Aunt Nita didn't mind if we looked at her Christmas cards. The cards were in all sizes and had Christmas and winter scenes. Some were in the traditional Christmas colors of red and green and said, "Merry Christmas and a Happy New Year." Others were mostly blue and said, "Silent Night" or "Peace on Earth." I was able to read most of the printed words, but I still couldn't read the signatures on the cards unless they were signed by Grandma's sisters.

Aunt Nita came home and said she thought she saw Santa and his sleigh going over the rooftop of the house across the street, so I hurried to the front door to see for myself. I stared at the rooftop until I started getting cold, but I didn't see him, so I went back to the kitchen.

"Aunt Nita, you're lucky. You're the one who always sees Santa."

"I don't think Santa wants children to see him; that's why he always comes after they've gone to sleep."

"I'll bet he was coming here, but he changed his mind because I wasn't in bed asleep," I worried.

"No, it's still early," Aunt Nita corrected herself. "I must have just thought I saw Santa. He probably hasn't even left the North Pole yet."

Grandma suggested, "You'd better let me take you upstairs so you can get ready for bed and try to be asleep when he comes."

I went to bed, but it seemed as though it took me forever to fall asleep. I even heard the dining room clock strike ten, which meant I'd been trying to fall asleep for almost an hour. Christmas Eve put a lot of stress on me. Instead of getting in bed at my usual bedtime of nine o'clock, I worried about everything I could think of that would keep Santa from coming.

I needed to pay attention and follow directions all year; then, I wouldn't be so worried on Christmas Eve. I could relax and fall asleep earlier if I thought I had been as good as I could be.

Christmas Holidays 1943

The next morning, Grandma and BeeWee woke me up and told me Santa had come. I put on my rose-colored chenille robe, with my matching corduroy slippers, and followed them downstairs.

There under the lighted tree, were the things that Santa had brought me. I shook with excitement as I saw a red scooter. That took the place of the tricycle I had outgrown. There was a new doll that had soft, lifelike skin. I knelt beside the tree and held her in my arms, rocking her back and forth as though she was a real baby. Then, to the far right of the tree, I saw a large box with a brown jumper and a yellow blouse, which I thought looked like what I had tried on in the store before Christmas. I didn't mind Santa bringing the clothes; I was just not looking forward to wearing them.

Grandma urged, "Go ahead. Pull out the clothes in that big box."

I didn't want Grandma to think I didn't like the clothes, so I set my doll back in her box and pulled the big box toward me.

As I held it up, I saw that it wasn't the dark chocolate-colored, stiff corduroy, size seven, straight as a board jumper I had tried on; it was a size 6X, milk chocolate- colored, soft corduroy, gathered at the waist, and with a pocket. The blouse was soft cotton in a buttery-yellow color, with a round collar that had a narrow ruffle around it that matched the narrow ruffles at the wrists of the long sleeves. Santa somehow knew just what I'd like to wear and brought me the perfect outfit.

By now BeeWee was wondering why Mama hadn't come for Christmas morning.

"Now Clarence, don't you get upset again about whether Florencie comes on Christmas morning. You can see that the baby's as happy as a lark, and that's what matters."

"You're right. That's what matters. I just wish Florencie wouldn't miss it." With joy in his voice again, BeeWee pointed out, "You've got a couple more boxes to open and a stocking hanging on the mantle, so let's get going."

My stocking never looked like any pictures of Christmas stockings I'd seen. It was a clean white sock with an apple, a tangerine, a banana, some English walnuts in the shell, and some broken hard Christmas candy, wrapped in waxed paper. I guess my candy got broken like Grandma said her toys were broken one year, but it was all right with me if my candy was broken. It would still taste the same.

Grandma fried an egg for me, buttered a slice of fresh white bread, and put apple butter on it, but I was almost too excited to eat. I ate slowly and sipped my warm, creamy coffee. Then I thought about my wonderful things under the tree and ate faster so I could soon get back to them.

Grandma said I needed to get dressed before I started playing again because someone might come since it was Christmas Day. I got dressed, played Mother and Child by myself, and rode my scooter in the house.

BeeWee sat in the high back chair, seeming to enjoy being in the room with the lighted Christmas tree and watching me play with my new things. "Sugie, how do you think the tree and the windows would look with all blue lights?"

Grandma told me BeeWee always wanted to have all blue lights one year. I knew Grandma thought they would make her feel sad, and I didn't want that to happen, so I tried to think before I spoke. I thought about what I liked best and suggested, "All blue would be pretty, but I'd miss seeing the colored lights."

"Sugie, I think you've hit the nail on the head. I'd never thought about missing the colored lights we've always had."

Grandma came into the living room and asked what kind of soup we wanted for lunch. BeeWee said he'd rather have pork and bean sandwiches, and she explained that they would be just as quick to prepare as the soup.

After lunch, BeeWee went upstairs to take a nap, and Grandma continued to prepare our Christmas dinner. I sat in the high back chair and read what I could from my new, big Bedtime Stories book. It had 365 short stories in it, one for every day of the year, but I knew I'd want to read more than one each day.

Everyone came around five o'clock for a delicious turkey dinner with all the trimmings prepared by Grandma with love for all of us. We sat around the table for a long time, eating as much as we could hold; and talking a lot, sometimes everyone talking at once. Then, the women cleared the table; the men went into the living room to sit, talk, and smoke, and I rode my scooter from room to room so I could be with all of them.

Grandma, as usual, shooed Mama and Aunt Nita from the kitchen to the living room so they could sit down and talk while she put the leftovers away. BeeWee and Daddy talked about their jobs with the railroad, and Mama and Aunt Nita talked about clothes, movies, and people they knew.

Grandma finally came into the living room and said it was time to open gifts.

Aunt Nita announced, "I want to give Daddy his gift first, so he can start using it."

Everyone said they knew it must be a carton of cigarettes, but when Aunt Nita brought it out and BeeWee opened it, it was a shiny chrome and black cigarette stand. "It's for the living room," Aunt Nita explained.

"It's good-looking and something I've needed for a long time. Thank you, Juanita," replied BeeWee as he set it beside his chair.

Everyone exchanged the usual handkerchiefs, socks, a carton of cigarettes for BeeWee, hose, slips, and makeup sets. BeeWee and Grandma gave Mama a small box that contained a gold pin shaped like a bouquet of flowers that had pretty, ruby-red stones. They gave me a small box that contained a pretty gold bracelet that I could adjust the way one would adjust a belt, so it would fit me for a long time.

Aunt Nita had begun to look sad because she knew she had told Grandma and BeeWee not to buy her a gift this year, and BeeWee had said they wouldn't give her a gift if she didn't want one.

BeeWee said, "Well, that's it. That's all the presents. Oh, wait. Here's something else." Then, he reached behind his chair and pulled out a wrapped gift that was obviously bedroom slippers because of the size and flimsiness of the cardboard box that bent inward a little as BeeWee handed it to Aunt Nita. "Juanita, your Mama, and I know you said not to give you anything, but after all these years, we couldn't let the day go by without giving you at least a little something."

Aunt Nita looked pleasantly surprised. She slipped the wrapping paper off the box, and there was tissue inside that I thought was covering bedroom slippers. Then, I was almost as surprised as Aunt Nita when she pulled out a jewelry store box and opened it to find a pin, gold like Mama's, but with garnet-red stones instead of ruby-red ones. She looked happy. "But you didn't need to…" she started.

Grandma jumped in, "Juanita, you should know we wouldn't think of not giving you a gift."

BeeWee just sat there and chuckled, pleased with himself for fooling Aunt Nita.

Everyone except Grandma sat and talked a little longer. She went back to the kitchen to wash the stacks of dirty dishes.

"Grandma, you never get through working," I noticed.

"Honey, I don't mind hard work. I've worked hard all my life."

"I wish you could be in the living room, talking with everyone else."

"I appreciate that, honey, but I'm happy just knowing that we could all be together for another Christmas."

Tears welled in my eyes when I thought of how hard Grandma had worked and was still working so we could have a wonderful Christmas. When I put my arms around her waist to hug her, I felt the dampness of the towel she had pinned around the front of her dress, where the dishwater had splashed on her from the sink. "Grandma, I love you so much."

"I love you, too, honey." She dried her hands on the damp towel and hugged me back. I knew I was a very lucky little girl to have the most wonderful grandmother in the world.

BeeWee smoked and used his new smoking stand, coughing every time the smoke drifted up in his face.

I played Mother and Child with my new doll, listened to everyone's conversations, and went in and out of the kitchen to see Grandma and to talk with her.

Mama said it was nine o'clock, time for me to go upstairs, put on my pajamas, and go to bed. She walked upstairs with me to see that I did what I was supposed to do, then she went back to the living room to be with the others.

It wasn't cold in the house. Grandma kept the fire burning in the stove since it was Christmas Day, and everyone was in the living room.

I lay there thinking about what a wonderful day it had been, but as thankful as I was, I suddenly remembered that I hadn't said my prayers. I threw back the sheet, the woolen blankets, and the chenille spread and knelt by the bed to pray for so long that I almost fell asleep there on the wooden floor.

It was fun having time off from school to play. I especially had fun with my new scooter—riding in the house and outside. The weather was so cold that I couldn't stay out for more than a few minutes before going back in with a cold face, cold hands, and cold feet, even though I was completely covered except for the center of my face. I thawed out by sitting with my back to the Arcola coal stove and sipping a cup of Nestles cocoa.

On New Year's Eve, Grandma and I listened to Guy Lombardo and his orchestra broadcasting from New York. They played a lot of dance music and talked about the crowd of people in Times Square who were waiting to see the New Year.

I felt sad about 1943 ending, but I knew I'd always remember it because I had wonderful memories of 1941 and 1942. What I wanted most in the New Year was probably what everyone in our country wanted. We wanted World War II to end.

Part IV — 1944

Observations

Our country had been at war for three years, and many changes had taken place during that time.

Thousands of our servicemen had been killed, and even more, thousands had been seriously wounded. More men were being drafted every day to take the places of those who would never fight another battle.

There had been so many casualties that the age of those who were eligible to be drafted had continually risen until Daddy could be drafted at any time. He was 29.

President Roosevelt had always said our success in the war depended on the continuous running of the railroads, so Daddy had been exempt from the draft, but many more men were needed overseas.

Older men, with more seniority on the railroads, like BeeWee, would have to work overtime to do the work of the younger men who would be drafted.

Some things did not change. Norfolk continued to have a housing shortage, despite the fact that more housing was built as quickly as possible.

A new navy housing project was built near the naval base, but they didn't build a school, so the children who lived there were bused to my elementary school.

When I first started school, I didn't know where any children lived except those who lived on Grandma's street.

Norfolk's population had steadily increased since before the war when President Roosevelt said we had to be prepared in case we were drawn into the war. Middle-aged men with families moved to Norfolk to take advantage of the good-paying civilian jobs with the navy and needed housing. The families of married servicemen whose home port was in Norfolk also needed housing.

When I began my second semester of first grade, I began to better understand the reason for the searchlights darting through the sky at night, the air raids, the blackouts, the dark green window shades, and the under-the-desk drills at school. We were preparing for an enemy air attack that could be a drill or the real thing.

New Pictures for the Mantle

This New Year's Day, Aunt Nita gave me some lined paper and a pencil and said I could write my own New Year's resolutions now that I was in school. Then she went to work. When she came home from work, she said I had done very well to write my resolutions by myself.

Not long after Aunt Nita's twenty-second birthday, on January 4th, she told me I could start calling her Nita instead of Aunt Nita. I was pleased to think she thought I was old enough and educated enough to address her as more of a peer than as an aunt.

The next night she had a date with a tall young sailor. As he walked in the door, she said, "This is Shirley, my older sister Florence's daughter." He had a full face and grinned broadly and pleasantly when we were introduced. I thought he seemed to be genuinely happy to meet us. Nita said his name was Baxter. Baxter often came to take Nita out on dates, and Grandma and Mama said they thought Nita liked him more than anyone she'd ever dated.

When they had their pictures made at a photography studio and exchanged them with each other, we were fairly certain they liked each other, but Nita would never say anything about him. Nita had copies of her picture made for Grandma and BeeWee, and Mama. Grandma set Nita's picture on the mantle in the living room. Nita looked just as pretty in the picture as she did on the night when she wore her pink angora sweater and her fur coat for the first time. In the picture, she was wearing a pale pink rayon blouse that had a round, ruffled collar.

Grandma asked Mama to have her picture taken so she could put it on the mantle, too. Mama said she didn't particularly want to have her picture made, but she did it eventually. It was a smaller picture than Nita's, but Mama looked just as pretty. She had her softly curled, shoulder-length, strawberry blonde hair combed slightly different from Nita's and was wearing a powder blue woolen pullover sweater with a string of pearls.

I liked looking at their pictures and at the picture of Nita's friend, which Nita had set on the opposite side of the mantle from hers. He had given her two pictures: one of him in his navy-blue uniform and one of him in his white uniform. She chose his picture in the navy-blue uniform for the mantle and set the other one on the mantle in her room.

My First Boyfriend

The teacher said we could exchange valentines on Valentine's Day, so I picked out valentines at Robbins' Confectionary for my classmates. We turned them in to her in the morning, and she gave them out to us in the afternoon. She called out our names to walk to her desk to receive our valentines.

There was one valentine that was larger than the rest, and I wondered who it was for.

Everyone noticed the large valentine, and there was whispering among some of the students who were curious about who would get it. The teacher finally took it from the box and called my name. I could hardly breathe when I walked to her desk to get it because I knew that all eyes in the room were on me.

I opened it and saw it was from Ted, the boy who had stood up for me on that day when he thought Miss Odum was making me nervous. I gave him a valentine, but it was the same size as the valentines I gave to everyone else in the class. I could hear some of the students saying I was his girlfriend and he was my boyfriend, but I didn't mind.

Sometimes we couldn't always go outside for recess after lunch because it was too cold or it was raining, but we still had a break from going directly back to the classroom. We went to the auditorium and watched newsreels like the ones we saw at the movie theaters.

On the first day that we had recess after Valentine's Day, I was walking with Patricia, and we passed by the monkey bars, enjoying the warmth of the sunshine on a cold day. Suddenly two girls in my class, who were sitting at the top of the monkey bars, started chanting, "Shirley and Ted, sitting in a tree, k-i-s-s-i-n-g, first comes love, then comes marriage, then comes Shirley with a baby carriage."

I didn't know exactly what it meant; I was just embarrassed to hear them chanting about Ted and me. Patricia told me that I should ignore them.

When I came home and told Mama, she explained, "You can't pay any attention to that. They did the same thing when I was in school."

I thought giving me that large valentine was a sweet thing for Ted to do. In fact, it was my happiest day at school.

My Seventh Birthday

One day, Mama let me know that I could have a birthday party and invite the children in the neighborhood again.

"Mama, can I invite someone from my class, too?"

"I think you can, as long as you invite just one girl. Who do you want to ask?"

"I want to invite Patricia."

"All right."

I was so excited that she said yes. "Can I invite Jerry instead of Darrell?"

"You can invite both of them, but you can't snub Darrell and invite just Jerry. After all, Darrell lives next door," she pointed out. "Don't you think he'd be disappointed if you didn't invite him?"

"I guess so."

"Then, it's settled. We'll invite both of them."

I thought about what she said for a minute, and then I told her, "You don't have to send Jerry an invitation because I know he won't come."

"We'll still invite him. He'd probably be disappointed if you didn't ask him." Mama planned the same party as she had the year before. The only difference was my being allowed to ask Patricia.

At my party, after I blew out the seven candles on my cake, we ate big slices of it with ice cream. Darrell still mixed his peanuts with his ice cream and seemed to thoroughly enjoy eating them together. Then, we went to the living room so I could open my presents. Mama had told me to hold up each gift so everyone could see it and to thank the person who gave it to me.

I was doing as she said until I opened the gift Patricia gave me. When I opened the box and saw two pairs of pink rayon panties, I knew I couldn't hold them up in front of everyone, especially Darrell. I put the lid back on the box, walked over to Mama, and whispered, "Mama, I need to tell you something in the hall."

"You need to tell me something in the hall?"

"Yes. I need to tell you right away." I grabbed her hand and started to pull her with me.

"All right, but make it quick."

When we were in the hall, I told her about my predicament.

"You will go back in that room, hold up those underpants, and say 'thank you' to Patricia," she insisted. "How do you think she'll feel if you don't thank her and hold up her gift?"

"She won't mind, Mama."

"Shirley May Dawson," she said sternly, pointing her index finger toward the living room, which meant I'd better get back in there and do what she told me to do. When she called me by my full name, I knew she meant business. My failure to obey her directions after she called me Shirley May Dawson would result in her slapping me on the top of my left arm, leaving it red, or switching my legs until they were scratched. When I went back to school, the children would say, "Look! Shirley has stripes on her legs." Then they'd want to know what I did to get the switching. I didn't want that to happen, so I went back into the living room and did as I was told.

Patricia looked so happy. "My grandmother picked them out, and she even bought me some just like them!"

Although I fully expected Darrell to laugh or snicker, he looked expressionless, so I realized I had made a lot out of nothing. He acted more maturely than I did. Grandma and BeeWee would have called my reaction to the gift "making a mountain out of a mole hill."

Baxter Receives Orders to Go Overseas

A few days after my birthday, Nita informed us that Baxter had received orders to go overseas.

"Well, I'm sorry, Juanita. Where does he have to go?" asked Grandma.

"He's not allowed to say where he's going," Nita explained.

Mama was surprised. "Does that mean that you can't write to each other?"

"We can write to each other, but we have to send our letters to the Fleet Post Office in New York. They'll read the letters and censor anything that refers to a place or a time because they don't want our enemies to find out anything that could interfere with battle plans and put our men in danger."

Nita never said she loved him, but she wasn't her happy-go-lucky self after that. She still went out with her girlfriends, but she didn't go out with any other servicemen.

I missed having the servicemen come to the house. Mama and Grandma said they wondered whether she should stop seeing other young men since she wasn't engaged to be married. Of course, they didn't say anything to Nita about it.

We thought she received letters from him because there were letters in the mail from the Fleet Post Office, but she probably still wrote to the servicemen that she'd written to before she met Baxter.

She looked worried when she saw the number of war casualties printed on the front page of the newspapers each day or when she heard about the casualties on the radio. She had no way of knowing where he was, if he had been wounded, or if he was still alive. When she received letters, she was always happier.

I was sorry that Baxter had to go overseas. I didn't know him very well, but every time he came over to the house to take Nita out on a date, he seemed nice and friendly to me. I could tell that Nita liked him better than the other servicemen she used to go out with. I hoped he would be safe and come back home.

Daddy Expects to be Drafted

One morning when we were eating breakfast, Mama said, "You might as well know that Bill's expecting to get his draft notice in the mail any day."

"I don't want Daddy to go to war."

"I don't want him to go either, but if he's drafted, he has to go," Mama explained.

"Well, Florencie, don't worry about it until the time comes." BeeWee tried to assure her, "I was drafted during World War I, but I didn't have to go to war."

Mama couldn't believe it. "How in the world did that happen?"

"I reported for my physical, and they disqualified me because they said I was underweight."

Mama sighed. "Bill's not underweight, though."

"You never can tell. They might find something else wrong," suggested BeeWee.

I'd been listening this whole time, and then I blurted out, "BeeWee, I don't want you to have to go to war either!"

"Thank you, Sugie, but don't worry; I don't think they'll get around to calling men my age. Besides, some of us have to mind the store at the railroad."

"There's a store at the railroad?"

BeeWee chuckled. "That's just a way of saying that the railroads need some of us to stay here and work."

"Don't be so sure. If the war keeps going on, they might call you, too," Grandma pointed out.

BeeWee smiled. "You wouldn't want me to be drafted again, would you?"

"That would be one of the last things I would want, Clarence. I just think it could happen if the war doesn't end soon. We all need to get down on our knees and pray that God will find a way for our country to end this war."

"Grandma and I have already been praying every night for the war to end." I didn't want Daddy or BeeWee to be drafted. I hoped that the war would end before that would be necessary.

The Insurance Man

Someone knocked at the front door, and Grandma asked Mama if she would see who was there. When Mama came back to the kitchen, she announced, "Mama, Mr. Scott's here to collect the life insurance premiums." Mr. Scott was the insurance agent for the Metropolitan Life Insurance Company. He was a tall, good-looking man with wavy black hair that was graying at the temples. Grandma and BeeWee had taken out insurance policies on the two of them, Mama and Nita. Insurance agents used to collect life insurance premiums at the doors of people who had insurance with their company. Grandma's and BeeWee's premiums were forty cents a week, ten cents for each policy, each week.

"Tell him I'm going upstairs to get my pocketbook, and I'll be right there." Grandma soon came back downstairs and handed four premium books to Mr. Scott. He pulled his pen out of his coat pocket and wrote in each book as Grandma opened her change purse and took out some coins.

"All right, Mrs. Daugherty, that'll be ten cents for each policy."

"Here's the forty cents, Mr. Scott." Grandma handed him the money.

"Thank you, Mrs. Daugherty. I'll see you next week." He turned to Mama, "Nice talking with you again, Florence."

"It was nice talking with you, too, Mr. Scott," said Mama as she closed the front door.

I didn't usually go to the door when men came to take care of business; I stood behind the heavy drapes that divided the front hall from the back hall and watched through the middle, where the drapes were slightly parted. The only exception was when the mailman, Mr. Austin, came. He arrived about the same time each day except Sunday. I liked the way he always smiled and handed the mail to me.

The Food Situation

Even though there was still a housing shortage in Norfolk, there was still not a shortage of food. The farms in Virginia still kept a steady supply of fresh vegetables and fruit coming into the city, and no ration coupons were necessary to purchase them.

We were fortunate that Grandma had access to fresh potatoes, onions, collard greens, cabbage, rutabagas, white turnips, fresh corn on the cob, and butter beans to cook. She knew how to make some of the most delicious meals with the fresh produce we had. Her lettuce and tomato salads in late spring and early summer were the best. Grandma shredded white cabbage and carrots for coleslaw that couldn't be better.

Processed foods were still rationed, so Grandma used ration coupons for the seasoning meat and butter that she used to flavor some of the vegetables and the mayonnaise that she used in the salads. She also had to use ration coupons for meats and canned vegetables, such as Campbell's pork and beans, soup, and Del Monte creamed corn.

I liked having Grandma's creamed potatoes and creamed corn. I put creamed potatoes on my plate, made a hole in the middle, and filled it with creamed corn. It was yummy.

Milk was plentiful in Norfolk. The local dairies still delivered bottles of milk to the door, and the chain grocery stores had bottles of milk in their dairy sections. We had plenty of eggs to eat each day, and BeeWee and I still dyed eggs on Easter morning.

We worried about running out of sugar and butter because they were always scarce. Even though sugar was scarce and rationed, candy was plentiful. If we had the money to pay for it, we could buy all the candy we wanted. Every restaurant, cafe, lunch counter, or other place that sold cups of coffee limited the amount of sugar that people could use, but we could buy unlimited fountain soft drinks, snowballs, milkshakes, ice cream sodas, ice cream, ice cream sundaes, and banana splits.

Cold bottled soft drinks, such as Coca-Cola, Pepsi-Cola, Dr. Pepper, Seven-up, Orange Crush, and Grapette, were always in a cooler near the cash register of every corner grocery store.

Nabisco kept the cookies coming. Grocery shelves were lined with boxes of vanilla wafers, animal crackers, sugar wafers, large, flat boxes of assorted cookies, and others. I liked all cookies, but I especially liked the little boxes of animal crackers with pictures of circus animals on the box and the string handle. It was nice to have my own personal box of cookies that I could carry around by the handle. I'd open the box and take out a couple of cookies, look at the animal shapes, and take small bites so they would last longer.

My favorite little round devil's food snack cake with the white cream between the two soft, moist layers was always available at the corner grocery store, but I never got them anymore. We used to pick out our favorite snacks on the way to Lynnhaven, where BeeWee fished, and we sat on the beach and ate lunch before the war. Gasoline was as scarce and rationed as it ever was.

I think BeeWee, Grandma, Mama, and I missed going to Lynnhaven more than anything else. I know I did. We hadn't been to the beach since the summer when I was four.

The USO Dance

I knew Nita was worried about Baxter being overseas, and Mama was worried that Daddy might be drafted.

I wondered if this war would ever end. I knew from listening to the news, reading the daily newspapers, and seeing the newsreels at the movies and during rainy day recesses at school that it wouldn't end in time for us to go to Lynnhaven on BeeWee's vacation in July.

Since people couldn't buy enough gas to go on long day trips, like Lynnhaven, or drive to visit distant relatives, they found other things to do. Reading, listening to the radio, listening to records, playing cards, playing board games, and going to the movies were my favorite pastimes. Those who had planted victory gardens spent time taking care of them.

Local young, single men were all serving in the armed forces, and we didn't even know where they were. They were still fighting the war on two continents: Europe and Asia. Before the war, many of those men had never been out of their own state. It was a hard way for them to see the world.

The servicemen who swarmed the streets of Norfolk were from all over the United States. Their time in Norfolk was temporary. They, too, would eventually go overseas. More than any of us, they needed to have pastimes to enjoy while they were on liberty.

Downtown Norfolk was the hub of activity for them as well as it was for the citizens. The YMCA and the USO (United Service Organization) were also located downtown. The USO held regular dances, and the single young ladies of Norfolk were welcome to attend.

When I read in a newspaper about the USO dances, I said, "I'll bet I know how Nita met her boyfriend. I'll bet she met him at a USO dance."

Grandma thought for a moment. "I don't know if Nita likes to dance."

If Nita wouldn't tell us how they met, I'd just use my imagination. I pictured Nita attending a USO dance with her girlfriends. They would be standing together when a tall, young sailor in a navy-blue uniform walked over, grinned broadly, and would invite Nita to dance.

She would say, "Oh, I don't know how to dance. I just came to watch everyone else."

He would take her hand. "Come on. I'll show you. It'll be fun."

Nita would see something in him that she liked too much to protest. "If you promise we won't dance too fast."

They would slow dance to *Moonlight Serenade* and then do a slow jitterbug to Glenn Miller's *String of Pearls*. Nita would realize that she liked dancing more than she thought she would.

Baxter and Nita would blend in perfectly with the other dancers and smile happily. When the band began playing *In the Mood*, the other dancers would begin dancing a fast jitterbug, and he would respect Nita's wishes by walking her back to her group of friends.

She would like that, so when he asked to see her again, she would agree.

It could have happened like that; I'd like to think so.

Grandma Worries About Nita

Nita hardly ever got to drive the 1941 Chevrolet that she and BeeWee had bought together before the war. She walked to the bus stop, a block and a half from Grandma's house, and rode the bus to work. She went to work so early in the morning that the buses were no more crowded than they'd been before the war.

Her girlfriends usually worked the same hours, so it was convenient for them to stay downtown after work to eat at the telephone company cafeteria or at a restaurant. Afterward, they would shop or go to a movie and ride the bus home.

Grandma was worried about Nita walking home from the bus stop by herself at night. Before we went to bed, Grandma switched on the front porch light, which was so bright it must have had at least a seventy-five-watt bulb in it. Sometimes when Grandma waited for me to go to sleep, she walked through the darkness of the inside of the house to go outside to see if she could see Nita walking home.

All the downtown department stores, five and dime stores, and shops closed by six o'clock every day. Drugstores, restaurants, and movie theaters stayed open later. The last showing of movies began around nine o'clock and ended around eleven o'clock. By then, the movie marquees were dark, and there was hardly any traffic except for the buses that drove everyone away from the area. The only constant light was from the streetlights and some of the stores that kept the lights on in their show windows.

The reason why I knew about downtown Norfolk late at night was that Nita drove downtown to pick up Mama from Whelan's drugstore. That was the only place that she ever worked, and she only worked there for about a month. Even then, I never liked the way the dampness set in at night, even fogging the car windows.

What a difference a few hours made.

Summer of 1944

Except for not being able to go to Lynnhaven, summer was the same for the children on Grandma's street. We played outside for as long as we could every day. I was outside by ten o'clock in the morning and went inside only to eat lunch, take a bath, and take a nap in the middle of the day. When I woke up, I dressed and went outside to play and waited for the popsicle man to come. Later, Grandma called me in to eat soup with bread and butter. Then she sat on the porch, and I usually played until nine o'clock.

The only exception was when Grandma took me to the neighborhood movie theater about once a week. They still showed three cartoons and a newsreel with every movie.

Bugs Bunny was still my favorite cartoon character, but they were all funny. As time went by, I realized they weren't showing Droopy cartoons anymore. I was sorry about that because Droopy was my second favorite. He was a funny brown dog with long, droopy ears and a slow, droopy-sounding voice. Grandma liked seeing the newsreels so she could keep up with the world news, even though most of it was grim during the war.

During the two weeks that BeeWee was on vacation, Grandma and I went with him when he went fishing after dark some nights but sitting on the bench to watch him didn't compare with sitting on the beach at Lynnhaven while he fished from the bridge. The best part of those evenings was still stopping for ice cream cones on the way home, not that I didn't like being with Grandma and BeeWee. I liked being with them anywhere.

As much as Grandma, BeeWee, and Mama liked going to Lynnhaven, they never complained about not being able to go. I didn't complain, either. I just reminisced about how much I enjoyed it.

BeeWee took us to the Ocean View Amusement Park again, and Mama took me on the same rides that we liked. I fished for ducks twice and got the same little prizes from the box under the counter as I had the year before. After what Mama told me last summer, I sort of knew I wouldn't win a nice prize from the shelves, but there was something about the dream of winning that was exhilarating. It might have been worth the nickel or dime to have the dream for a few minutes once in a while.

The Two Dimes

One hot July night, when Grandma and I were sitting on the front porch, I asked her if she would order ice cream cones from the drugstore. I don't remember ever asking her before because I thought she would suggest it if she had the money.

"Ice cream cones would certainly be good right now, but I don't think I have any money. Let's go upstairs, and I'll look and see if I can find any change in the bottom of my pocketbook." Grandma turned on the overhead light in the back bedroom, and we sat on the edge of the bed as she rummaged through her pocketbook. I looked over her shoulder, hoping she'd find some money, but there wasn't even a penny in the bottom of her purse. "Wait a minute. I know of one more place to look. I think I might have two old dimes in the top drawer." She found the dimes right away.

"Is there still time to call the drugstore before they stop delivering?"

"Don't worry; there's still plenty of time. We'll go back downstairs, and I'll call." She walked toward me, clutching the dimes in her hand. "What kind of ice cream do you want?"

"I'd like to have chocolate." I could already almost taste how good the creamy ice cream and the crunchy cone would be.

"It's so late I think I'll skip the cone tonight and get a scoop of vanilla in a Dixie cup," Grandma decided.

"Can I see the old dimes, Grandma?"

"Sure, honey. Here they are." She handed them to me carefully.

The dimes were definitely old because they were worn thin. I knew they must have some special meaning for Grandma.

"When did you get the dimes, Grandma?"

"My mother gave them to me when I was a young girl, just going to my first job. She wanted me to keep them in a safe place in my pocketbook in case I needed them for an emergency."

"Grandma, you saved these dimes for a long time. I don't need to have ice cream tonight. I'd rather for you to be able to keep your dimes."

"I don't need them anymore. It's more important to me now for my sweet granddaughter to have an ice cream cone. Come on, honey. Let's go downstairs so I can call the drugstore."

When we were halfway across the bedroom floor, I turned toward her. "Here are the dimes, Grandma."

As I reached out to hand them to her, they slipped out of my hand. It was amazing how they got away from me and rolled so quickly across the floor. I hurried after them and reached to pick them up, I couldn't believe how fast both dimes were still rolling, and they slipped right through the cracks in the floor.

My eyes were moist with tears, and I had a lump in my throat from trying to keep from crying. It wasn't about the ice cream anymore. It was about losing Grandma's dimes. I started crying my eyes out to the point of blubbering. "Grandma, the dimes were important to you and...."

"I'm not worried about those dimes, honey. You're more important to me than those dimes could ever be."

"Grandma, I love you so much."

"I love you, too, honey," she said, leaning over to hug me as hard as I was hugging her.

I knew I would never forget that night.

Beginning Second Grade

In August, Mama took me for my new school shoes, and, as usual, my new shoes were a half size or a size larger, and they looked three sizes larger to me.

After Labor Day, I went back to school with quiet resignation, hoping I would have a nice teacher but not taking it for granted. I knew that after what happened last year, I would have to stay in school regardless of what happened. I didn't even want to leave school again because I didn't want Mama to spank me.

My second-grade classroom was across the stairway from my first-grade classroom, and my teacher was Miss Gray, an older teacher who wore her nearly white hair in a large bun above the nape of her neck. She wore rimless bifocals, no makeup, and she had a kind face. Unlike the other teachers, she wore dresses that looked like the cotton housedresses Grandma wore at home. I liked that because it gave her the appearance of being grandmotherly and less intimidating than the other teachers. She wore hose and black laced shoes with wide two-inch heels.

I was going to do my best to pay attention, follow directions, and do my work in any teacher's class, so I didn't think I needed to feel threatened all the time or be yelled at.

I liked my first-grade teacher Miss Odom, but I felt silly tiptoeing down the hall with my finger over my lips.

Miss Gray didn't threaten, yell, or have us tiptoe down the hall with our fingers over our lips. I had the same classmates that I had last year, and everyone was good and did their work, as far as I knew.

I felt comfortable about school for the first time since I'd started first grade with Miss Trueheart. I could tell from the first day I was going to like second grade because I liked Miss Gray.

President Roosevelt Runs for a Fourth Term

That fall, President Franklin Delano Roosevelt was running for his fourth term as president, and Grandma often mentioned that he was a good man. On the news, they said that no other president had run for a fourth term.

President Roosevelt had been president my entire life. I couldn't imagine anyone else being president. I liked his wife, First Lady Eleanor Roosevelt, too; I thought she was a good first lady.

President Roosevelt was a Democrat, but BeeWee was a Republican. BeeWee was the only one in the family who voted, so every chance she got, Grandma put in a good word to him for President Roosevelt. I wanted to put in a good word, too. "BeeWee, I wish you would vote for President Roosevelt. He's such a good president."

BeeWee would only say, "I know President Roosevelt is a good man, but I've always been a Republican, so I'll have to think about it."

I thought I was getting somewhere with him, so I didn't dare say anything else except, "BeeWee, I'm glad you're going to think about it." After he went to work, I spoke with Grandma. "Do you think BeeWee will decide to vote for President Roosevelt?"

"I don't know, honey. He's always told me he's a Republican, but I'm sure he likes President Roosevelt."

"Does that mean he'll vote for him?"

"I don't know, honey."

All during the war, I'd thought we'd get through it with the help of God and President Roosevelt. I didn't think that President Roosevelt was a god, but I thought that God was working through him.

On Election Day, BeeWee dressed in his suit and hat and went to the polls to vote. Grandma, Mama, and I rode with him and waited in the car. He drove to a large tan brick house and parked the car. The voting was taking place in the garage. We watched as BeeWee and other men in suits and hats lined up to vote, which led me to believe that voting was for men only.

BeeWee would never tell us how he voted. He had a little twinkle in the corner of one of his eyes that told me he was not only happy to vote but happy to keep us guessing.

I couldn't wait to see the newspaper the next morning to see if President Roosevelt had won. When Grandma came to my bed with my cup of coffee, the first thing I said was, "Did he win, Grandma?"

"He won, thank the Lord!"

I was happy to hear it from Grandma, and I could hardly wait to hear it on the news.

When I look back now, it makes me sad that Grandma wasn't voting, too. She was so informed about all world affairs, and she always thought that Franklin D. Roosevelt was an excellent president. I can't imagine what she must have been thinking, knowing that her husband was likely not voting for the person she thought would be the best fit. Grandma had the right to vote, but they probably couldn't afford to pay the poll tax at the time for them both.

Thanksgiving and Christmas Traditions

We had our usual wonderful Thanksgiving dinner. Grandma always gave our family a lot to look forward to. We never had to wonder what we'd do or what we'd eat on Thanksgiving. Grandma would see to it that we gathered together for excellent food and togetherness as a family.

When it was close to Christmas, my same classmates who said they would give me presents last year and didn't start to tell me that they were getting me a gift this year. Remembering what Mama taught me, I explained, "That's all right. I don't expect you to give me anything because I don't have the money to give you anything." I couldn't believe that was Shirley Dawson talking. I was excited to tell Mama how I'd handled that situation this year.

"Now you're getting smart!" Mama declared. I was happy with myself and even happier that we didn't have to spend time and money shopping for gifts and wrapping them. I also wouldn't have to go through the embarrassment of being taken for a fool this year.

Before we left for the holiday break, Miss Gray said that after Christmas, we were going to start practicing for her annual George Washington's birthday play that we would present in the auditorium. I'd never been in a play, and I was looking forward to it. BeeWee kept up the tradition of buying and putting up the ten-foot-tall tree, and Nita and I decorated it, though we still couldn't turn on the tree lights at night. The faded tinsel was even more faded, but Nita and I still put it on the tree.

Mama put the window lights in the front living room windows. She and Grandma decided it would be all right to put in all blue lights this year since we couldn't turn them on anyway.

"Look BeeWee. The window lights are all blue this year."

BeeWee laughed. "They think they're fooling me, but I know they only put in blue lights because we can't turn them on."

Nita's Package

One day a package was delivered to the house for Nita. It was about twelve inches square and two inches high. The return address was the Fleet Post Office, so we knew it was from Baxter.

Grandma and Mama said they bet he had sent her a Christmas present, and we all wondered what it was.

"Can I hold the box to see how heavy it is?" I asked.

Mama hesitated. "You can hold it for a minute."

"It feels kind of heavy. Maybe it's a box of candy," I guessed.

"I don't know. It feels too heavy, to me, to be candy," Mama said doubtfully.

"Can I shake it?"

"No. Give me the box," Mama insisted. "I'm going to set it on the living room table by the door, so Nita will see it when she walks into the room."

"It doesn't matter what it is; it's the thought that counts," Grandma added.

"That's right. I'm sure Nita will be happy that he sent her a present, no matter what it is," Mama agreed.

"Grandma, do you think Nita sent him a present?"

"Nita wouldn't tell us if she did, honey."

"I think I'll ask her," I decided.

"No, you won't. If she wants us to know, she'll tell us," said Mama firmly.

Grandma laughed. "That's something we'll never know."

Later that afternoon, as we were eating our soup, I mentioned it to Grandma again. "I can hardly wait for Nita to come home and open the present."

"Don't expect Juanita to open the present in front of us. I've known her long enough to know she would never do that."

"Do you think she will show it to us?"

"I don't know, honey. We'll just have to wait and see."

Nita must have opened the box when she came home that night because Grandma said she showed it to her and told her to leave it out so we could all help ourselves to the dried fruit.

When Mama came to Grandma's that morning, she and Grandma wondered if sending the fruit was a way that Baxter was trying to tell her where he was, but after thinking about it more, they decided he could have bought a box of dried fruit almost anywhere because gift boxes like that were always for sale at Christmas time.

Grandma was right. Nita never told us whether she sent her boyfriend a gift.

Unexpected Christmas Guests

Christmas morning was as exciting as ever for me.

There was a surprise for us on Christmas Day. Mama and Daddy came in the late afternoon with Daddy's brother, Don, and his girlfriend. His brother was a few inches taller than Daddy, and he was wearing his army uniform. It was the first time Grandma, BeeWee, Nita, and I had met him. His girlfriend was a tall, attractive brunette who sat on the arm of the living room chair that he was sitting in, with her arm draped around his shoulder.

Poor Grandma was scurrying around between the kitchen and the dining room to put two more place settings and two more chairs at the table. I knew that Grandma, BeeWee, Nita, and I would have to eat less so there would be enough for the two unexpected guests. They seemed to enjoy the dinner and went back to the living room to smoke. With four people smoking, the room was very smoky.

This Christmas morning was one of the only mornings that BeeWee didn't get emotional about Mama not coming early enough in the day to see me open my gifts. To think that when they finally arrived that day, they brought guests that we hadn't even met without warning, I can't imagine how BeeWee and Grandma would have felt. It was completely inconsiderate, and I was shocked that Mama and Daddy would not have respected that Christmas Day was one of the two times a year when we all got together as a family for a meal.

As a little girl, I remember feeling particularly sad for Grandma that she had to work even harder to accommodate two more people.

Part V – 1945

Shooting Baskets

New Year's Day was on a Monday. I sat in the living room and wrote my usual resolutions, and wished for the war to end soon. I liked having off from school on Monday, but I looked forward to returning on Tuesday to start practicing for George Washington's Birthday program. At the time, the day we now know as President's Day was called George Washington's Birthday.

We began practicing on our first day back. Miss Gray had us try out for the parts, and I hoped to be either Betsy Ross or one of the minuet dancers. She showed us the pretty long cotton dresses the girls would wear, and I wanted to wear one of them. We practiced the parts at school, and I practiced in the living room every afternoon. Afterward, I went to the backyard to shoot baskets.

One day when I was shooting baskets, an older girl with long, dark brown curly hair came into the yard. She asked if she could shoot baskets sometimes. She was wearing a pale pink blouse, a navy-blue unbuttoned cardigan sweater, dungarees, and black and white saddle shoes like teenage girls wore. Although she seemed to be a nice girl, I couldn't believe a girl who was obviously several years older than I was would want to shoot baskets with me.

"You're probably wondering who I am. My name is Diana, I'm eleven years old, and I'm visiting my cousin, Adrienne, who lives in the apartment building next door. I've been watching you from her window."

I was surprised. "I didn't know anyone was watching me. Which apartment does your cousin live in?"

"She lives up there, on the third floor." She pointed toward the apartment building next to Grandma's house.

"Adrienne is a beautiful name. Your name is pretty, too."

Diana smiled. "Thank you."

As we talked, I found out she didn't really want to come and shoot baskets with me. She wanted to shoot baskets by herself when she came to visit her cousin. I didn't know when she thought she'd be able to shoot baskets by herself because I shot baskets every day when it wasn't raining. She certainly had a lot of nerve. I started to question her. "If you're visiting your cousin, why do you want to shoot baskets? Does she want to come over here, too?"

"No. Adrienne has a lot of homework to do, and her mother works, so she has to help with the housework and the cooking."

"I stay with my grandmother, and this is her yard, so I'll have to ask her. If you want to wait, I'll go inside and ask her now," I offered.

"Okay, I'll wait. Do you mind if I use your ball to shoot baskets while you ask her?"

I couldn't believe she was bold enough to ask me that. I handed her the ball and went inside to ask Grandma. When I did, Grandma knew exactly what to say. "Tell her she's welcome to play with you when you're in the yard, but I can't accept the responsibility for other people's children to play in the yard alone."

Diana said that would be all right, and we took turns shooting baskets for the rest of the afternoon. Even though I knew she wasn't there because she wanted to be my friend, I liked her, and I had fun.

January 20th was right around the corner, as Grandma would say. President Roosevelt was about to be inaugurated for his fourth term.

Diana came over to shoot baskets with me more often than I thought she would. We were quiet at first. I didn't know what to say to a girl her age, but she eventually started talking to me. One day she asked, "Do you have a boyfriend?"

"Yes. I have a boyfriend in my class at school. Do you have a boyfriend?"

"No. I don't have one." Diana quickly thought of another question. "Do you have any older brothers?"

"I'm an only child," I replied.

"I am, too."

I thought it was odd that Diana would bring up a boyfriend with a girl so much younger than she was, but I enjoyed having someone to shoot baskets with every once in a while.

George Washington's Birthday Program

Miss Gray finally announced who she had chosen for the program, and I was surprised I didn't get a part. I didn't want Grandma and Mama to know, so I still practiced the parts after school.

A few days later, Miss Gray took us to the auditorium and had several of us stand on the stage in front of the heavy burgundy stage curtains. She handed each of us a strip of white paper with one sentence to read about the flag. My sentence was, "The white stripes stand for purity."

I wasn't happy about reading only one sentence in the program when I'd hoped to be Betsy Ross or dance the minuet. I still wondered what Grandma and Mama would think when they came to see the program and saw other students in the parts, I practiced every afternoon.

That wasn't the worst thing that would happen, though. The worst thing was that I couldn't pronounce the word "purity" correctly. I said "purrity" and no matter how much I practiced at home and at school, I still couldn't say it correctly. I was discouraged because I didn't usually have a problem pronouncing words.

I wished Miss Gray would give the sentence to someone who could pronounce the word, but she didn't. I thought *Woe is me. I'll stand on the stage in front of an auditorium full of people and mispronounce a word in the one short sentence I have to say.*

Miss Gray had some of us march on the stage to the song *Stars and Stripes Forever,* and she said she'd choose one boy and one girl to lead it and carry the flags. I liked the march better than the minuet, but I didn't expect to be one of the leaders. She said a boy would be first and a girl would be second in the march. She chose a boy named Hugh, and I was surprised she chose me.

I was happy to be one of the leaders. I wouldn't have been disappointed about not getting one of the other parts if I'd known about the march.

One day, we stopped our rehearsal to exchange valentines, and I was nervous because I wasn't sure whether Ted still thought I was his girlfriend. He wasn't the type of boy who chased me around on the playground, kissed me, or passed love notes to me. At recess time, he was usually with one of the other boys, and I was with Patricia. When we happened to look at each other, he always gave me a little smile, and I smiled back. He was always nice to me, but he was nice to everyone.

Another boy in my class started passing little folded slips of paper to me. When I unfolded them, I saw that he'd written "I love you," but I never wrote notes to him.

When it came time to look at our valentines, there was a big valentine in the box, and I was happy it was from Ted to me. I was glad we were still boyfriend and girlfriend.

The day after Valentine's Day, after days of practicing more than a hundred times, I learned to say "purity." Grandma smiled and said, "I've always said practice makes perfect, and you proved it by learning to say that word."

On the morning of our program, the audience liked our march. We got a lot of applause, and the principal asked Miss Gray to let us perform the march for the upper elementary students in the afternoon. I was surprised and happy that we did so well, and Miss Gray said she was pleased with our performance.

She got us ready that afternoon, and we marched again. I don't know if we were just tired by that time or if we didn't start with the record, but we were out of step with the music. A couple of students' crepe paper sashes came loose and hung down, so I know we looked pretty frazzled. Miss Gray was disappointed in us, and I was disappointed, too.

That afternoon Mama brought up the subject of the play parts. "I knew the teacher wouldn't give so many parts to one child, so I went to the program not knowing what to expect."

I didn't want to go into all the disappointing details, so I just said, "I liked practicing all the parts."

When I thought about it later, I was glad I practiced the parts. I'd enjoyed playing the part of Betsy Ross and dancing the minuet in the living room every afternoon.

Mumps

About two days after the program, the glands in my neck started aching, and Mama called the doctor. He told her it sounded like the mumps on both sides of my face. He said my cheeks would swell, and I'd have to stay away from other children until the swelling was gone in about two weeks.

The doctor said it would be all right for me to play by myself in the backyard, but I should stay away from adults who hadn't had mumps. Everyone in my family said they'd had mumps, so I could still be around them.

My cheeks swelled, and the glands in my neck ached when I swallowed, ate, or drank. It was painful to chew meat, so I didn't eat it. I slowly ate things like soft-fried or soft-boiled eggs, Cream of Wheat, and mashed potatoes, but swallowing was still painful.

I stayed inside for the first couple of days, so Diana came to the door to find out why I wasn't outside shooting baskets. Mama told her I was going to begin playing again that day, but she wasn't allowed to come in the yard because I had mumps, and it was a contagious disease.

Diana insisted, "I know, but I had mumps years ago, so I can't catch mumps from Shirley."

"I'm sorry, but I'll need to have a note from your mother saying you've had mumps; she knows Shirley has mumps, and it's all right for you to play with her," Mama explained.

Diana came to the door the next afternoon with a note for Mama, and we shot baskets. We played together two or three more times while I was at home. She told me there was a new boy in her class and she liked him. She said she hoped he'd like her, too.

"Maybe he'll end up being your boyfriend," I said.

She smiled and happily agreed, "Maybe he will."

After that, I didn't see her for the rest of the time I was at home.

On the day I returned to school, I was at the front door of Grandma's house when I happened to see Adrienne coming from school carrying an armful of schoolbooks, so I asked her about her cousin.

"Oh, Diana doesn't come over anymore," Adrienne explained. "She was already mad with me because I didn't have enough time to spend with her, and now she's mad because she has mumps."

I thought to myself that I wasn't too surprised, but I told Adrienne, "Mama told her I had mumps, and she wasn't allowed to come in the yard. She and her mother said she'd already had mumps."

"I know, but she and her mother forgot she'd only had mumps on one side, so now she has mumps on the other side." Adrienne continued on, walking into the apartment building with her books.

The day after I went back to school, my class was coming inside from Big Recess, and we lined up in the hall beside our classroom. I stood too close to the radiator, and my leg came in contact with it, causing me to say, "Ouch."

Only a couple of students heard me and whispered, "What's wrong?" and "What happened?"

I glanced at my ankle, just above the cuff of my sock, and saw a big, red burn, but I didn't want to attract attention to myself, so I said, "Nothing's wrong."

Since we'd already had Big Recess, I knew school would be out in about two more hours, and I thought I could endure the pain until then.

We hung up our coats in the cloakroom and walked toward our seats. One of the girls who knew something had happened to me suddenly said in a loud voice, "Miss Gray, Shirley has a big red burn on her leg. She burned it on the radiator in the hall."

Miss Gray had the school nurse call Mama, and she came right away with a tube of Unguentine, a burn ointment. I went out in the hall with Mama and watched as she squeezed out a big blob of the ointment, which was sort of colorless and greasy, and rubbed it on my burn. She was as gentle as she could be, but the stinging nearly killed me.

We stood there while Mama screwed the cap on the tube and put it in her pocketbook. I looked at my ankle once again and saw that a blister, about an inch high and as big around as a quarter, had covered the burn like a dome. Mama told me to go back in the room but to be careful not to pop the blister because that would make it burn more.

I was embarrassed for the teacher and my classmates to see me with that big blister on my ankle, but they all seemed to be very sympathetic. When I got to Grandma's that afternoon, I asked her if I could pop the blister with a needle to let out the fluid so I wouldn't have to go around with a big bubble on my ankle.

"You have to let nature take its course, honey. It's nature's way of healing the burn. If you leave the blister alone, it will go away by itself, and the burn will heal."

Although I was tempted to pop the blister, I didn't because I knew I could depend on Grandma to know best.

No Birthday Party, but a Surprise

The New Year had gotten off to a busy start. Time seemed to be going by faster than usual, but that was all right with me. It was close to my birthday, and I could hardly believe I'd be eight years old in a few days.

Mama said since my birthday was going to be on a Saturday this year, she'd appreciate it if I didn't have a party and invited other children. I told her I didn't mind because the children never had a birthday party and invited me. There were also the hard feelings between Darrell and Jerry that always kept Jerry from coming to my parties. Worst of all, I'd had to hold up the gift of the pink underpants for the other children to see.

I thought I'd miss having a birthday cake, but Mama said I'd have one with the family. When it got closer to my birthday, Mama asked if I'd mind having the cake on Friday instead of Saturday. I didn't mind at all having it a day earlier.

On Friday, March 16th, after school, I had cake, ice cream, and ginger ale, but no peanuts, mints, "Happy Birthday" cups, plates, little mint and peanut baskets, and party favors. There was just Grandma, Mama, and me. Nita and BeeWee were at work.

Mama put eight candles on the cake, and I made a wish, but it was harder than ever to blow them out. Then, she handed me a small, simply wrapped package. "This is your only present from all of us. It's expensive, so we all chipped in."

I had no idea what it was until I took off the wrapping paper and saw a box from the jewelry store. When I opened the box, I was thrilled to see a wristwatch.

"It's a nice Gruen watch. It's an adult's watch, but because it has a cord band, the jeweler has adjusted it to fit your wrist," Mama pointed out. "You know how to tell time now and you've proven that you take good care of your things, so we thought it was time for you to have a watch."

Mama, Grandma, Nita, and BeeWee had been teaching me to tell time for as long as I could remember, but I never expected to get a watch. It made me feel good to think they noticed I took good care of my things and they thought I could accept the responsibility of wearing a nice watch.

Mama came over and put on the watch on for me. "Never take it off at school for any reason, Shirley. You can't get it wet, or it'll be ruined. Take it off before you take a bath, be careful not to splash water on it when you wash your hands, and don't let it get wet in the rain."

From the time Mama put the watch on my wrist, I could hardly stop looking at it. A gold watch with a black cord band was very stylish. Nita had one almost exactly like it. Daddy had a round gold railroad pocket watch, similar to BeeWee's, and Mama had a watch that she hardly ever wore.

I was concerned that Grandma didn't have a watch, but she said she didn't want one. She never wore any jewelry except a gold wedding band and a pretty Tiffany-style diamond engagement ring, which was a gold band with a single, raised diamond in the center.

Mama had an engagement ring with tiny chip diamonds and a matching wedding band, but they irritated her finger, so she hardly ever wore them. Mama said she didn't care whether she wore the rings because Daddy didn't have a wedding band. He said he didn't want to wear a ring because he might get it caught on something and injure his finger when he was working on automobiles.

I only took off my watch before I took a bath. I even slept in it.

I wore that same watch all the way through school and for about a year after I was married. I loved that watch, and I kept it in my jewelry box even after I stopped wearing it because it brought back pleasant memories.

A Sunny, but Sad Spring Day

After the cold winter we'd had, the milder spring weather was a relief. It was cool but comfortable enough on a sunny afternoon to wear just a sweater over our clothes.

Martha had invited me over, and I was putting on my sweater to get ready to go to her apartment when they interrupted one of the soap operas to announce that President Roosevelt had died suddenly of a cerebral hemorrhage in Warm Springs, Georgia.

We were shocked to hear it, but Grandma said, "I didn't think he looked well in the picture with Churchill and Stalin at the Yalta Conference. The poor man has been through so much, working hard to get the country out of the Great Depression and trying to get us through this war."

When I got to Martha's, we went out on her porch to swing. It was nice swinging on the second-floor porch in the cool air and warm sunshine. We were quiet for a while before I asked, "Did you hear about President Roosevelt?"

"I heard it on the radio just before you came over. Did you like him?"

"I liked him a lot, and I'm sorry he died."

"I'm sorry, too."

Tears rolled down our cheeks.

We continued swinging and crying, each of us holding on to the swing with one hand and putting our free arms around each other's shoulders.

I'd always thought a lot of Martha and wished she felt the same about me. I felt terrible when she said things that hurt my feelings, and she snubbed me after she started school. Our mutual admiration of President Roosevelt and our sadness about his death seemed to bring us closer together as friends.

When I went back to Grandma's, I found out that Harry S. Truman, President Roosevelt's vice president, was now president of the United States. I was worried about how we'd get through the war without President Roosevelt's leadership.

Easter Sunday and Easter Monday

I didn't get a new Easter outfit last year because I could still wear the one I got the year before, except for the shoes. Mama took me shopping to buy a new outfit, and we went to the shoe store first to be sure they'd have the shoes in stock. Last year, I'd seen Martha wearing white patent leather shoes, and some of the girls in my Sunday school class had started wearing them, but I didn't know if the store would have the shoes in my narrow width. We were lucky they had the shoes in my size, so Mama bought them, and we went to the department store to look for the rest of my outfit. It didn't take long to find a navy blue, lightweight wool coat, a light blue dress, a white patent pocketbook with a shoulder strap, and a white straw hat.

On Easter Sunday, I dyed eggs with BeeWee, and then Grandma and BeeWee gave me a basket with a big, white stuffed rabbit. We went to Sunday school and came straight back to Grandma's, the way we always did on Easter. Grandma and BeeWee put the dyed, cooled eggs in my basket, and BeeWee took pictures of me with his Kodak box camera as I stood on the front steps.

Afterward, I sat on the steps in the sun while Grandma prepared lunch and BeeWee took a nap. It was nice sitting in the sun, eating a hardboiled egg and a yellow marshmallow peep, but I missed Crissy. I wondered why I hadn't seen her lately. Maybe it was because I'd been spending more time shooting baskets in the backyard. Grandma eventually told me lunch was ready, and I went into the house to eat.

After lunch, I sat on the steps with my basket again, and I was surprised when Martha came over and sat with me. She was wearing the same colors. I guess they were popular for girls this year. She also had a big Easter basket and a big, white stuffed rabbit, like mine. I wished she'd been here earlier, so she could've been in the pictures with me. We sat and talked and ate candy from our baskets all afternoon, the way Crissy and I used to do. It was fun, but I still wondered about Crissy.

Grandma took Martha and me to City Park on Easter Monday. We had fun playing on the playground. Grandma got a Coca-Cola and peanuts, and Martha and I got cola snowballs and popcorn, and we sat on a bench to eat our snacks. Then, we played some more and went to the duck pond. I didn't roll down the hill by the duck pond this year, though; I just looked at the ducks.

Good News and Bad News

On April 28th, we heard that Mussolini, the former Premier of Italy, was captured and killed by a firing squad of Italians. A few days later, it was announced that Russian troops had captured a government building in Germany, where Adolf Hitler was hiding in a bunker. He knew he'd been defeated, so he committed suicide. After hearing the second news broadcast, I asked, "Does that mean the war is over, Grandma?"

"I don't know, honey. I guess it depends on whether Hitler has anyone who can take over for him."

"Do you think there could be someone else who is as mean as Hitler?" I was anxious to know.

"I don't know, but I certainly hope and pray that there isn't." Grandma sighed.

In May, we heard that Germany had surrendered. May 8th was referred to as V-E Day, which meant Victory in Europe Day. One of the generals who seemed to receive a lot of publicity in newsreels was General Dwight D. Eisenhower. I finally realized it was because he'd been the Supreme Allied Commander for the invasion of Europe since 1944. I thought victory meant the war was over, but Grandma said it was over in Europe, but it was still going on in Japan.

"Oh, that's right. Japan was the country that bombed Pearl Harbor, and that's why we went to war in the first place." I couldn't believe I had forgotten. After seeing the graphic newsreels of our troops and the Japanese troops fighting in the war, I often thought about it when I was trying to fall asleep at night.

As a very young child, I didn't understand why Japan, Germany, and Italy had declared war on our country. I did know from seeing the newsreels that Hitler was the leader of the Nazi party in Germany, and he was considered to be the meanest man in the world. Until the day he died, I thought he'd eventually invade our country and torture us.

As an adult looking back on these times, I think that it's terrible that a little girl would have to be so afraid. It was bad for me in the United States, but it was far worse for the children of Germany, Japan, and the other countries that were affected by the violence more directly – many of them and their families lost their lives.

Going to the Movies

It seemed to me I went to see more movies in 1945 than in any other year. Grandma took me to a movie at the Rosna Theater about one night a week during the months when the weather was mild enough for us to walk the three blocks to get there. Those months were usually May through September.

Grandma and I still liked musicals best because they were often in Technicolor, and we enjoyed the singing and dancing. We saw *Anchors Aweigh*, with Frank Sinatra and Gene Kelly. They played the parts of two sailors on leave, who had a good time and did a lot of singing and dancing. Another evening, we saw Betty Grable and June Haver in *The Dolly Sisters*. It was about the lives of two sisters who sang and danced in vaudeville in the early 1900s. I liked the movie, and I sang the songs *I'm Always Chasing Rainbows,* and *I Can't Begin to Tell You* from the time I left the theater until I went to bed that night.

One of my favorite movie musicals was *State Fair*, with Dana Andrews, Vivian Blaine, Jeanne Crain, and Dick Haymes. It was a movie about an Iowa family's experiences at the state fair. The music was by Rodgers and Hammerstein, who composed music for Broadway shows. The songs *It's a Grand Night for Singing* and *It Might as Well Be Spring* were beautiful and perfect for the movie, which was one of the best I'd ever seen. As usual, I sang the songs from the time Grandma and I left the Rosna Theater until my bedtime. The musicals made me happy, which was a good way to leave the theater.

I also liked the way they still showed three cartoons with every movie. Even though I still didn't laugh aloud the way some people did in the theater, I thought they were funny. The previews of coming attractions, the newsreel, and the cartoons were shown before the main attraction, the movie.

I saw in the newspaper, on the movie page, that a movie with Margaret O'Brien, a child star who was about my age, was coming to a downtown theater. Since Edward G. Robinson, one of Daddy's favorite actors, was in it, I asked Mama if we could go to see it. She said she'd ask Daddy, and he said yes. So, one Sunday afternoon, we stood in front of the theater with a long line of people, including many men in uniform, to see *Our Vines Have Tender Grapes*. I could tell Daddy wasn't happy about standing in the line. I'm certain we were only there because Edward G. Robinson was in the movie. When we finally got inside, there was standing room only. Some people didn't leave as soon as the movie was over. If they liked the movie and had the time, they watched it again. I hoped it would be a good movie, but not so good that everyone would watch it again.

Just before the movie began, most of the people who had seen it got up and left. The ushers showed us to the seats, but some people still had to stand. There were almost always people standing at the back in the downtown theaters. I noticed the rows of seats were closer together and not as well-padded as the seats in the Rosna. Mama told me it was because the Rosna was a newer theater.

When the movie started, I could tell it wasn't going to be the kind of action-packed gangster film that Edward G. Robinson was usually in. It seemed to be about a little girl growing up in a farming community in Wisconsin. I couldn't believe it. I liked the movie, but I missed some of the beginning of it, worrying that Daddy was going to be mad with me and want to leave. I didn't want to miss seeing Margaret O'Brien, but Daddy fell asleep in five minutes and slept through the entire movie, so I didn't have to. Thank goodness he didn't find out he'd stood all that time, and it wasn't even the kind of movie he liked.

On another day, Mama and Daddy took me to see *To Have and Have Not*, a movie based on an Ernest Hemingway novel. I wasn't old enough to read his books, but I knew he was a great writer. I'd noticed that movies based on successful books were usually good. The stars were Humphrey Bogart and Lauren Bacall. It was her debut in the movies. It was the kind of movie Daddy liked, but he still fell asleep. I didn't understand some of it, but I enjoyed watching Lauren Bacall and Humphrey Bogart. Not long after we saw the movie, Nita read in *Photoplay* magazine that they'd gotten married.

I liked drama better if I could understand it. Grandma and I went to see *A Tree Grows in Brooklyn*, a movie that was based on a book by Betty

Smith. I wanted to see it because Peggy Ann Garner, a child star, was in it. Dorothy McGuire and James Dunn were in the movie, too. It was about a young girl growing up under difficult circumstances in a tenement in Brooklyn, New York. I completely understood it, and I thought it was the best drama I'd ever seen.

Imagine an author being able to write a book that was good enough to be made into a movie, I thought. I looked forward to the time when I'd be old enough to read the books.

Important Events

While I worried about our country being at war with Japan for such a long time, I wondered if or when the war would ever end. Scientists in the United States were making an atomic bomb. In July, Grandma read that it was tested in an isolated spot in New Mexico.

Later in the month, we heard on the radio that a U.S. Army B-25 bomber airplane crashed into the Empire State Building in New York City, killing three people in the plane and thirteen people in the building. I didn't know until then that the Empire State Building was 102 stories high. We heard later that the accident occurred because the pilot was unfamiliar with flying in New York City.

In August, a United States Army Air Force plane dropped an atomic bomb on Hiroshima, Japan, and the United States demanded that the Japanese surrender. When several days passed and our government received no reply from the Japanese, a U.S. Army Air Force plane dropped an atomic bomb on Nagasaki, Japan.

The Japanese surrendered, and the surrender papers were signed aboard the battleship Missouri in Tokyo Bay on September 1, 1945. That day was designated as V-J Day, which meant Victory over Japan Day.

All of these events took place when I was getting ready to start third grade.

Mama took me to buy my usual brown leather oxford-type school shoes, which were still the only school shoes in my narrow width. The new shoes were always a size larger than they were the year before. I never liked them until they were a little worn and scuffed, which I thought made them look smaller.

I got the clothes I needed to replace anything I'd completely outgrown. I tried on the winter coat Mama bought me in the first grade, and it still fit because it was a size eight. In fact, the way the coat was made, it was still too big. I might be able to wear it until I left elementary school, after the seventh grade, which was fine with me because I liked the coat.

Martha and I still played together and talked about how glad we were that the war was over and how happy we were to start the next grade in school. She'd been nicer to me since April, even looking my way when we passed each other in school and playing with me sometimes after school. During the summer, we played together more than we ever had. I hoped she'd still be nice to me after school started.

I was so happy; it felt like a major reminder that God loves America. It was as if a big burden had been lifted off my shoulders. I would have been even more worried and scared about the war if I had known about what people experienced in the countries where the war was being fought; I learned about that much later. Although I had been happy in my life, our whole country had the weight of the war present all the time.

Everyone Played an Important Part in the War

Women played important roles during the war. Thousands of women served in the Navy as WAVES (Women Accepted for Voluntary Emergency Service), in the Army as WACS (Women's Army Corps), in the Coast Guard as SPARS, and in the Women Marines. Now they had to decide whether to make the service their career.

It wasn't the first-time women had served in a war. They'd been nurses, telephone workers, and clerical workers, and they still served in those positions, but in World War II, they were pilots, truck drivers, and airplane mechanics as well.

Women who'd never worked outside their homes before did amazing jobs of taking men's places on assembly lines in defense plants to make airplanes, tanks, parachutes, and every other kind of war equipment that was desperately needed. Those jobs were expected to be temporary, wartime jobs, but now many were no longer needed. The men who held the jobs before they enlisted were coming home, and many would expect their old jobs to be waiting for them.

Women and men volunteered at the USO to provide entertainment and an enjoyable gathering place for the servicemen and other community members. Men volunteered to be air raid wardens, who walked through the streets in helmets and knocked on doors to chastise anyone who had even a sliver of light showing through the side of a window shade.

While many people were directly involved in the war or working in defense plants, at the Naval Base, and at the Navy Yard, others played important roles by keeping the home fires burning and supporting the war effort.

Women took care of their families, and worked as long-distance telephone operators, nurses, teachers, salesladies, waitresses, secretaries, maids, part-owners and operators of 'mom and pop' grocery stores, elevator operators, and many other jobs.

Men who weren't fighting in the war were needed at home to keep the railroads and public transportation running, to mine coal and load it on ships, to work on farms, and to do the necessary mechanical work to maintain all private and commercial vehicles and machines. There were also other important jobs, such as bakers, doctors, insurance agents, mail carriers, ice men, truck drivers, and construction workers, to build housing projects. Our cities needed workers like trash collectors, telephone repairmen, utilities and bank workers, police officers, and firemen, among others, to keep things running.

All of those people who kept things going at home did everything they could to make life seem normal, especially for the young children during the war years. As children, we were aware of what was going on because the news was everywhere: on the radio, in the newspapers, in Life magazine, and in newsreels at the movie theaters or at school during rainy day recesses.

Beyond that, life continued on the home front. People were proud of the troops and glad to have had the scrap metal drives, rubber drives, and victory gardens. They sold war bonds, bought war bonds, and did work they never thought they'd do.

During the war, keeping up the morale of those in the service overseas and everyone in the country was important. We all looked forward to having something to do when we weren't working or going to school. The entertainment industry provided plenty of entertainment for everyone in the form of a variety of radio programs, movies, and records. Big bands traveled all over the country to play music for listening and dancing.

Bob Hope, the comedian and movie star, kept up the morale of the troops who were overseas by organizing USO shows with popular stars to entertain them. The shows were broadcast on the radio so we could listen to them at home. Bob Hope was very funny, and his jokes were tailor-made for the troops. It was good to hear the jokes, but it was even better for us to hear the laughter of our troops. The newsreels showed parts of the USO shows, so we could see the expressions on the troops' faces as they watched the shows.

We took pleasure in doing what we did for the war effort. There was the attitude that our troops were fighting for us, and we had done everything we could to help them.

Starting Third Grade

Starting the third grade was a nice new beginning, and it was even nicer not to have to worry about the war anymore. Although I was happy to start back to school, I was always apprehensive about starting a new grade. I worried about whether I'd like my new teacher if she'd like me, and if I'd have the same classmates as I had the year before.

I walked to school by myself on the first day. It would have been nice to walk with Martha, but we never seemed to leave home at the same time.

My new teacher was Miss Young. I wasn't good at figuring out an adult's age, so I estimated; she looked older than Mama and Nita, who were in their twenties, so she must have been in her thirties. She was a pretty brunette of medium height and build. She seemed to like the class, and I think everyone liked her.

I was happy to see mostly familiar faces and a few new ones in the classroom. A new girl was sitting beside me. I didn't know if she was new to the school or if she'd come from another class in the same building. Since she looked even older than Martha, I didn't think she'd want to have anything to do with me.

When the teacher had to leave the room, the girl started talking softly to me. She asked me my name and said her name was Lillian. She had long, medium brown hair that was curled on the ends, hazel eyes, and freckles. She said she was probably older than anyone else in the class because she was supposed to be in fourth grade.

I whispered to her, "I thought you looked older, but you seem too smart to have to repeat a grade."

"When I was in first and second grade, I had perfect attendance because I didn't get the childhood diseases that the other children got. I thought I'd never get them, but from the beginning of third grade, I got all of them, one after another," Lillian explained. "Since I missed so much of the school year, I have to repeat the whole grade."

"That's a shame, but I'm glad you're in my class, Lillian. I had chicken pox before I started school when I was four. That's why I have a little white scar on my face, and I missed two weeks when I had mumps last spring."

The teacher came back into the room, so we stopped talking.

During Little Recess, we walked around together on the playground and talked some more. She asked me if I had sisters or brothers, and, of course, I said no. I asked her if she had sisters or brothers, and she said she had two of each, but they were much older. The youngest one was a teenager.

I liked third grade better than any grade yet. I mostly liked that I could read so many good books. My classmates were nice, and I already knew most of them from first and second grade, although the new ones were nice, too.

I was too young yet to know what I wanted to be when I grew up. At that time, I thought that if I could ever be a teacher, I'd like to be just like Miss Young and teach the third grade, too. She made me feel the way I had hoped to feel from the time I started school—happy to be learning!

My New Friend and My Old Friends

Lillian and I seemed to talk naturally with each other during every recess. We never ran out of things to say. We especially liked to talk about movies and movie stars. She could carry on a conversation better than any child I'd known since I first met Jerry. Even Jerry didn't carry on a conversation after the first few times we talked.

I still liked Crissy better than any friend I'd ever had, and I enjoyed all the time we spent together. Although we didn't have conversations, we had a wonderful rapport and enjoyed each other's company. I think we always genuinely liked and understood one another. She was a true friend. I just wished we could play together more often, but she wasn't at home much anymore.

My other classmates were all nice, but we didn't talk a lot to each other. Ted and I were supposedly boyfriend and girlfriend, but we never talked enough to get to know each other. I thought he was nice, and I guess he thought I was nice. We always smiled, almost as though we shared a secret when our eyes met, and I didn't smile at just any boy. We, of course, shared no secrets since I knew next to nothing about him, and I doubt he knew anything about me. It was no secret that we liked each other.

Sometimes the teacher had the whole class play dodgeball on the grassy area between the basketball courts and the white clapboard church next to the playground. One day, when we were running around fast to keep from getting hit by the ball, a girl named Virginia and I tripped and fell on the grass at the same time. As we were getting up, she said, "You know what, Shirley? You'd have a good figure if you weren't so skinny." I just looked at her because I had no idea how to respond to such an unusual remark.

Martha and I still liked playing paper dolls together on her living room rug on some Saturday afternoons. We kept playing together sometimes after school, too. We didn't play in dresses and skirts anymore. As soon as I got to Grandma's after school, I went upstairs and changed to blue denim dungarees, rolled up to a few inches below my knees, and a red plaid flannel shirt. I wore my school shoes and short white socks, cuffed at the ankles. Martha dressed the same way, except that her shirt was blue plaid.

There was a lot we could do outside, but we often stuck to one thing all afternoon: hopscotch. The front of the apartment building had no grass, so Martha drew the hopscotch squares in the hard dirt with a stick. Some of us who played hopscotch liked to have our own playing piece that we used all the time. I had a pretty piece of dark blue glass that was flat and smooth around the edges. Martha played with a smooth piece of green glass. Other children would just pick up the nearest rock they found on the ground.

I don't know when Martha learned to skate, but she and I started skating together on the sidewalk some afternoons after school, one of us behind the other. I thought we skated pretty well because we didn't fall. We skated to the end of the block, turned left at the corner, and skated to the end of that block. Then we turned around, skated back, and sat on Grandma's steps. After two or three minutes, we got up and skated again. We would repeat that pattern for the rest of the afternoon.

Martha was still nice to me. Sometimes she even shot baskets with me in the backyard. Since we had started spending more time together, she would look at me even more often if we passed each other in the hall at school.

I hadn't seen Jerry since I started third grade, probably since I was in school all day and I played outside with Martha most afternoons. Since his mother kept him inside the apartment, I'd hardly ever see him on weekends. Over the summer, almost every child in the neighborhood, even Jerry and the teenagers, would play Hide and Seek, but we always stopped playing after Labor Day because the school-age children went back to school and had to do homework in the evenings. Even though I was spending more time with Martha during the week, Darrell and I still played Tarzan, Cops and Robbers, or Cowboys and Outlaws on Saturday afternoons in the backyard.

There are some things that I never outgrew, like the games that I played in the backyard with Darrell, but I really enjoyed how I had grown into games that the older children played. Lillian could always tell such creative stories, and Martha opened up to playing all kinds of games, not just Mother and Child. It was nice to have Lillian at school and Martha, Crissy, and Darrell after school, who all shared so many of my interests in games to play; we were always entertained.

Servicemen are Coming Home

I thought because the war was over, everything would immediately go back to normal, but I think everyone in the country soon realized it would take more time than we had anticipated. There were so many men overseas that it took time to transport all of them back to the United States.

One day, Grandma said that Nita told her Baxter was planning to come back to Norfolk instead of returning to his home state, but Nita didn't know exactly when he would return.

We were glad Baxter had survived the war, but we hadn't known him long or been around him to get to know him. Nita certainly hadn't told us anything about him. I just knew she seemed serious after meeting him. Even when he was away in the service and she went out with her girlfriends, she didn't seem like the happy-go-lucky girl she had always been.

Grandma and Mama said they had noticed a change in her, too. "Maybe she's in love," Mama wondered.

"Well, Florencie, if she is, I sure hope we get to know the young man she's in love with."

I felt as though he was already a member of the family because of the picture of him on the living room mantle and a picture of him on the mantle in Nita's room. The only other pictures on the living room mantle were those of Mama and Nita. There was also a "Christ is the Head of this Home" dark green cardboard sign in the middle of the top shelf of the mantle.

When I was a child, I thought that Baxter would return to Norfolk and that he and Nita would eventually get married, even if they didn't know each other very well.

October 1945

We were happy that rationing was over, but there were still shortages of the same things that had been scarce during the war. I asked Mama if she thought they'd made Halloween costumes this year.

"I don't know," she said as if she didn't really want to talk about it.

I always looked forward to Halloween because I liked to go trick-or-treating. "Do you think we could go to the store to see if they have any?"

"Your Dutch Boy costume will probably fit you perfectly this year since it's a size 8-10," she said, intending to end the conversation right there.

I felt like crying, but I bit my lower lip to try to hold back the tears as I walked from the kitchen to the living room and sat in the chair beside the radiator. Mama didn't know I was sad, and I didn't want her to know. After sitting there, fighting back tears for a couple of minutes, I was all right. After all, they might not have had the materials to make costumes yet; then I'd be crying over nothing.

I still wondered if they made costumes this year. I don't know why but for as long as I could remember, I'd wanted to be a gypsy on Halloween. If they didn't make costumes, I wouldn't be disappointed because it would be impossible for me to get one. If they did make costumes and even made a gypsy costume, I'd be even more disappointed.

In the meantime, everything was going very well at school. Miss Young had told us in September that her class would put on a program around the middle of November, and we had to begin practicing in October. After my experiences with the second-grade program, I wasn't excited about being in another program. I knew I was just another person in the class, and there was no reason for me to expect to get a particular part. If I got a part, I'd tell my family and practice just that one.

When Miss Young said the play would be *The Sleeping Beauty*, I never expected for one second that I'd have a part. She called on one boy and one girl at a time to read the parts of Sleeping Beauty and the Prince together. The class watched intently as each girl and boy took their turn. I was last.

When it was my turn, I saw that I was paired with a new boy named Victor. He was a nice-looking boy with wavy black hair and blue eyes. As he read the part of the prince, I thought he looked like a prince, but it never entered my mind that I looked the part of Sleeping Beauty.

After we read, Miss Young announced that Victor and I had the parts. She showed me a yellow crepe paper dress and said I could either wear that or one of my own dresses. I told her I thought the crepe paper dress was pretty and I'd like to wear it. I was surprised to get the part, but the class seemed to approve of her choices because they were all smiling.

That afternoon, as soon as I took off my coat and walked into the kitchen, I told Mama and Grandma about the part.

Grandma said, "That's nice."

Mama didn't say anything.

"Miss Young has a pretty yellow crepe paper dress for me to wear, too," I beamed.

"That's good," said Mama as she turned to continue listening to her soap opera.

We practiced for the play at school every day, and I practiced my part in the living room for a few minutes every afternoon. Then, I played outside.

One afternoon I went to the backyard and climbed to the woodshed roof to play Tarzan. After playing for a few minutes, Darrell came into the yard and said his uncle took him to buy something, and he wanted me to guess what it was.

"I don't know. Why don't you just tell me?"

"I'll give you a clue. It's something I've never had before," he said excitedly. I'd never seen Darrell have anything but a pair of rusty old roller skates that his uncle had given him, so I still couldn't guess. He finally told me his uncle had bought him an Indian costume for Halloween.

"Your uncle bought you a Halloween costume?"

"Yes. He took me to the store to pick it out. It's my first Halloween costume, and it's exactly what I want to be. My mother told me to ask you if I can go trick-or-treating with you."

"Sure, you can," I said, thinking how horrible it would be for me if the weather was not cold enough to require a coat.

When I went in the house that afternoon, I told Mama I knew they had Halloween costumes in the stores this year because Darrell's uncle bought one for him.

"You don't need a new costume until you've outgrown the one you have," she said sternly.

"Mama, I'm eight years old, and I've never picked out a Halloween costume. I've already worn the Dutch boy costume on four Halloween nights. The only reason why it still fits is because it's size 8-10."

"I'll think about it," said Mama, trying again to stop the conversation.

Grandma said softly, "Florencie, if you are running short...."

Mama interrupted, "That's not it, Mama. Shirley has a good costume that should fit her perfectly this year. She doesn't need a new one."

"Florencie, the child has never had the pleasure of going to a store to pick out a Halloween costume that she likes."

Seeing that Grandma was putting herself in the middle to try to help me and Mama was becoming irritated with her, I chimed in, "That's all right, Grandma. I'll wear the Dutch boy costume again this year. Then, maybe next year, I'll be able to get a new costume." Mama had obviously made up her mind, so Grandma and I didn't say anything else.

I tried on the Dutch boy costume, and it did fit me this year. Now that it fit, it wasn't bad looking.

I tried on the hat that came with the costume. I'd forgotten about the hat because I'd never worn it before; it'd been too big, and it was always so cold, so I wore my woolen hat. The Dutch boy hat actually looked kind of cute!

Mama said if I wore my Dutch boy costume this year, she'd definitely buy me any costume I wanted the next year. It's a good thing it finally fit me because Martha said her mother bought her a gypsy costume, and she wanted to go trick-or-treating with me.

Martha and I put on our costumes when we got home from school because Mama wanted to take a picture of us. Now that I'd grown to fit my costume and it looked cute, Martha thought it was new, and I didn't tell her that it wasn't. I didn't see Darrell and Crissy, and Mama wanted to take the picture while it was still sunny, so she just got a picture of me and Martha in our costumes. When the picture was developed, and I saw myself in the costume, I realized the only reason I'd never liked it was because it'd been too big for me.

The weather was mild enough for us to walk around in our costumes all afternoon. When I went inside to eat supper, Martha went home to eat. We agreed to meet in front of Grandma's house after supper with our big, brown grocery bags to go trick-or-treating.

The sun had gone down, so it was chilly enough for Martha and me to wear our navy-blue cardigan sweaters over our costumes, but we didn't even have to button them. Darrell didn't wear anything over his costume because it was big enough for him to wear clothes underneath, which made him look heavier than he was. Mama went with us to all the houses in our block and a few others that were nearby.

Children who appeared to be young teenagers were trick-or-treating by themselves because there wasn't a strict rule about not trick-or-treating after the age of twelve. No one cared if they still wanted to go trick-or-treating.

We got all different kinds of candy. Some people gave us small red apples, and one person invited us in to help ourselves to freshly popped popcorn from a big bowl. We each grabbed two handfuls and dropped the popcorn in our bags.

It was getting cool and damp, and we had to go to school the next day, too. So, Mama saw that Darrell and Martha got back to their houses safely, and I sat in the middle of the living room floor, opened my bag, and peered in at the loot that filled about a quarter of the big bag. Grandma said she would wash the apples.

Daddy came to pick up Mama, but he didn't come inside. Mama said he didn't care anything about Halloween because he'd never celebrated when he was a boy because he lived in the country and there were no other houses nearby. Mama and Nita had talked about having fun trick-or-treating with their neighborhood friends when they were children. Grandma and BeeWee never said whether they celebrated Halloween when they were children.

After I handed the apples to Grandma, I ate some of the popcorn. Then I ate the Hershey's bar that Grandma gave me. I closed my bag and carried it with me to the kitchen, where Grandma and I listened to the radio until nine o'clock, and then I went to bed. It was the best Halloween I'd ever had. Mama said I could pick out any costume I wanted next year, and I already knew what I wanted. Next Halloween, I wanted to be a gypsy.

A Package Arrives

There was still a slow return of the servicemen from overseas and a continuing shortage of the same necessities that had been scarce during the war.

Nita looked forward to Baxter's return from wherever he'd been during the war. I wondered if he'd be allowed to tell her where he'd been now that the war was over.

He'd told her months ago that he'd give her a late birthday present because he was waiting to get to a certain place to get her a special gift. A package finally came in the mail, and Nita took it to her room to open it. In the package was a rust-colored, medium-sized alligator pocketbook with what was supposed to be a real, stuffed baby alligator on the top.

We hadn't seen pocketbooks like that before. Then, as more servicemen came home, we began to see other young women carrying them; and we knew their boyfriends or husbands had been overseas.

Nita carried her alligator pocketbook every day. When Baxter came back to Norfolk, she carried it when she went on dates with him, even when she wore her mink-dyed muskrat fur coat. I hardly knew what to think of the alligator pocketbook. I think it would have looked great without the baby alligator. The design was nice, a nice clutch bag. The alligator made it look more like a novelty than a serious-looking pocketbook, but Nita loved it.

He'd gotten a job and a place to live somewhere nearby, but Nita didn't tell us what he did or where he lived. I didn't understand why she was so secretive about it.

War Bonds

They stopped selling war bond stamps to schoolchildren. I'd filled my ten-cent stamp book and started a twenty-five-cent book, but I'd only bought a few of those stamps. Mama said the quarters they'd given me for the second book were money down the drain because they couldn't cash in a book until it was full.

When Daddy went to the bank to cash in the ten-cent book of red stamps for a war bond, he was told he could still buy the twenty-five-cent stamps to complete the book and cash it in for a bond, but I guess he thought it would have been too expensive to finish filling the book all at once, so he lost about $2.50. It would have been nice of the bank to refund the $2.50 worth of war bond stamps already bought.

I had enjoyed buying both the ten-cent and twenty-five-cent stamps to fill up my war bond books. Looking back, I think it was a great way to get children involved in the war effort and for them to have the good feeling of contributing. I was sorry, though, that while Daddy was trying to do something good, he ended up losing $2.50, which was a lot of money back then.

The Sleeping Beauty

In school, we were about to present our play, so I invited Mama, Grandma, and BeeWee. Daddy was never able to come because he either had to work or he had worked all night and was sleeping. Nita always had to work.

When the play was over, we received a lot of applause, and Miss Young said she was very happy with the way we performed. I could see Grandma, Mama, and BeeWee smiling afterward, so I knew they liked it.

After school, when I went to the kitchen to talk with Grandma and Mama, I asked if they liked the play, and they said they did. Mama said she was surprised that I had the leading part in the play. "Mama, I told you about it a long time ago, and I practiced every afternoon."

"You told me, but I didn't know what to believe after you practiced everybody's part in last year's play," she explained. "If I'd been sure you had that part, I could have bought you a nice dress to wear."

"You didn't think the dress I was wearing was good enough? I liked it."

"It was pretty, but it was made of paper," Mama pointed out.

I thought Mama made it sound as though I was wearing a dress cut from a sheet of newspaper when the yellow crepe paper was made very pretty, with a round neckline, trimmed with a gathered, round collar and short sleeves. It was fitted at the waist and had a gathered skirt that was the same length as my dresses. I could see that it had been nicely stitched on a sewing machine. I wore my underskirt, which was a slip, under it, and I wore my Sunday school shoes and socks. Mama could have bought a dress made of cloth, but I don't think she could have found a prettier dress. Grandma said she thought the dress looked fine, so I didn't worry about Mama being concerned about my wearing a crepe paper dress in the program.

It made me feel great that the teacher said that she was proud of our performance. I was thrilled to have gotten the opportunity to play Sleeping Beauty, and I felt confident in the pretty handmade crepe paper dress. Looking back, it makes me wish that I had been able to have more opportunities to be in plays, but back then, there were not as many organizations and programs for children to be involved in theater as there are now.

Happy Days

I went upstairs, changed my clothes, and went outside to jump rope with Martha. She tied a long, old piece of clothesline rope to one of the railings on the first-floor apartment porch. We took turns turning the rope for each other to jump, and we counted aloud to see how many times we could jump without missing. This was a lot more fun than jumping by myself with my jump rope with the red wooden handles. After about an hour, we got cold and went inside our houses.

At school, we started learning songs that I liked a lot. The first one was called *Sweet Betsy from Pike*. Our class sang it at school every day, and I sang it at home all the time. Then, about a week before Thanksgiving, we sang *Over the River and Through the Woods*, which was also a favorite song of mine. I sang it at home, too.

Third grade was so much fun. I liked going to the school library, which was on the second floor of the building. It was a large room with shelves of books and sturdy oak reading tables and chairs. The librarian, Miss Braswell, appeared to be about forty. She had medium-length dark brown hair that curled around the edges, and she wore glasses. She insisted on our being completely quiet. She walked around shushing us even when we were already quiet, but she was nice, and I liked her.

I enjoyed looking at the books and deciding which one to check out to read at home. Some of my favorite books to read were the biographies of George Washington, Abraham Lincoln, and Dolly Madison.

One day, Miss Braswell handed me a book and said she thought I would enjoy it. The name of the book was *The Secret Garden*. I'd been flattered to think that Miss Young thought I was capable of handling the leading part in *The Sleeping Beauty*, but Miss Braswell flattered me even more by suggesting that book to me. She would never know how much she built my confidence by letting me know she thought I was capable of reading a book on a higher reading level. I checked out the book, and I thoroughly enjoyed reading it at the kitchen table every night while Grandma was washing and putting away the dishes.

After Grandma had noticed my new pattern, Grandma told me, "Your mother used to read all the time, too. She'd sit in the living room with her nose buried in a book almost every day. I had to call her three or four times to come to eat because she didn't want to put the book down."

I wasn't surprised to hear that Mama liked to read when she was a child because I knew she liked to read love story magazines. I liked that Grandma could see similarities between me and Mama when she was a child.

Thanksgiving

As usual, Grandma spent a lot of time cooking our delicious Thanksgiving dinner. Everything was the same, except she cooked more because Nita had invited Baxter to dinner, and she told Grandma he was a big eater. He enjoyed the food, and he complimented Grandma on her good cooking.

Afterward, everyone except Grandma sat in the living room and talked. Like BeeWee and Daddy, Baxter smoked cigarettes. I'd never seen him smoke before because he'd only been in the house long enough to pick up Nita to go out on a date. He and Daddy found out they were both from North Carolina, but they were from different sections of the state. Baxter was born closer to the center of North Carolina, and Daddy was born closer to the Virginia line.

I soon went back to the kitchen to talk with Grandma, as I usually did, and I decided to ask Grandma if I could dry some dishes and set them on the shelves.

"You don't have to do that, honey."

"But I want to learn how to do it, Grandma."

"Well, all right. Here's a dry dish towel, but remember you can stop when you want to." I wish I could say I was doing it just to help Grandma, but I really wanted to do it. Like all girls at that time, I knew I'd be expected to get married someday, so I'd have to learn to do things like drying dishes. It might have seemed like something silly for an eight-year-old girl to think about, but after observing Grandma and Mama, I already knew how old I wanted to be when I got married. I wanted to be twenty-two, the age Grandma was when she got married.

Once I started, I found that I liked drying dishes and putting them away. I wanted to dry all of them, but Grandma said we had to stop to go into the living room to spend time with the family.

An Unexpected December

Just as we had learned other songs earlier in the year, we sang *Silent Night* at school, and Miss Young sometimes played a recording of music from *The Nutcracker* by Tchaikovsky. It was really beautiful.

As soon as Santa Claus was in the W.G. Swartz department store window again, Mama took me downtown to see him. Another afternoon, we looked at clothes, and Mama held up some skirts and blouses in front of me. She let me put some change in one of the Salvation Army Santa's black kettles. Newspaper boys still sold papers on downtown corners, and I noticed that the buses, streets, and stores were as crowded as they'd been during the war.

We always looked forward to the day after BeeWee's payday when he bought the Christmas tree. I hurried to Grandma's after school to see it. He had strung the tree with lights, and it was ready for Nita and me to decorate.

After we hung the ornaments on the tree, Nita showed me the flat boxes of tinsel she'd bought. She pulled a handful of the shiny, silver strands from a box and showed me how bright the tinsel was compared with what we'd had to use during the war when they weren't making it. Before we could even get started decorating, I went to the kitchen to get Grandma, so she could see it too. As we stood there, talking about the new tinsel, we heard a hissing sound.

"Let's be quiet so we can try to hear where it's coming from," Grandma whispered.

Nita set down the tinsel, and we followed the sound to the kitchen, where we saw what was making the noise. Steam was sizzling from the tall, cylinder-shaped, aluminum-painted hot water heater beside the Arcola coal stove.

"Oh, my Lord, have mercy!" Grandma uncharacteristically shouted. "Juanita, you and Shirley need to stay in the living room but go upstairs first and get our coats in case the boiler explodes and we have to leave the house. I'm going to call the piers and tell them we have an emergency, and we need your Daddy to come home."

I was scared because I'd never known Grandma to call BeeWee at work. Nita and I went upstairs together to get the coats and then sat on the edge of our seats in the living room. Grandma came into the room, but she didn't sit down. She paced the floor, wringing her hands and nervously sniffing. Nita was nervously sniffing, too. I was too petrified to speak.

"The man who answered the phone said they'd get word to your Daddy right away, but it would take longer if he was unloading coal from his pier car to a ship. It's a shame something like this had to happen when the two of you were enjoying decorating the tree."

"Don't worry about it, Mama. I'm just glad it didn't happen when you and Shirley were here by yourselves or during the night when we were all asleep."

In a few minutes, BeeWee pulled the car into the driveway, hurried through the front door that Grandma held open for him, and went directly to the kitchen. We followed him but kept our distance in the back hall.

He opened the bottom cabinet doors and pulled out the round, galvanized dish pan, and placed it under a faucet at the bottom of the tank. He turned on the faucet to allow some of the hot water to drain into the pan. Then, he pulled on a pair of long, heavy work gloves. When the dishpan was three-quarters full of water, he turned off the boiler faucet and emptied the pan of hot water into the sink. He repeated that procedure several times until the hot water stopped sizzling at the top. Then, he took a long wrench from his toolbox and turned a valve at the top to shut off the boiler so the water would stop heating. "I've turned it off now, so it won't cause any more trouble. We just won't have hot water until the tank is fixed, if it can be fixed. I have to go back to work now. I'll see you later, at my usual time." Having averted a possible disaster, he took off his heavy gloves and rushed to his car to head back to the piers.

After he left, Nita and I started putting the new tinsel on the tree. Grandma followed us into the living room. "I don't know when I've ever been so nervous. I need a dose of Spirits of Ammonia. Do you want one, Juanita?"

"No thanks, Mama. I'm fine."

Grandma left and came back with a small glass of water with Spirits of Ammonia mixed in it. "Shirley, if you feel nervous, you can inhale this before I take it, and it will help to settle your nerves." I wasn't nervous, but I inhaled the Spirits of Ammonia because I liked to smell it.

Nita rolled her eyes and shook her head. "You're not nervous, Shirley."

I didn't say anything.

Grandma sat down and sipped the liquid in the little glass. "I know one thing. I'll never have another boiler in the kitchen."

"Don't worry, Mama. A plumber can probably fix it," Nita reassured her.

"You don't understand. I won't have another boiler and have to go through this again," said Grandma firmly.

"What will we do for hot water?" asked Nita in disbelief.

"I'll heat water in the kettle on the stove," said Grandma decisively.

We finished putting on the tinsel; Nita stood on the chair, reached to place the star on the treetop, and turned on the lights. It was wonderful to have shiny tinsel and to turn on the tree lights at night again.

I always liked decorating the tree with Nita because it was the only time she spent the evening with us. Grandma had baked Nita's favorite meal of steak, potatoes, and onions in gravy all afternoon, and we'd enjoyed eating it when Nita came home from work.

"Mama, would you like to hear my new record?"

"Sure, Juanita; what is it?"

"It's *Sentimental Journey* by Doris Day."

"That's a pretty song. I need to listen to some soft music like that to calm my nerves."

"I do, too, Grandma."

Nita rolled her eyes, shook her head, and said, "You don't have any nerves." She took the record out of the wrapper, put it on the turntable, and carefully placed the record player arm with the needle under it in the first groove of the record so the song would start at the beginning. She was trying to be careful not to scratch the record, too.

I hadn't heard of Doris Day until she recorded that song, and it became so popular. We liked the song so much that we asked Nita to play it again. At nine o'clock, I had to go upstairs to bed, but as I lay there waiting to fall asleep, I enjoyed listening to Nita's other records.

When Mama came over the next day, she was surprised to hear about the boiler.

BeeWee wanted Grandma to call a plumber, but she was adamant about not wanting to have a tank of hot water in her house again. She heated water in the large aluminum kettle and poured it into the sink to wash dishes. Then, she heated another kettle of water to rinse the dishes. When it was time for me to get ready for school, she told Mama to heat the kettle of water and take it upstairs for me to bathe at the sink. It was different and awkward, but I managed.

She heated a kettle of water and took it upstairs for BeeWee to shave and wash his face. He still took a shower at the piers every night after work to wash off all the coal dust, but he'd always enjoyed soaking in a nice hot bathtub of water on Saturday night, which required that Grandma heat several kettles of hot water and make several trips up and down the steps.

We all figured that Grandma would get tired of that and call someone to fix the boiler, but she didn't.

Christmas & New Year's Eve 1945

When Mama asked me what I wanted Santa to bring me, I said I wanted a bride doll because that was the new doll this year. I'd never had a grown-up doll, so I was excited about getting one. I didn't know what else to ask for because I thought I had everything anyone my age could want. I'd like to have something to ride, but I was at an in-between size: too big for a tricycle and too small for a two-wheel bicycle.

I listened to Santa's radio program from the North Pole, and I decided to write a letter to him this year. I hadn't written to him before because I didn't think I could write well enough, and I knew Mama would somehow let him know what I wanted.

They played the same Christmas music on the radio that they played every year, and I still liked the same songs. This year they also played a new song that I liked a lot called *Let it Snow! Let it Snow! Let it Snow!* by Les Brown and his Band.

I felt the same joy on Christmas morning that I always felt when I awoke and went downstairs to see what Santa had brought me. The bride doll was beautiful, and I got a few new clothes, a game, a watercolor set, and a book to paint in. My usual lumpy, clean, white work sock stocking was hanging from a big nail on the mantel, and I wouldn't have traded it for all the Christmas stockings in the world. I knew what would be in it before I looked, and I wouldn't have wanted it to be any other way.

When I took out each piece of fruit, each English walnut, and the broken pieces of hard Christmas candy wrapped in waxed paper, I felt loved.

The scents of the big, fresh Christmas tree in the living room corner, the turkey and dressing roasting in the oven, the tangerines and apples in the cut glass bowl on the dining room table, and even the coal burning in the Arcola stove in the kitchen intermingled to form one very special scent: Grandma's and BeeWee's house on Christmas Day.

We had our usual delicious meal with the family, and Baxter, who I suspected, even more, was a potential future member of the family. I enjoyed playing with my bride doll, especially combing her long, blonde hair and painting with my watercolors.

On New Year's Eve night, while I was sitting in the kitchen with Grandma, listening to Guy Lumbardo's music on the radio, I became as nostalgic as I always did at the end of the year. I knew I'd always remember 1945, just as I remembered the years before it.

When I made my New Year's resolutions tomorrow, I wouldn't have to start by wishing the war would end soon. That wasn't a resolution, but I always thought about that before I wrote my two resolutions. I'd have to think about what they would be next year.

Part VI – 1946

A New Year Surprise

I wrote two New Year's resolutions: "I want to continue doing well in school" and "I want to continue being a good girl."

The third grade was my best year in school so far, and I wanted it to stay that way. I liked my teacher, Miss Young, better than any teacher I'd had yet. She was nice, and I felt comfortable in her class because she was fair and didn't yell at us. I liked my classmates, too. Lillian was still my best school friend.

Being a good girl became easier every year. As I learned more in school and learned from my experiences, I learned more about what was right and wrong, too. After all, I was eight years old. I'd be nine on March 17th.

Aunt Nita would be twenty-four in a few days, on January 4th. It didn't seem so long ago that I was three and she was eighteen. Time seemed to go by slower when I was younger.

January 4th was on a Friday, and I was surprised to see Nita in the kitchen with Grandma, BeeWee, and Mama when I went downstairs to eat breakfast.

"Nita, I thought you'd be at work. Now I get to wish you a happy birthday!" I was thrilled that she was there so early.

"Thank you, Shirley. This is an especially happy birthday for me because I have some good news. I switched my hours with another telephone operator so I could tell all of you at the same time. Mama, I want you to sit down."

When Grandma sat down, Nita announced, "I'm engaged!" She extended her left hand over the table so we could have a good view of the ring. It was a pretty yellow gold band, with a single diamond in a Tiffany setting, just like Grandma's engagement ring, but with a slimmer band and a smaller diamond.

"Oh, it's beautiful! The diamond is sparkling," I said, aware of the awe in my own voice.

Everyone commented on what a beautiful ring it was.

"When did you get it?" asked Mama. She couldn't wear her own rings because the thin metal engagement ring and wedding band collected soap and water underneath and caused her finger to break out.

"I can't tell you that," said Nita in her usual secretive way.

After Nita didn't answer Mama's question, we were quiet. I guess we figured Nita had said all she wanted to say. I thought it was nice that she told all of us at the same time about her engagement and showed us her ring.

Then, I was surprised when she said she was getting married in two months and was going to have a private wedding in a minister's study. Only her best friend, Paulette, and her husband, Arthur, would be there to be witnesses. Not even the family would be invited.

She also told us they would go on the Old Bay Line steamboat from Old Point Comfort to Baltimore on their honeymoon and rent a furnished apartment in Norfolk to move to after the wedding.

Grandma, Mama, and BeeWee sat in shocked silence. I was silent too, but thinking about how happy I was and that I knew this was coming

Nita explained, "Mama, you know how self-conscious I am. I could never get married with people watching me."

"That's all right, Juanita. It's your wedding, so you should have it the way you want it," Grandma reassured her.

"Bill and I ran off to North Carolina to get married," Mama added. "Bill's cousin and the wife of the justice of the peace were our only witnesses, so I'm not one to say anything to anybody about their wedding."

BeeWee broke his silence, "Well, that's nice, Juanita. I'm going to the woodshed now to paint some fishing lures." BeeWee stood up and walked out the backdoor.

I'm sure BeeWee meant what he said. He must have been glad that Nita graduated from high school, worked at a good job for several years, and told the family about her plans ahead of time.

As Nita was leaving to head out to work, Mama, Grandma, and I each gave her a big hug, and then I went upstairs to get dressed. I was excited for Nita to be getting married.

A Time for Change

At first, I was happy about the engagement, the ring, and the fact that Nita was happy. I didn't have time to think beyond that because I had to finish my breakfast and go to school.

I was thinking about it the whole morning while I was sitting in class, but I didn't want to interrupt the lesson to tell anyone. Finally, during Little Recess, I told Lillian that my aunt was engaged to be married and had a pretty ring, but I was too busy to think about it again until I got home that afternoon.

When I went upstairs and changed from my school clothes to my blue denim dungarees and red plaid flannel shirt, it hit me that Nita was soon moving away from this house, and I knew I'd miss her a lot.

I hurried up and went downstairs before I started feeling sad. Mama and Grandma were in the kitchen, listening to the soap operas as they did every weekday afternoon. I thought that maybe playing with Martha could help, but Martha and I hadn't planned to play outside together because it was too cold.

As I was thinking about what would help cheer me up, I realized that I was hungry, so I asked Grandma if I could make myself a catsup sandwich, and she said I could. I opened the loaf of Nolde's bread and took out a soft, white slice. It was so good to have sliced bread again after the war was over. I shook some Heinz catsup onto the middle of the slice of bread and folded it over. That was my sandwich.

After I ate it, I picked up the morning newspaper from the top of the stack of papers Grandma kept on the chair by the back door and took it to the living room to read. I sat in the chair by the radiator and pulled the chain on the floor lamp to turn on the seven-and-a-half-watt bulb. As I read, my sad feelings about Nita started to go away.

I read that television had progressed to the point where manufacturers were making television sets, and although they were expensive, some people were buying them for their homes. I'd never seen one, but I thought it must look like a radio, with a place for a picture on it. I wasn't excited about television sets because I didn't think we'd ever have one.

On the next page, I saw that the cost of living had risen thirty-three percent since the bombing of Pearl Harbor. I hadn't learned about percentage yet, so I didn't know how high it was. Thousands of steelworkers went on strike to demand higher wages.

Another article talked about how some of those in the service were still in the process of coming home. They were going to need low-priced housing. A law called the G.I. Bill of Rights became effective in 1944 that guaranteed G.I.'s low-interest rates on loans for homes and for education.

There was a whole page dedicated to rations, and it said that gasoline rationing had ended, so there was a lot more traffic on the roads. The government planned to build expressways to speed up the flow of traffic. Sugar was still rationed because it was scarce. They expected it to be scarce until 1947. For the first time, I found out it was rationed because the government wanted the service personnel to have plenty of sugar and candy. They also used it to make rubber, gunpowder, and plastics. No wonder I could buy all the candy I wanted during the war. Since it was readily available for those in the service, it was available for the rest of the country, too.

I was amazed at how many things were going on since the war ended. It seemed to me that we had not only picked up where we left off before the bombing of Pearl Harbor, but we were moving at a much faster pace.

I stopped reading the news and turned to the funnies. After I read those, I turned to the movie page to see which movie was playing at the Rosna Theater tomorrow. Maybe Grandma would take me in the afternoon if the weather wasn't too cold. Then, I decided not to check the movie page because I knew the weather wasn't going to warm up for a long time.

When I went into the kitchen to put the newspaper back on the stack, Grandma and Mama were talking while there was a soap opera on that they didn't listen to. I put a kitchen chair beside the Arcola stove and sat with my back to it.

Grandma noticed. "Are you cold, honey?"

"No. I just like to feel the heat from the stove on my back."

She chuckled and asked me how school was that day.

"It was fine. I told my friend Lillian that Nita was engaged to be married, and she had a pretty ring." As I told Grandma about what I had said to Lillian, I started to feel a little bit sad again.

"That was nice. I hope you're not too disappointed that we're not going to see Juanita get married."

"Don't worry. I'm not disappointed about that. I'll just miss her after she moves."

"Well, she won't move very far away, and I'm sure she'll come to see us when she can," Grandma reassured me.

"I know you'll miss her, too, Grandma."

"I will, but Juanita's best friend, Paulette, is married now, and Juanita had always said she wanted to be married before she was twenty-five years old."

A few days later, shortly after Nita's announcement, Baxter applied for a job with the railroad, and BeeWee gave him a good reference. He got the job, but he didn't have a car yet, so he started coming to Grandma's every day to ride to work with BeeWee.

Nita was still working as a long-distance operator at the C & P Telephone Company, and she told us that she wanted to keep working there even after she and Baxter got married.

It was exciting to hear about Nita's engagement. Her dreams came true, and I was happy for her. Time goes by so quickly, and you just don't think about someone you love leaving until they do. My happiness for Nita outweighed my sadness about her leaving. Nita had always been a wonderful aunt to me. I wished her the happiness she deserved.

February 1946

The Monday before Valentine's Day, Miss Young made a pretty box for us to put our valentines in on Thursday, Valentine's Day. It was white, with strips of red, ruffled crepe paper around the top and the bottom edges of the box. There were red paper hearts on the sides and a wide slit in the box top for us to put in our valentines.

As usual, I spent the time leading up to Valentine's Day wondering if Ted would give me another big Valentine. It was too much for me to expect that he would still be my boyfriend in the third grade. I had sort of prepared myself not to be disappointed if he didn't give me one this year. After all, he still played with the boys, and I played with Lillian and our other girlfriends at recess. I knew no more about him than I knew in the first grade, and I didn't think he knew anymore about me. He'd never even chased me, passed a love note to me in class, or given me a quick kiss on the cheek and run away, the way a few boys had from the time I'd started first grade. We still smiled at each other, though.

On Thursday afternoon, when it was time to exchange valentines, Miss Young gave us cups of vanilla ice cream first. She asked me to take a cup of ice cream next door to Miss Rawls. She was a fourth-grade teacher with the best classroom in the building. It had practically floor-to-ceiling windows that overlooked the playground, and it was on the sunny side of the building.

When I returned to my room, we ate our ice cream. Then, Miss Young took the lid off the box and called our names to come to her desk to get our valentines. We were all happy when our names were called. If Ted didn't give me a big valentine, or he gave a big valentine to another girl, everyone would notice, and some children would comment on it. Even if they did, I planned to smile and say, "That's all right."

The suspense was almost too much for me. I almost wished he'd never given me the biggest valentines in first and second grades, so everyone wouldn't notice if he didn't give me one this year.

Finally, my name was called, and the big valentine in the box was from Ted. We smiled at each other, and I was very happy.

I didn't really think Ted and I were boyfriend and girlfriend anyway. That was something the class made up, probably because of the big valentines. I think he just thought I was a nice girl, and I thought he was a nice boy.

March 1946

It was still cold, but there were already signs of spring on March 1st. The daffodils poked through the cold soil in Grandma's front yard first, the way they did every year since my great-grandmother had planted them. I liked that because I felt as though a part of her was still here in the pale-yellow daffodils, the blue hydrangea, the purple wisteria, and everything else she planted.

Her presence was still here through the effort she made to buy the new house in Norfolk, plant pretty flowers and flowering trees, and cook good things to eat to make a home for her four young daughters after the heartache of losing her husband and twenty-one-year-old son within two years of each other. Grandma said the losses hurt the girls deeply, too. They all loved their father because he was a fine man, and they felt the same about their brother, who was a fine young man. She was able to do it because she had good girls who went to work and helped her. I was proud of my grandmother and my great-grandmother because they were strong women.

In March, I usually thought mostly about my birthday, but this year I thought more about Nita getting married. I wondered what she planned to wear. I knew it would be something nice. I tried to picture what she'd wear, but I couldn't because I'd never seen a wedding, even in a movie. One afternoon I asked Mama, "What do girls wear at their weddings when they're in the minister's home?"

"I think they wear white or light-colored suits. I remember what I wore to the justice of the peace's house when I got married. I wore a long-sleeved pullover, yellow woolen sweater and a woolen skirt, with a string of pearls."

"I'll bet you looked pretty, Mama."

"I tried to look my best before I left home, but it was a long drive, and I was a nervous wreck. Mama was the only one I'd told, so I knew Daddy would be mad when he found out. By the time we stood in front of the justice of the peace, my knees were knocking, and my hands were so sweaty I was trying to dry them with a handkerchief before your daddy put the set of rings on my finger."

I knew Nita would look pretty with her softly curled brunette, collar-length hair, dark brown eyes, and perfectly shaped red lips. She'd smell nice in her perfume. It was nearing the end of winter on her wedding day, March 10th, but the weather was still cold, so I figured that she'd wear her full-length, mink-dyed muskrat coat over her clothes to the minister's house and on her honeymoon.

As I thought about the wedding, I thought once more about how Nita would be moving out and started to get a little sad again. To get my mind off of missing Nita, I began to think about my ninth birthday. I could hardly believe that this would be my last year in the single digits.

Mama asked me what I'd like to do for my tenth birthday, and I said I'd like to go to The Acropolis restaurant to get a chef salad with Thousand Island dressing, drink iced tea, and play one of my favorite songs on the jukebox. Mama and Daddy had taken me there to eat supper with them one time, and I really enjoyed the salad.

March 17th came on a Sunday this year, so Mama said she'd like to take me to the restaurant after school on Friday, which was fine with me. I'd feel more comfortable with just Mama than if Daddy came with us. I loved Daddy, but I didn't get to know him, and he didn't know me because we didn't spend much time together. He was very quiet, probably because his father raised him to believe children should be seen and not heard, especially at the dinner table. I was afraid to try to talk with him while we were eating. On the few occasions when I went to wherever he and Mama were living, he sat in the living room chair and fell asleep.

Anyway, Mama and I had a nice time at The Acropolis restaurant together. I enjoyed the chef salad with hearts of lettuce and tomato cut into bite-size pieces, small cubes of ham and cheese, and creamy Thousand Island dressing. It was fun to sit in the restaurant with Mama, talking and playing songs on the jukebox. While we were eating, Mama said there were some new pants out called pedal pushers, and she was going to buy me a pair for my birthday, but she wanted me to try them on to see if I liked them.

We left The Acropolis restaurant and went to the children's department of a downtown department store. I tried on the pedal pushers, and I liked them. They were cotton turquoise and came a few inches below the knees to about the length that I cuffed my dungarees. The cotton wasn't as heavy as the denim dungarees, though.

At the end of March, Nita and Baxter returned from their honeymoon and went to live in an apartment in a nice section of the city. It was a part of someone's house, but they had the same privacy as they would have in an apartment house. They invited us over to see it as soon as they got settled, and we all liked it.

As I was sitting next to the Arcola stove reading the newspaper later that same week, I noticed that it said the divorce rate had doubled since 1940. Although Mama and Daddy were once separated for a short time, I never heard Mama say anything about getting a divorce. I'd only heard of celebrities, like movie stars, singers, and band leaders getting divorces.

Reading about marriage and divorce made me think about how I wanted to get married someday and live happily ever after, the way they did in fairy tales I'd read, like Cinderella.

The Promise of 1946

On April 1, 1946, we were all sitting in the kitchen when we heard on the news that the miners and coal workers went on strike to demand higher wages, safer working conditions, and health benefits. More than 400,000 coal miners walked off-site. Although Daddy had more seniority now, he was still laid off.

"I'll go back to work with my tools until it's over," he assured us. Daddy never forgot his automobile mechanic's skills, and by continuing to buy a few tools at a time, he'd built up a large collection.

Baxter, who'd just started working for the railroad, was also laid off, but Nita was still working, and Baxter said he would make money during the strike by painting people's houses.

Later that week, Mama took me shopping for new black patent leather Mary Jane shoes for Easter, but they didn't have my narrow size in stock. They ordered the shoes but couldn't guarantee they'd be in by Easter.

"Here we go again," I thought out loud, remembering the time a few years ago when Mama ordered the shoes, and they didn't come in until two days before Easter.

Mama explained, "I'd gotten used to shopping for your shoes earlier when they had a few narrow widths in the store, but the time slipped up on me this year because we were all thinking about Nita's wedding."

My coat and dress from 1944 still fit me. Mama always bought my clothes a little too large, sometimes a lot larger, so I'd get more wear out of them. I grew taller, but I didn't gain so much weight that I couldn't still fit into the clothes. Although my dress was now hitting above my knees, I didn't think anyone would notice because girls were still wearing their dresses above their knees even though clothing manufacturers were beginning to make ladies' dresses longer.

The Thursday before Easter, we got the call from the department store that my shoes came in, thank goodness! I am so glad that I wouldn't have to wear my old ones because my toes were pressing against the end of the shoes, and they were uncomfortable. Also, they looked bad because of the scuff marks and grass stains that couldn't be cleaned off of the white patent leather.

Just as we did every year on Easter morning, BeeWee and I dyed hardboiled eggs, and I went to Sunday school with Grandma and BeeWee. That afternoon Martha and I sat in the sun on the front steps and ate hardboiled eggs and candy from our baskets. I noticed Martha was still able to wear her clothes from the Easter before last, too.

On Easter Monday, Grandma took Martha and me to the city park, and we had a good time playing on the playground. We took our usual break to sit on a park bench and munch on our popcorn and the crushed ice in our snowballs while Grandma ate her nickel bag of peanuts and drank her small Coca-Cola.

In May, after 59 days on strike, President Truman and the leader of the United Mine Workers of America struck a deal known as The Promise of 1946, which met the demands of the workers, providing them with health care, higher wages, and pensions. Daddy and Baxter soon went back to their regular railroad jobs.

Pinocchio and a New Dime

In June, Mama and Daddy took me downtown to the Colonial Theater to see Walt Disney's *Pinocchio*. The Colonial was one of the theaters on a side street downtown. The admission price there was the same as at neighborhood theaters because they didn't show first-run movies.

Pinocchio was Walt Disney's second feature-length animated film. It was a wonderful movie, and *When You Wish Upon a Star* was one of the prettiest songs I'd ever heard. Listening to that song was like being lifted to the stars. I looked up at the silver-colored sprinklers in the ceiling and pretended they were stars.

Mama said she'd taken me to see the movie when it first came out in 1940, but I was only three years old, and I couldn't sit still and concentrate. I walked up and down our row and played with the seats.

She talked Daddy into taking us to see *Pinocchio* so they could see one of the shorts, which were short films that I thought they showed only at that theater. They were often comedies with Laurel and Hardy or The Three Stooges. Daddy liked those comedies so much that he laughed out loud at them. I'd hardly ever heard him laugh at all. Sometimes there were western shorts, with a group of cowboys singing and playing music. Mama and Daddy hoped to see some of their musician friends, whom Daddy had met while working at the automobile dealership, in those western shorts, but I don't think they did.

A new dime was in circulation with President Franklin Delano Roosevelt's picture on it. The Mercury-type dime had been in circulation through 1945, and it would still be used, but from now on, they'd only make Roosevelt dimes. I was glad President Roosevelt was honored in that way because I thought he deserved it.

Whooping Cough

I was happy that summer was here, but I already missed being in school. I didn't miss the routine of getting ready for school and doing schoolwork. I missed being with the other children in my class, especially Lillian. The girls in my class either lived on the other side of the busy Hampton Boulevard or rode the bus from Navy housing, so we didn't see each other during the summer.

The weather was warm, and I liked being able to go out in the backyard every morning to enjoy the warm, sunny weather, the colorful flowers, and the sweet scent of honeysuckle.

I still liked to climb up the wisteria vine to the woodshed roof and sit with my feet and legs dangling over the edge. They dangled a lot farther down now than when I'd climbed up there for the first time.

BeeWee still made his fishing lures in the woodshed. When he stepped outside to smoke, he was coughing more now than ever. I soon began to cough, too. I wondered why I was coughing like BeeWee, so Grandma told Mama she should call the doctor and tell him about my cough.

The doctor said I probably had whooping cough because he'd heard of a lot of cases of it this summer. He said I'd have to stay at home, away from other children, until I stopped coughing. At least I was out of school for the summer, so I didn't have to miss a lot of time.

I nearly coughed my head off. It wasn't that I was coughing all the time; I'd be fine for a long time and then start on a coughing jag that I could hardly stop. It was like getting a tickle in your throat and not being able to stop coughing until you drank some water. Unfortunately, water didn't always help when I had whooping cough, and that was especially frustrating. A few times, I coughed until I lost my breath, which was scary. I'd seen BeeWee do that, so now I knew how he felt. It also gave me a better understanding of how Nita felt when she had an asthma attack as a child.

Like chicken pox and mumps, whooping cough lasted about two weeks, and then I was fine. Now I'd had all the childhood diseases that most children got these days except measles. After I was well, it was good to be able to play with the other children, go to movies, and go out with Grandma and BeeWee on payday again.

An Unexpectedly Dangerous July 4th

We never celebrated July 4th. It was one of the quietest days on Grandma's street. Since it was a holiday, Daddy had the day off, so Mama spent the day with him. BeeWee and Nita always had to work on July 4th. The day was so quiet that the popsicle man didn't even come by.

When I went into the backyard that morning, it was already hot, and everything I tried to do, like shooting baskets, made me hotter. Baxter not only came to ride to work with BeeWee every day, but he also came to eat lunch, so there were no leftovers for supper.

Grandma and I had Campbell's soup with bread and butter and then sat in the dark green rocking chairs on the front porch. There were no children playing Hide-and-Go-Seek, and no one was going for a walk.

Since the time I'd asked Grandma if we could get ice cream cones and I lost her dimes in the cracks of the floor, I'd never asked for ice cream cones again. Besides, even if she ordered them from the drugstore, they'd be melting by the time the delivery boy brought them to us. I still liked my ice cream hard and cold, so I could hold the cone and bite into the ice cream instead of licking it as it rolled down the cone onto my hand.

I rocked in the rocking chair and played the cars game by myself. I guessed what color car would drive by next, and I kept a mental record of how many I guessed right. It was hot on the porch, but it was even hotter in the house, so we couldn't go inside and listen to radio programs.

A car pulled into the driveway and stopped. Mama and Daddy got out and came up on the porch. At first, I thought it was nice that they'd dropped by to see us. Then I saw they were upset, and I knew something must have happened.

Grandma told them to have a seat on the glider. After they both sat down, Mama told us what had happened. She said they rented a fishing boat at Lynnhaven that afternoon and went out for Daddy to fish. I was surprised to hear that because I didn't know Daddy had ever fished.

Mama said Daddy rowed the boat pretty far out, but they could still see the shore. Daddy dropped the anchor in the water, which was still at the time. Daddy fished for a while, but they were hot, and the fish weren't biting, so they prepared to leave. Daddy pulled up the anchor and began to row back to shore. They felt a little breeze, which they welcomed at first because they were so hot. The breeze became steady and strong, and the current was carrying the boat toward the pilings under the railroad trestle. Daddy could no longer use the oars to guide the boat, so he stopped rowing and pulled the oars into the boat.

Daddy told Mama they'd each have to grab a piling and hang onto it when the boat went under the trestle. Somehow they were able to grab the pilings. Their arms were scratched, but they stopped the boat. They climbed up slippery rocks covered with wet, green seaweed to get back to shore. Then, they walked back to the boat rental place and told them where they could find the boat.

Mama and Daddy said they'd never go out in a small boat again.

Grandma and I listened to their story without saying a word because I think we were both shocked.

Grandma found her voice. "Well, I'm thankful you're both alive after a dangerous experience like that."

Mama and Daddy got up to go.

"You're welcome to sit here on the porch with us," Grandma offered.

"Thanks, but we have to go because Bill has to go to work in the morning. We just stopped by to tell you what happened to us."

"Well, I'm just glad you're all right," said Grandma, still in disbelief.

BeeWee's Vacation

Several days later, everyone except Daddy happened to be in the kitchen together. Since BeeWee always took his vacation in July and there was no gas shortage this year, I thought everyone would be anxious to go back to the beach at Lynnhaven. I decided to bring up the subject while everyone was here together. "You want to go to Lynnhaven to fish, don't you, BeeWee?"

"I always like to go fishing, but Lynnhaven's a long way to go." BeeWee took a sip of his coffee from his saucer.

BeeWee was such a good fisherman; he could catch fish in any water that had fish. He often kept his fishing gear in the trunk of the car and fished from the coal piers when he got off from work.

"Grandma, don't you want to go?"

"Well, I don't know. It seems like a long time since we've been to Lynnhaven, and too much sun gives me a sick headache," she reminded me.

"Mama, you want to go, don't you?"

"I don't want to go to Lynnhaven anymore," she said firmly.

I couldn't believe what I was hearing. "You don't want to go to Lynnhaven? I thought you'd liked going there since you were a child."

"I liked it until Bill, and I went out in that boat on the Fourth of July."

Aunt Nita said she couldn't go because she hadn't been feeling well lately, and that worried everyone. Grandma was able to persuade Nita to make an appointment with the doctor.

I was disappointed about everyone's lack of enthusiasm about going back to the beach, but like the rest of the family, I was concerned about Nita.

When BeeWee's vacation came, BeeWee fished at the same place where he'd fished during the war. Grandma and I went with him, and we stopped for peach ice cream cones on the way home. I always liked to do that.

He also took some time during his vacation to paint, as he always did. I was glad he was painting the outside of the house since the fumes from the oil-based paint sometimes gave me a headache when he painted inside. I watched him paint, and then I skated on the sidewalk before it got too hot. Sometimes Martha skated with me.

I understood why Mama and Daddy wouldn't want to go back to Lynnhaven so soon, and I knew that Nita wasn't feeling well, but I still wished that we had been able to go to Lynnhaven during BeeWee's vacation. It was one of the only fun family outings that we still hadn't done since the war ended. I still had a nice time going with BeeWee to his wartime fishing spot and going to get the peach ice cream cones together with him and Grandma.

Summer Friends and the Final Dare

Darrell and I were older now, but we still liked climbing up the wisteria vine to the woodshed roof and playing Tarzan. We often galloped around Grandma's yard on brooms, pretending to be cowboys, outlaws, or lawmen on horses. I liked imagining we were riding in the west, with nothing but wide-open spaces and blue sky, as I'd seen in Western movies.

I hoped my summer friend from Pennsylvania would come back to visit her grandparents in the apartment building since the gas shortage was over, but she hadn't come yet.

Crissy and I sat on Grandma's steps and talked some Sunday afternoons. Grandma lowered the awnings in the summer, so the dark green and white striped awning over the steps provided shade on a hot afternoon.

On some hot or rainy afternoons, Martha would invite me to her apartment to play with her paper dolls.

For all of June and most of July, I'd only seen Jerry when all the children on the street played Hide-and-Go-Seek after supper. Then, one day when I was leaving Martha's, he cracked open the door to his apartment and whispered for me to come to the back of the building.

I remembered our past conversations and looked forward to talking with him again, but he just said he wanted to show me something.

Jerry slipped out of his house and joined me on the sidewalk in the back of the apartment building. "Would you like to see something I can do?"

"I guess so. What can you do?"

"Stay right where you are, and I'll show you."

As he walked up the black iron steps to the second floor, I thought, *Here we go again. Jerry must have forgotten the time he'd slid down the railing from the second floor and dared me to do it.*

He reached the second floor, climbed the steps to the third floor, and slid down the railing.

"That was good," I said, although I was not really that impressed.

"I'll bet you can't do it," he dared.

I remembered when he'd dared me to do dangerous things when I was a lot younger. I'd done everything he'd dared me to do except to slide down the rail from the third floor.

"Why should I do it?" I couldn't think of one reason.

"If you can do it, you should prove you can," he pressed on.

"To tell you the truth, Jerry, I don't want to do it," I said firmly.

"You're just saying that because you know you can't do it."

"Maybe I can; maybe I can't." I turned around and walked to Grandma's.

Someday, I might decide to go up to the third floor of the apartment building to try to slide down the pole, but I would do it because it was something I wanted to do, not because Jerry dared me to do it.

Back to Lynnhaven

BeeWee and Grandma finally decided to go to Lynnhaven one day later in the summer, but we went later in the afternoon when the sun wasn't as bright, and it wasn't as hot. On the way, we saw the tall sand dunes and marveled over the view of the beach and the water from the top of the bridge. We went to the beach on the other side of the road from where we used to go so BeeWee could fish from the water's edge. Grandma could easily see him and let him know when we were ready to go. I liked watching him cast his line in the water.

Sitting on the sand, watching the waves roll in and out over the shoreline, and smelling the salt air reminded me of why I'd missed going to Lynnhaven for the past few years.

After we were there for a couple of hours, I had to go to the bathroom, so we went home.

I was glad Grandma and BeeWee took me back to Lynnhaven, although they didn't particularly want to go. I would have been disappointed if we hadn't gone at all that summer. It was a nice feeling to be able to do something that we hadn't been able to do for so long because of the war; it felt like things were returning back to normal.

Not long after that, Nita finally went to the doctor and told us she was expecting a baby in January. We were all happy to hear the news.

Grandma told me that it meant that I would be a cousin soon, which was very exciting for me. I was so happy for Nita to have a new baby, and I was excited for our family to grow.

Starting Fourth Grade

Mama and I soon shopped for school shoes again—the same brown leather, laced shoes that I got every year. Most of my classmates wore brown leather shoes, but they had a choice of styles.

I was happy to get Miss Rawls as my fourth-grade teacher because she had the best room in the building. I liked the almost floor-to-ceiling windows that overlooked the playground, not that I was going to gaze out the windows all day. I liked the brightness they gave the room.

Miss Rawls was a tall, middle-aged teacher with light auburn hair pulled back into a bun. She wore glasses, cotton dresses, and black laced shoes with wide two-and-a-half-inch heels.

Most of my classmates were back, including Lillian and most of the girls I'd known and had played with at recess since first grade. Ted, the boy I liked best, the only one I'd thought of as a boyfriend, wasn't in my class this year. I guess he must have moved during the summer.

There were some new students in my class. I thought a boy with auburn hair and freckles was nice and would make a nice boyfriend, but he had already liked a new girl in the class who had naturally curly hair and wore red lipstick. I thought they both lived in Navy housing. There was also a nice, cute girl named Fay, who lived in Navy housing, too. She played with us at recess.

In a few weeks, a nice boy named Tommy joined our class. He resembled Ted because he was the same size and had brown hair, except that he had a crew cut, and Ted didn't. When I received a little folded scrap of paper that said, I love you, Tommy, I knew I had a new boyfriend.

I wasn't fickle. If Ted hadn't moved, I'm sure I would have ignored Tommy's note. Anyway, wherever Ted was, he probably had a new girlfriend who would be the lucky recipient of his big valentines from now on.

Fourth grade wasn't just about having friends at school. I enjoyed learning about Virginia history. The fact that eight United States presidents were born in Virginia was very impressive.

My Favorite Halloween Costume

Around the first of October, Mama took me to buy a Halloween costume. It was fun and exciting to shop for my costume. I wanted to find a size 12-14 gypsy costume, which was the largest size they had, so it would last for the rest of my trick-or-treating days.

We found one Halloween costume and took it out of the box. I held it up in front of me to be sure it wasn't too long. The length was just right. It was a much larger size than I needed, but there was elastic in the short sleeves and at the waist, so it wouldn't look baggy. I tried it on when we got back to Grandma's and showed it to her and Mama. They liked it and said they'd look in the dresser drawers for old jewelry for me to wear with it.

Shopping for a Halloween costume for the first time was amazing. The old jewelry Mama and Grandma found for me was perfect. I could hardly wait to put on my costume when I got home from school. Darrell and Crissy came over. He was wearing his Indian costume, and Crissy was wearing a gypsy costume. Mama took a picture of us in front of Grandma's house. We went to our houses to eat supper, and then we met again to go trick-or-treating. Each of us carried a large brown grocery bag in anticipation of receiving lots of treats.

We went to as many neighborhood houses as we could before the night air became too chilly and damp. We said goodnight to each other and went to our houses to check our loot. I sat on the living room floor and ate the popcorn that one of the neighbors always gave me and the milk chocolate Hershey bar that Grandma always gave me. Then, I got ready for bed because I had to go to school the next day.

Being a gypsy was so much fun! I like still having Darrell and Crissy to go trick-or-treating with, too. I was so lucky to have my costume and my friends.

November 1946

In school the next day, the teacher had changed the Halloween decorations to cardboard turkeys and pumpkins for the upcoming Thanksgiving holidays.

At Grandma's, there was the annual lace curtain washing, starching, and stretching. Although I was a bit older and might have been able to help, the tradition remained a two-person operation with Mama and Grandma. Every year, Mama continued to prick her finger over and over, seemingly hundreds of times, and each time shouting, "Ouch!" I watched and learned, confirming that I still did not want to have these curtains when I grew up.

Nita had gradually been gaining weight as her baby got larger, causing her back to hurt more. In her job as a long-distance telephone operator, she had to work at a switchboard. At that time, telephone operators didn't stand, but they did sit on high chairs, like the ones you would sit at around a counter. The high chairs were hard on the telephone operator's backs, who weren't already in the family way, and Nita's ended up hurting so bad that she needed to quit her job at the telephone company.

We all enjoyed being together for Grandma's delicious Thanksgiving dinner. Mama, Daddy, Nita, Baxter, Grandma, BeeWee, and I all celebrated the day together. Next year, we would have my new cousin joining us as well!

I was happy to have the Friday after Thanksgiving off from school. I skated in the house after breakfast, and when it got sunnier and a little warmer, I went outside and skated on the sidewalk. I was surprised that Martha came out and skated with me for a while.

She hadn't been as friendly to me since she'd started fifth grade, which was on a different floor than the fourth-grade classroom. I wasn't too surprised that she became uppity again when she moved upstairs and had made a new friend at school.

However, my feelings weren't hurt this time because I had my own school friends now.

Mama and BeeWee said they wanted to take me to the bike shop so I could sit on the bicycles to see if I was big enough to ride one. I sat on a bicycle, but it was too big for me, so I still couldn't ask Santa to bring me one for Christmas; maybe I could next year.

December 1946

Mama took me downtown to see Santa Claus, and I listened to him on the radio. I wrote him a letter, but I didn't know what to ask for because I wasn't big enough to ride a bike.

BeeWee bought another ceiling-high Christmas tree, put it in the old iron stand, and strung lights on it. He'd added a new string of lights that just came out this year. They were Noma bubble lights. The lights were shaped like candles and were in the same colors as the other lights. When they had been on for a couple of minutes, the liquid inside would bubble. I liked that.

I looked forward to decorating the tree after school that day. Nita was at Grandma's to help to decorate the tree that afternoon, and Mama was putting the bulbs in the window lights. Grandma brought the ornaments downstairs.

This year, I was the one who stood on the chair to put the ornaments on the upper branches of the tree because Nita couldn't stand on the chair. She handed the ornaments to me. Mama put the ornaments on the hard-to-reach back branches and put the star on the treetop. I stood on the chair to put tinsel on the top branches. Then, Nita, Mama, and I put it on the rest of the tree. It was finished, and Grandma said it looked as pretty as ever.

We celebrated Christmas Day the same wonderful way that we always did, but this year there was a lot of talk about the new baby that Nita expected in January. Mama said this would be the last Christmas and the last year I would be the only grandchild in the family. She said I'd have to get used to the family paying attention to the new baby. That was all right with me. I was looking forward to paying attention to the baby, too.

Grandma and BeeWee always made the Christmas holidays special for the family in a nice, quietly exciting way. I'll never forget the feeling of anticipation leading up to Christmas Day that made me so happy.

They were memory-makers, and what wonderful memories they were. I'll always remember BeeWee's enthusiasm for the season, especially everything he did to get the big, live Christmas tree every year and string the lights on it for Nita and me to decorate. Grandma always cooked all day on Christmas Eve and into the early hours of Christmas morning so we could enjoy the wonderful food in the late afternoon as we sat around the dining room table together. I loved when the family got together like that. All of these things that they did to make us so happy, they did to keep our family traditions alive. I was very fortunate to have my grandparents to help me to see the importance of traditions and gathering together as a family.

I was happy for Nita, and I thought about the baby very often; mostly, I wondered whether it would be a girl or a boy. There had been no boy in the immediate family for many years, so I wondered how it would turn out this time. I looked forward to seeing the baby, and I could hardly wait until he or she could talk. I liked the idea of having a cousin that I could talk to and play games with, simply enjoying each other's company.

I grew so much in the past year. I was so happy to have been able to read full chapter books now; I especially loved biographies and The Secret Garden. My confidence grew so much this year, and I am excited to see how much more I grew in 1947. Because Nita got married and started her family this year, I have begun to think a lot about how I want to be when I grow up, and this year when I make my New Year's resolution, I will think about how I can work to achieve my goals.

Looking Back and Looking Forward

Many people might think children have no worries because they're young and they don't have the responsibility of adults. Like everyone else, I had my own worries, though, plus worries about the United States being bombed by one country and being invaded by another country. Living near one of the largest naval bases in the world made me feel uneasy because I knew it was a prime target for bombing. I was relieved when those countries were no longer our enemies.

It was so nice the way that Grandma and BeeWee thoroughly enjoyed making the Thanksgiving and Christmas holidays wonderful for all of us, no matter what was going on with the war. They put in a lot of work and love to make us happy. It was our tradition, something we looked forward to all year. I loved it when the whole family was together.

As time went by, I knew there would be inevitable changes. From the morning that Nita made sure we were all together over a year ago to tell us she was getting married, the changes happened quickly. In January 1947, we were all excited with the birth of Nita's son.

While Nita's life was moving forward, I started to think about what my life would look like when I got older. My role models were close to me. They were Grandma and Nita. I admired them for everything they were, and I wanted to be like them in every way.

I would be ten on my birthday in March, and so far, I didn't have many plans, but I knew that I wanted to graduate from high school and get a job like Nita. In 12 years, I would be 22, the age that Grandma got married, and I decided that I wanted to get married then, too. I was looking forward to the changes in my own life. I wanted to eventually have what my grandparents had: marriage, my own home, and a family. To have that, I had to take it one step at a time.

At first, I thought I couldn't have a regular family because my mother and father were always moving around and didn't seem to care about me. It took me all these years to realize that I had a wonderful family, and it was a complete family—BeeWee, Grandma, Nita, and me.

At going on-ten, I was happy with my life. My childhood wasn't ruined by the war, and it wasn't ruined by having young parents who moved all the time. I enjoyed being a child, doing the things that children do. I was blessed to be able to live with Grandma and BeeWee. Their house, yard, and neighborhood were perfect for raising children. Although they'd already raised their own, Grandma loved children and had a big enough heart to take on one more, thank God.

I appreciated everything that my family did for me more than I can ever find the words to say, but God got me through the toughest times and provided me with the angel that I so desperately needed: Grandma.

Acknowledgments

A special thanks to my daughter and granddaughter, Susan and Katie Baskerville, for the countless hours they have devoted to working with me in our "book sessions". Thank you to Susan for her determination and passion for igniting the editing process and for coordinating the culmination of our final product. Thank you to Katie for always bringing her creativity and love to our sessions, for collaborating with me, and for helping her "Maga" work on this book about her own experiences as a granddaughter.

I would like to thank my daughter, Beth Johnson, for encouraging me throughout my writing process, for sending me so many books on writing, and for helping me consolidate my files onto one computer. Thank you to my grandson, Eric Baskerville, for his tireless efforts in locating old photographs and notebooks and for his love and support during the process. Thank you to Susan Abrams for her time, care, and effort spent as the first person to photocopy everything that I had written and compile all my stories and chapters into one large binder. Thank you to my son-in-law, Steve Baskerville, for his time and dedication spent bringing together the final publication of the book and for making sure I always had each new draft printed and available to work on whenever I needed it. Thank you to my son, Lee Johnson, for inspiring me all those years ago to write my first story and for always being supportive of my writing.

Thank you to Aunt Nita for being a role model for me. And finally, thank you to BeeWee for providing a home, making time for me, and teaching me about nature.

About the Author

Shirley Johnson is a mother of three, a grandmother of three, and a retired elementary school teacher who has been writing for more than 40 years. She has lived in Norfolk, Virginia, for her whole life and wanted to share her experience as a little girl living in a city with one of the largest naval bases in the world during World War II. Shirley graduated from high school and went on to be the first in her immediate family to go to college. She received both a bachelor's degree in elementary education and a master's degree in education. She taught for more than 30 years in both public and private schools in Norfolk. Shirley enjoys carrying on the family traditions that her grandmother and great-grandmother started, including having her great-grandmother's turkey dressing recipe annually at Thanksgiving and Christmas. For nearly 50 years, she has taken a family vacation to the Outer Banks to bring together her immediate family.